ENVIRONMENTALISTS

If you find yourself in a hole, stop digging.
– Will Rogers

ENVIRONMENTALISTS

An Eyewitness Account from the Heart of America

Steven D. Paulson

Printed by CreateSpace, an Amazon.com Company
Available from Amazon.com, CreateSpace.com, and other retail outlets.
Available on Kindle and other devices.

Environmentalists: An Eyewitness Account from the Heart of America
Steven D. Paulson. -- 1st ed.

ISBN-13: 978-1514264447
ISBN-10: 1514264447

ACKNOWLEDGEMENTS

I owe a great debt of gratitude to the many people who gave of their time and thoughtfulness to be interviewed or to correspond with me. Without them, this book would not have been possible. They include:

Irv Alderson, Jeanie Alderson, Gayla Benefield, Bev Borer, Sam Clauson, the late Anne Charter, Steve Charter, John Davidson, Nancy Davidson, Andrew deGarmo, Jennifer Ferenstein, Mary Fitzpatrick, Mark Fix, John Gatchell, Nick Golder, Paul Hawks, Denis Hayes, Cesar Hernandez, Dena Hoff, Jerry Iverson, Frank James, Jim Jensen, Beth Kaeding, Jim Kuipers, Margie MacDonald, Amy McBride, Clint McRae, Wally McRae, Eileen Morris, Roger Muggli, George Nickas, Julia Page, Richard Parks, Ellen Pfister, Jim Posewitz, Linda Rauser, Nicole Reisner, Wade Sikorski, Arnold Silverman, Arlo Skari, the late Les Skramstad, Jeanne Souvigney, Dave Strom, Mark Trechock, Jack Tuholske, LJ Turner, Helen Waller, Sandy Weiss, Kevin Williams, Charles "Boomer" Winfrey, and Janet Zimmerman.

The people I've worked with at the Northern Plains Resource Council and, years earlier, at the Black Hills Energy Coalition taught me more than I can account for here – about courage, tenacity, justice, and many other values that I hope all Americans hold dear.

For their valued help with research, I must express my appreciation to Emily Forrette Paulson, Lawrence Perry, Becca Fischer, and Dar Anne Dunning. My gratitude also goes to Wade Sikorski for his advice and encouragement in steering through the publishing process.

I offer my thanks to Karen M. Olson for her cover photo, which expresses so much of what I mean to say on these pages.

Thanks also to Kristal Lohse for her cover design.

I am indebted to Candace Forrette, Paula Berg, Colin Lauderdale, Teresa Erickson, Svein Newman, Olivia Stockman Splinter, Ted Lange, and Emily Forrette Paulson for their edits and their insights on the manuscript. My wife Candace has extended many indulgences to a husband who spent too many evenings and weekends on this project.

For Candace

Table of Contents

ENVIRONMENTALISTS

You get as hard-boiled as you want to, but in the long run, we're going to get you. We are bigger than you and we can last longer.

– coal company executive

CHAPTER ONE

Make the World a Better Place

When Eileen Morris was a young girl in Billings, Montana, her family ran a neighborhood grocery store. They lived in an apartment at the back of the store and, from that apartment, Eileen got to know her community and the people in it very well.

She joined the Girl Scouts as a second grader and, later in life, worked for the organization. The Girl Scout Law includes an admonition to "use resources wisely, make the world a better place," and this ethic has stayed with Eileen throughout her life.

Eileen is eighty-three years old now, with bright white hair. Her late husband grew up on a ranch south of Ashland, Montana, and the family still owns that land. Cowboys used to trail cattle herds up there from Texas for grazing. Eileen is a great-grandmother, and is busily retired.

An asthma sufferer, Eileen has an especially personal stake in clean air. She was very aware as the air quality in Billings deteriorated in the 1970s due to the sulfur dioxide pollution from two oil refineries, a coal-fired power plant, a sugar beet processing plant, and other industrial sources of air pollution.

Eileen had a friend, Nettie Lees, who also suffered from asthma and, together, they helped form a local citizens' group to push for reducing the air pollution in Billings. They convinced the state Air Quality Bureau to draft enforceable air quality standards that would protect public health, and they persisted, against strong industry lobbying, to convince the state legislature to enact these standards. At the same time, though, the major polluters persuaded the legislature to enact a special provision in those standards that exempted the polluters in Eileen's county. The poor air quality of her county was the very reason to enact those standards in the first place, but now the standards wouldn't apply there.

It took ten years before the state legislature would repeal that exemption, and Eileen and friends would lobby at all levels for improved practices at the refineries and other industrial facilities that were the major sources of that pollution.

When Eileen and Nettie were driving home from one of many meetings in Billings with the chief of the state Air Quality Bureau, they drove through a plume of refinery stack pollution that was at ground level due to an air inversion. The plume affected Nettie the worst, triggering an immediate asthma attack, shutting down her respiratory system. By the time she arrived home a few minutes later, Nettie was unable to speak. She had rescue medication and a nebulizer at home, but she did not recover. Nettie Lees died the next day. When Eileen works for a cleaner environment today – for less air pollution or less coal mining – she does it for her old friend Nettie and for all the other people – especially kids – whose health is affected by polluted air.

CHAPTER TWO

I Was Born and Raised

I'm an environmentalist.

I'm also a husband and a father.

I'm a taxpayer.

I'm a wage-earner, the son of a wage-earner.

I love my country.

I'm a member of the Mayflower Congregational United Church of Christ in Billings, Montana.

I love the fact that Americans have improved our country when it was necessary... that we ended slavery (although it took decades of effort and America's bloodiest war to achieve it), and that we stopped denying women the right to vote (although it took more than a lifetime of struggle to attain it).

I was born and raised in South Dakota.

Today, I work for a Montana organization called the Northern Plains Resource Council. I'll be referring to Northern Plains in this book because I'm familiar with the work it does and I know quite a few of its people. But I do not speak for the organization... I'll also be writing about other issues, places, and people; I'll be writing about events that took place before I ever heard of Northern Plains.

I take a dim view of politicians who lie, or who wrap themselves up in the flag.

I strongly dislike extremism of all kinds: right-wing, left-wing, religious, environmental, whatever. Barry Goldwater famously said that extremism in the defense of liberty is no vice. Yes it is. Extremism in the defense of anything leads people to give up on reason; eventually it leads people to violence.

When I see people in faraway lands carry signs that say, "Death to America," I feel the same way inside that you must feel.

When I visited Washington, D.C., my favorite places there were the Lincoln Memorial and the Jefferson Memorial.

I've operated a couple of small businesses in my life, and worked for several others. I love the entrepreneurial spirit that draws people to find new ways to do something, to find new ways to support their families and, sometimes, to make the lives of other people better. However, this is different from the brand of capitalism we're supposed to accept without question nowadays.

I try to buy local whenever I can. Other things being close to equal, I prefer that my dollars support local businesses and employ local people. On a broader scale, I'd rather pay a few dollars more for an item and help keep a job in this country than pay a few dollars less and send that job to China.

I spent a lot of time in retailing, and I know there's no excuse for poor customer service.

I detest seeing jars on store counters asking people to drop in coins to help someone get treatment for cancer or get a needed operation, or get medical treatment after an injury. When did we decide that our country is better off if people have to beg for coins to save the life of a child with leukemia?

I appreciate to my core that I live in a country with freedom of religion. Some countries have state religions, and none of them are places where I'd want to live. A lot of Americans don't realize how lucky they are not to live in such a place.

I treasure many American places. The ones that are most deeply rooted in my heart are the Desert Southwest and the Black Hills and Badlands of South Dakota.

I place a high value on the night sky in places far from town where the sky is dark and the stars are brilliant.

I enjoy the sound of bluejays and running bison and a crowd cheering an extra-base hit by the home team.

Election Day is most special to me. I love the ceremony of it, the ritual. I like those people who work at the polls. I even like the poll-watchers for the political parties. I know that many people these days prefer to vote by mail, and I can understand why. But it means a lot to me to stand in line with my countrymen to share this civic ritual.

All things being equal, I prefer a sandwich that's sliced diagonally.

I think baseball is a wonderful sport, though I sure don't understand how Major League players can be paid so much to play it. And I don't think the designated hitter is real baseball. I prefer sitting on the third base side.

I'm proud to live in the nation that was the first place on earth to think of national parks.

When I hear about how various idiots have crashed drones in Grand Teton National Park, or into the Grand Canyon, into Yellowstone Lake, even into Yellowstone's world-famous Grand Prismatic Spring, the largest and prettiest hot spring in the United States (and it's still in there; they can't retrieve it)… when I hear about some jackass using a drone to harass a herd of bighorn sheep in Zion National Park, I just shake my head.

I admire the authors of the American Renaissance: Emerson, Thoreau, Hawthorne, Poe, Whitman, and so on.

I'm not merely a consumer. I am a citizen of my country.

CHAPTER THREE

Nature Fascists

"Hungry and out of work? Eat an environmentalist."
- Bumper sticker in Colorado

………………………………………………………

Engebret Paulson and Johanna Johannesdatter, a pair of young farm work-ers, married in Stjordalen, Norway, in 1880. They later followed Enge-bret's brothers to the American Midwest, eventually settling and raising a family in Dell Rapids, Dakota Territory. Engebret and Johanna were my grand-parents. My father, Harold Paulson, was the ninth of their ten children.

If you ever go through Dell Rapids, South Dakota, you'll see a historic downtown area, much of it solidly built by the Paulson brothers – Chris, Ole, Gundar, and Engebret. They used the mauve-colored Sioux quartzite that was quarried just outside town, and most of these quartzite buildings still stand to-day.

My father never took up the family business, but he stayed in the construc-tion trades all his life – as a skilled house and interior painter and wallpaperer. It was honest work, but not particularly steady.

When I was in grade school, I would take a couple dimes (or sometimes a quarter) to school each week, and purchase stamps for a savings bond book. When the book was full, I would trade it in for a $25 savings bond. I can re-member the time Dad had been out of work so long that he had to take my sav-ings bonds and cash them in just so we could get by for a while.

Dad stayed in South Dakota pretty much his whole life.

He was married once before he married my mother. As a young child, I asked him why that marriage hadn't lasted. After a short pause, he softly told me, "Well, I drank a lot then." That was all he ever told me about his first mar-riage.

But he never took a drink during my lifetime. He beat a serious alcohol problem on his own, and he never slipped up.

He and Mom married in 1950, and I was born the following year. But they divorced when I was young, and Dad raised me on his own. He was nearly 50 when I was born, and I know from being a parent myself how hard that must have been. He wasn't a warm man, but he loved me more than anything, and he wanted the best for me. My growing up was strictly working-class, but Dad taught me about the importance of fairness, being responsible for myself, getting an education, plus a little about baseball and fishing along the way.

There were a few things my father taught me that I later learned were wrong. I don't know where he picked it up, but the word "nigger" was a consistent part of his vocabulary. When I was a boy, in the late 50s and early 60s, the Civil Rights Movement was in full swing. Dad didn't think very highly of the people who led it, nor those who expressed support for it.

But by then we had gotten a television set and, even from South Dakota, I could see for myself what was happening. I could hear for myself what Rev. Martin Luther King, Jr., was saying. As a 12 year-old, I watched the televised coverage of the 1963 March on Washington, and I listened to King's speech about his dream for America. It wasn't just a dream for black people – it was a dream of a better country for all of us.

Dad would never listen to King's words. To him, King was just a "dirty nigger." He told me that King had a big mouth, and that someone was going to shoot him one day.

It's funny - hardly any black people live in South Dakota. To this day, I don't know where Dad got his ideas. I don't understand why he spewed such hatred for a group of people he never even knew.

It wasn't just African-Americans that he talked about this way. He didn't like Catholics, and he rarely used the word "Indian" without the word "drunken" in front of it.

Whoever it was that taught my dad to hate African-Americans and Native Americans and Catholics – whoever did that certainly did him no favors. My father was a good person, and repeating hate speech was his biggest weakness as a man.

The way he spoke about people he didn't know reminds me of the way Rush Limbaugh attached the word "wacko" to the word "environmentalist." Talk like that is based on something besides race or religion, but it's hate doing the talking, just the same. It's the same way someone taught my dad to use the word "nigger," and taught him to hate people he knew nothing about.

In this case, though, the hate speech is aimed at me. I'm an environmentalist, a conservationist. (Some people use the word "Green," though that's not something I've ever called myself.) Rush Limbaugh's hate speech is directed at me. And he's not the only one who talks about me that way. People talk about me that way who have never met me, who don't know what I think about anything. And they've been saying things like this about me for years.

"nature fascists"
- Ron Arnold[1]
"…environmental al-Qaida…"
- Stan Adelstein[2]
"Don't be fooled by the word 'conservationist.' It stands for 'green Nazi.'"
- John Stokes[3]
"the Fourth Reich"
- John Stokes[4]
"The Greens, at heart, are Despots… the Greens are the Taliban of America."
- Alan Caruba[5]
"Preservationists are like a new pagan religion. They worship trees and sacrifice people."
- Chuck Cushman[6]
"Environmentalism is part of a plan 'to dismantle industrial civilization' and must be destroyed."
- Ron Arnold[7]

"The United States is being taken over by terrorists. And it is not Iraq, Iran or foreigners. It is called extreme environmentalists. They have the state of Montana and Washington, D.C., on their knees. And we all better wake up and smell the coffee."

    - John O. Morris[8]

"Environmentalism regards man as a spreading cancer that must be eliminated at any cost."

    - David Holcberg[9]

"There are two groups of people who have made environmentalism their new home: socialists and enviro-religious fanatics. With the collapse of Marxism, environmentalism has become the new refuge of socialist thinking."

    - Rush Limbaugh[10]

"Environmentalists want man shackled to government regulations on behalf of animals, trees and rocks. The aim of the anti-capitalist protesters is self-evident: a socialist-anarchist state anchored in rubble. They do not want freedom; they want freedom destroyed."

    - John Lewis[11]

"Their goal is simple: They want to stop production of all natural resources on public lands in the United States."

    - People for the West brochure[12]

"Help our government destroy America. Join an environmentalist club."

    - Bumper sticker displayed on a state-owned vehicle in Montana

"From many years of studying environmentalists, I have come to the conclusion that they are unyielding religious fanatics. They are also seriously mentally ill. This makes for a dangerous combination."

    - Samuel Gipp[13]

"...the real motives of the environmentalists: not clean air and water, but the demolition of technological/industrial civilization. Their goal is not the advancement of human health, human happiness, and human life; rather it is a subhuman world where 'nature' is worshipped like the totem of some primitive religion."

    - Michael Berliner[14]

"The core of environmentalism is a hatred for mankind. They want mass infanticide, zero population growth, reduced standards of living and vegetarianism. Most crucially, they want Americans to stop with their infernal deodorant use."

    - Ann Coulter[15]

"...a bunch of commie peace queers."

    - a coal miner in Tennessee[16]

"These people are not honest, nor are they interested in factual science or the environment. What they are interested in is left-wing socialism that will dominate the lives of all Americans."

    - Donald Kopp[17]

"We should be fingerprinting environmentalists."

    - Ann Coulter[18]

"The obstructionists are at it again. Heaven forbid that Montana may get some more jobs. It's time to hunt these people down, and hang them."

    - Anonymous post on *Billings Gazette* website[19]

"Shoot the son of a bitch!"

    - an elderly Nevada woman yelling from the visitor's gallery when a Republican state senator testified against a Sagebrush Rebellion demand that federal lands be given to the state[20]

"...if the troubles from environmentalists cannot be solved in the jury box or at the ballot box, perhaps the cartridge box should be used."

    - James Watt[21]

Most Americans say they support environmental protection, but they've rarely made the environment a dominant force at the ballot box. If environmentalists were fanatics or extremists, nothing else but protecting the environment would matter to them, and politicians wouldn't dare ignore them like they do.

In raising my own daughter, one of the most important skills I tried to teach her is the ability to tell when she's being lied to. Whether she's being lied to by a politician, or by a gossip, or by a company that's trying to sell her something – knowing when she's being lied to is a vital skill that she'll need in life.

It's a skill we all need, and not just when discussing environmentalists. We need to use that skill whenever we hear someone generalizing about "teenagers," or "greedy businessmen," or "women drivers," or "rich white people," or "drunken Indians," or "hippies" or "rednecks" or "Papists."

"The Fourth Reich?" "The Taliban of America?" Get real.

CHAPTER FOUR

What This Isn't

This book isn't the voice of anybody but me. It's not the point of view of any organization, including the one where I work. I don't represent anybody, I don't speak for anybody. I'm not an expert, a scholar, a journalist, or an academic. I'm not a "mover and shaker" among environmentalists.

And I'm not trying to convince you to be an environmentalist. But I'd like you to understand who this particular environmentalist is, where I came from and, most of all, what motivates me, because – at one time or another – you'll hear someone say terrible things about me because I'm an environmentalist. I want you to know the truth.

CHAPTER FIVE

What This Is

This is just me talking to you, one American to another. I'll tell you as well as I can how I came to be an environmentalist. I'll tell you about some of my experiences, my concerns, my opinions, my beliefs, and people I've met. Along the way, I've asked a few other people about their own experiences and beliefs, and about what they are after – I'll tell you some of what they told me. It's important for all of us to understand what motivates American environmentalists.

I'll also tell you, as well as I'm able, what I want and why I want it.

I'm tired of being told that America will be a better nation:

- If we pollute more of our rivers;
- If we get rid of our wild country;
- If we allow more mercury, particulates, and carcinogens in the air that our children breathe;
- If we let our economic and political lives become dominated by corporations that have no loyalty to our people or our nation;
- If we upset the climate of the planet we live on (the only planet we <u>can</u> live on);
- If money becomes the main way we measure things.

I hope we can meet someday at a ball game, at work, maybe at a car show, and talk about how to make our country once again a place where people are brought together instead of a place where we're torn apart. It's critical in these times that we be able to talk to each other.

Maybe we'll meet in one of America's great cities or in the Great Sand Dunes. Maybe we'll meet at Zion National Park or inside the Lincoln Memorial. Maybe we'll meet at the Gettysburg Battlefield or on a Montana ranch that's targeted to be torn up a coal company.

There are a lot of places in this big, beautiful country where we're still trying to figure out how to do it right. But we'll never, ever, figure it out if we can't talk to one another.

CHAPTER SIX

The Narrative

The "Narrative" about the United States has moved millions of people in the Muslim world to hate America. It's a story that some radical Muslims tell each other – and tell young Muslims who don't know any better – about America. It says that Americans want to destroy the religion of Islam. It describes our nation and our people in ways that you wouldn't even recognize.

Thomas Friedman, in a 2009 column in the *New York Times*, described The Narrative as "the cocktail of half-truths, propaganda and outright lies about America that have taken hold in the Arab-Muslim world since 9/11. Propagated by jihadist Web sites, mosque preachers, Arab intellectuals, satellite news stations and books — and tacitly endorsed by some Arab regimes — this narrative posits that America has declared war on Islam, as part of a grand 'American-Crusader-Zionist conspiracy' to keep Muslims down."[1]

Friedman quotes a Jordanian-born counterterrorism expert who told him that "This narrative is now omnipresent in Arab and Muslim communities in the region and in migrant communities around the world. These communities are bombarded with this narrative in huge doses and on a daily basis. [It says] the West, and right now mostly the U.S. and Israel, is single-handedly and completely responsible for all the grievances of the Arab and the Muslim worlds."

But most of the Muslims being killed in the world are being killed by other Muslims. Whatever mistakes America has made in dealing with the Muslim world, I know that my country is not and has never been on a crusade to destroy Islam. I'm convinced – as was Friedman in his column – that The Narrative is a cynical tool being used by Islamic radicals to find a scapegoat for whatever people in the Muslim world may see wrong in their lives. Most of them, from what I understand, don't buy it. But many do.

It's a lie, of course. But what do we do about it?

The remarks that I quoted a few pages ago reflect another Narrative, a Narrative about environmentalists. This Narrative is spread in ways similar to the Muslim Narrative – websites, speakers, articles, cable news, books. And what are the elements of the Narrative? What do people say about environmentalists?

They don't all say the same thing, but here's some of what I hear:

- Environmentalists hate humanity, and want to destroy civilization.
- Environmentalists worship trees and rocks.
- Environmentalists are anti-business socialists who don't believe in private property.
- Environmentalists are against science and technology, and grossly distort information in order to gain attention.
- Environmentalists are always telling everyone else how to live.
- Environmentalists don't care about the lives of everyday people. They are members of the "leisure class," they don't have to worry about making a living, and just want to protect their personal favorite places to backpack.
- Environmentalists hate farmers and ranchers, and they are against hunting and fishing.
- Environmentalists are hippies and vegetarians. Or worse, vegans.
- They are radicals, or at the very least, liberal Democrats.
- Environmentalists are lawsuit-happy, and want big government to run people's lives.
- Environmentalists get all their money from liberal foundations on the East Coast.
- Environmentalists are obstructionists who are against everything, and not for anything.
- There are a lot of eco-terrorists out there.

CHAPTER SEVEN

A Sampling of Environmentalists

I was never considered an economist or a social engineer, I was
categorized as one of those "damn environmentalists."

....

S o who are environmentalists, really? And what do they really want? Here...
meet some of them.

(I should tell you right here that not all these people would want me to call
them "environmentalists." Many of them are well aware of The Narrative about
environmentalists, and they do not like being associated with it.)

Sandy Weiss, of Billings, Montana, got involved with a local organization
when she discovered the ground water beneath her house had been poisoned by
dumped dangerous toxic wastes that were traced to a nearby chemical company.
In the years that followed, Sandy discovered that it's not easy for citizens to get
public agencies to act on their behalf. It's easy to get reassurances, she learned,
but it's not easy to get information, and it's even harder to get action.

....

Dena Hoff grew up in western North Dakota, where she remembers learning
to value nature, as contrasted with "dirty big-city living" (with "big city" referring
to the state capital, Bismarck). Today Dena and her husband, a retired railroad
worker, run a farm near Glendive, Montana. She became active in an environmental organization for the first time when coal strip mining came to her home
town back in North Dakota. It was low-grade lignite coal, and it contained high
levels of uranium-bearing material.

Dena's environmental involvement has always been part of her love for farming. For many years, Dena chaired the Dawson Resource Council, a local affiliate
group of the Northern Plains Resource Council in Montana, which also elected
her as chair for a time. She was long active in her local irrigation district, and

currently serves on the board of the National Family Farm Coalition. To her, environmental issues and family agriculture go hand-in-hand.

....

Dave Strom moved his family from Chicago to Rapid City, South Dakota, in the early 1970s to get away from the people and traffic. He had been to the Black Hills on hunting trips when he was younger, and decided it was a better place to raise a family than Chicago. He joined the local chapter of the Sierra Club as a way to meet people who shared his interests in hiking, camping, and hunting. Eventually, he grew into a leadership role with the Club's local group, but he also worked in collaboration with other area organizations. A longtime sheet metal worker, now retired, Dave was active in a rural volunteer fire department for several years until heart trouble forced him to back off. Then he helped build houses for Habitat for Humanity.

It was Dave who once told me how having an ongoing organization is like having someone to tend a campfire, how it's a lot easier to get a good fire going if you don't have to start from nothing – making a new bed for the fire, gathering fuel, constructing it, and getting it started. Sustaining an organization even when things are quiet is like having someone there who is tending the fire for you, keeping a small fire ready for when you need a bigger one.

....

Mark Trechock was a Lutheran minister for years, and he had long tried to reduce his own pollution by reducing waste, lowering his thermostat, burning less gasoline, and so on. Later, he worked for more than 15 years as the executive director of the Dakota Resource Council, a community organization in North Dakota that addresses environmental and family agriculture issues. By the time Mark retired, his organization was at the middle of the gigantic oil boom in the Bakken Formation, trying to help landowners and other local residents deal with an invasion by oil drilling companies, oil field workers, and company men, along with legions of the heavy trucks hauling equipment as well as loads of chemicals and water for "fracking" the oil wells. (There also came an invasion of crime and inflation that actually drove many local residents from their homes because they could no longer afford to live there... the influx of oil workers had driven up rents that much.)

....

Bev Borer is a retiree in Billings, Montana. She has spent more than 20 years volunteering for the local Catholic hospital. Bev grew up on a farm and she attributes her lifelong concern with the environment to her farm upbringing. She first got involved with an environmental organization when two volunteers knocked on her door and talked with her about their work. She's a devout Catholic and the kind of dedicated, behind-the-scenes volunteer that any organization considers itself lucky to have.

....

The first time I met Irv Alderson was after a picnic he had hosted at his Bones Brothers Ranch on Hanging Woman Creek. The picnic was a fundraiser, raising money to fight a coal-hauling railroad that was being planned for the Tongue River valley in southeast Montana. At that time, Irv's ranch near Birney would have been bisected by that railroad – he said if the railroad were built, he'd end up with two bull pastures, one with grass and one with water.

After the picnic was over, a few of us sat and talked under the night sky on his patio. Irv recited a few of his favorite cowboy poems. The land at the ranch was homesteaded in the late 1880s, partly by Irv's great aunt and her husband, and partly by Irv's grandfather. Irv is a very soft-spoken man; it wasn't until later that I learned he had been a rodeo competitor of some note during the 1950s-70s.

Far from the nearest town, the Bones Brothers Ranch was a landmark on old aviation maps of the area; until just a few years ago, the barn roof was painted with the word "BONES" to help pilots of small aircraft find their location above the Montana plains.

That night on Irv's patio, I was a brand-new employee at the Northern Plains Resource Council, and I took notice when Irv talked about his deep loyalty to the organization, telling us that only Northern Plains had helped him in his years of struggle to keep his ranch from being torn apart by coal development and this proposed railroad.

Years later, Irv talked to an audience in Billings about getting through the lean years in agriculture. "The land has taught us what we can do and what we can't do. You can find values and knowledge there that you can't find in an EIS." Though Bones Brothers is strictly a cattle operation these days, it survived for years by "wranglin' dudes." That capacity to diversify has long been a staple of families who survive in agriculture, and Irv is concerned that "it'll be hard to do if the Tongue River Valley has been turned into an industrial park."

He describes his ranch this way: "My main assets are grass and water and my neighbors."

....

Irv's daughter, Jeanie Alderson, lives on the Bones Brothers Ranch with her husband, Terry Punt, and sons Carson and Gerrit. She and Terry work hard to protect the historic ranch they call home – ranch work and "activist" work. They've driven many thousands of miles and sat through days and days of meetings to keep Bones Brothers a viable cattle ranch and a good home, through the many years that energy companies have sought to drill it and cut through it. The ranch is more than a livelihood to this family.

Jeanie and Terry have worked out quite a partnership. Both of them have been heavily involved Northern Plains' work for many years. Both of them have testified many times to public officials who have the power to determine what happens to ranch families like theirs. And every fall, both of them – joined by family and neighbors – ride out across hillsides and gullies of the Bones Brothers Ranch to gather their cattle.

....

Arlo Skari came to Montana as a youngster in 1947. He and his wife raise grain and hay on his operation near Chester, Montana. They also raised two sons, one of whom is a partner in the farm. Growing up on farms (in Minnesota before the family moved to Montana), Arlo told me erosion "always bothered the hell out of me." His thinking about the environment as a political issue crystallized when he saw news coverage of the Cuyahoga River on fire near Cleveland (June 22, 1969) because of all the chemical waste it contained. He says he also has trouble with the fact that the U.S. consumes a quarter of the world's energy supply, even though we only have 4-5% of its people. "Just because we are energetic, well-educated, and historically productive doesn't mean that we have to be gluttonous," he told me. Arlo is very concerned about climate change, but is excited at our capacity to improve things, once we set our minds to it.

··

Ed Gulick aims to improve things. Raised in Billings, he trained as an architect specifically to build – literally build – a stronger future for his community and his country.

Ed's an idealist, motivated by a profound love of Montana's landscape and a strong sense of duty to protect it. This love and these principles pushed him to become active in his community as a young man, taking on increased responsibility within Northern Plains, eventually chairing the organization for two terms. But they also drive his work as an architect. Northern Plains' LEED Platinum "Home on the Range" building (see "Building Energy Independence") was Ed's first experience as a project manager. He credited that project with jumpstarting a local movement to buildings that make us more independent of fossil fuels, more independent of waste and pollution, more independent of the myth that we can't change anything.

··

The late Anne Charter fell in love with a cowboy when she was a young woman. She and her cowboy struggled to buy a ranch in the Bull Mountains of Montana, and they raised a family there.

An active Methodist, Anne first got involved in environmental issues when coal companies were speculating on lands where she and her husband Boyd ranched. The coal companies wanted to pursue the same strategies they had employed in much of Appalachia – buy out the surface owners and have a lot less trouble with citizens and regulatory agencies because they own everything. And the coal companies used some of the same strategies on landowners that they had used back east; they told landowners that their neighbors had already agreed to sell out, even when they hadn't.

Anne and Boyd talked with their neighbors, forming a small organization – the Bull Mountain Landowners Association (changed later to the Bull Mountain Land Alliance) – and then co-founding a statewide group, the Northern Plains Resource Council.

You can read Anne's story in her memoir, *Cowboys Don't Walk: A Tale of Two*. In her book, she quotes her husband Boyd, who died in 1978:

I said once that when we die America dies. I'm not trying to insinuate that if Anne or I or any of our neighbors die, America dies. We're not that important to America. But when it comes to people who have respect for the land and are trying to save the land from being destroyed, when people like us die, who will stand up here and fight for it... turn their money down and stand for what they think is right? When people like us die, America is dying.[2]

It was Boyd who told a coal company man, "You will always be $4.60 short of the price for my land."

Anne and Boyd are no longer with us; their son Steve runs the ranch now. And he continues to fight coal companies that are still threatening the land and water where he ranches. In particular, a large underground "longwall" mine is damaging water resources beneath the Bull Mountains. That mine is expanding and the corporation that owns it wants to develop a strip mine, too, and ship that coal to prospective customers in Asia. The Charter ranch stands to be wounded, perhaps fatally.

....

Ellen Pfister is a neighbor of the Charters. She raises cattle in the Bull Mountains north of Shepherd, Montana, and tries to do the best for her own land. In 1984, a grass fire burned up 90% of the ranch. Ellen and her late husband Don Golder had to put up 35 miles of fence the following summer. In the late 1990s-early 2000s, their main struggle was keeping their land productive through a persistent drought.

She described her own experience as a girl. "In 1955, my folks and I went to Clarion County, Pennsylvania, where my mother's people originated. She had been out to her great-grandfather's farm in the 1920s and she wanted me to see it. We found our way out to there, and there was nothing but a spoil pile. It had been strip mined, and nothing was left... We talked all the time on the ranch about how the grass was doing. It was a matter of great concern, and there in Pennsylvania there was nothing. I couldn't believe people would do that to the land."

When modern coal strip mining came to Montana, Ellen and her mother were determined not to let the same thing happen in the Bulls that had happened in Clarion County. Ellen lobbied to get the Montana legislature to pass a reclamation law. (She has a law degree from the University of Mississippi.) They did pass a law, but it proved too weak (which ranchers in affected areas had predicted). She worked also for enactment of a federal strip mine reclamation law. Congress eventually passed a law, but it was vetoed by Presidents Nixon and Ford. In 1977, the federal strip mine law was again passed, but this time it was signed into law by President Jimmy Carter. However, that enactment was not in itself a solution... Ellen knew that agencies tend to become "captured" by the industries they regulate, and persistent action by citizens is needed if this is to be prevented.

Ellen was an early Chair of the Northern Plains Resource Council. Later, she chaired the Citizen's Coal Council, which works with impacted citizens in coal-producing states. Some of the angriest people she's met at CCC meetings are those who have been "long-walled," which is an underground mining technology that uses large machines instead of people to completely mine out the coal seam, leaving no supports behind. This results in ground subsidence after a time, as well as disastrous impacts to the flow of ground water.

Now, Ellen's ranch – Dunn Mountain Herefords – is being long-walled. There is a lot of coal beneath the ranch, coal that the federal government owns. The government leased some of that coal to a long-wall mine, and now the results are visible on the surface. Cracks are opening on slopes at her ranch, cracks up to 15 feet wide and 40 feet deep. Cracks like this aren't exactly something you want on your cattle ranch.

"Land and water quality are tied together intimately," she told me. "The long-term health of humanity depends on the two. In addition to health, the long-term economy of an area is tied to land and water quality."

....

Boomer Winfrey of Lake City, Tennessee, is a retired newspaperman who learned long ago to be skeptical of coal industry assurances. He majored in geology in college at the University of Tennessee / Knoxville. While still in college, Boomer and other geology majors were given a "grand tour" of a Cities Service mine and smelter operation at Copper Hill, Tennessee. He told me they were "escorted into the mines, fed a big meal, and more or less recruited as aspiring mining geologists."

Boomer's second trip to Copper Hill was an eye-opener for him. His zoology class took a field trip to study the effects of air pollution on plant life near a smelter. This time, Cities Service had its private police surround the class, threatening to arrest the professor. The private police escorted the class off their property.

Strip mining had become pervasive in parts of Appalachia. "All I had to do was step onto my parents' front porch," Boomer said, "and look at the mountain that in my childhood had been beautifully forested and, by 1971, looked like a war zone."

....

When Beth Kaeding was a child in Kansas City, her family had no garden and never really got out of their urban setting. She came west for the first time on a family vacation when she was 15, through the Black Hills and on to Yellowstone National Park. From then on, she was determined to live and work in the West. After high school, for summers during college, Beth worked as a hotel housekeeper in Yellowstone.

College took her to Montana State University, where – in the 1970s – she was the first woman to earn a master's in Fish and Wildlife Management. In those days, she got a lot of resistance from the department's "old guard," who didn't want a woman there. That was one of many experiences that honed Beth's keen sense of justice.

I met Beth in the 1990s when she worked for the National Park Service in Yellowstone. Her path there took her through years of field and lab research and other positions in the Canadian Arctic; Colstrip, Montana; Salt Lake City, Utah; Flagstaff, Arizona; and Colorado National Monument. Along the way, she expanded upon her professional work by getting involved with local organizations trying to protect water resources and ecosystems in the West. She also learned to love elk hunting and bird watching. Every week for years, she has delivered Meals-on-Wheels to elderly people in her community.

In the early 90s, Beth joined a local group affiliated with Northern Plains. Working with people who live on the plains of eastern Montana, she developed a deep appreciation for that part of Big Sky Country... its wildlife, its rivers, its working landscapes. Eventually, she chaired Northern Plains and, since then, has continued working hard on our issues and to keep it a healthy organization.

Trained as a wildlife biologist, Beth cares about a broad range of big subjects – climate change, loss of ecosystems in the world, loss of plant and animal species, out-of-control population growth, and war. But she also cares about whether farmers and ranchers will be able to earn a livelihood on their land, whether citizens are treated fairly by the lawmakers who are supposed to represent them, and whether the Tongue River can persist as a healthy prairie river.

"I am determined to fight to my last breath," she once told me, "against ignorance and greed and abuse of power, and for the natural world." This includes fighting for the people whose farms and ranches stand in the path of coal companies, coal railroads, and oil and gas drillers. She has traveled all over Montana to speak up for these people because of that sense of justice deep down in her bones.

....

Helen Waller, who farms near Circle, Montana, never expected to become involved in environmental issues. She had married her high school sweetheart and they were busy raising five children, as well as wheat and cattle. But she got very personally involved in the 1970s, when a pair of companies announced plans to develop coal strip mines in her county. The companies told landowners that it was their patriotic duty, their "contribution to society," to allow their land to be strip-mined.

Working with her neighbors to find out what they were really facing, Helen discovered that the coal was of such low quality that it couldn't be economically shipped out of the area... coal-fired power plants would have to be built right there. Then, using the industry's own figures, Helen demonstrated that the company couldn't even show a need for the electricity they proposed to generate from the coal.

Helen read 2-inch thick environmental impact statements and other documents to become an expert on coal mining, its impacts, and the laws pertaining to it. Why did she do it?

In 1979, Helen wrote to the members of the Northern Plains Resource Council that, "I cannot separate my work with Northern Plains and the struggle we are engaged in from my convictions and principles as a Christian."[2]

In 2006, she told the Montana Council of Catholic Women that God "expects us to be stewards of the land – good stewards and caretakers. We dare not fail."

"God's word," she told them, "is profoundly clear as to what our responsibility is in the care of the earth and its occupants."

It was no small task. Helen had a family to raise and a farm to operate with her husband Gordy. Because her involvement frequently took her away from home, she said, "It was a case of having to give up enjoying what was important to me in order to preserve it for future generations."

....

Richard Parks of Gardiner, Montana, was a teenager when the U.S. Forest Service decided to spray for spruce budworm on roughly a million acres of the Absaroka and Beartooth Mountains, along with neighboring sections of Yellowstone National Park. His father, a fly-fishing guide, protested but, at the time, there were no laws like the National Environmental Policy Act (enacted 12 years later in 1969) to ensure that the public could participate in such land management decisions. "The spray job was done in late June to early July," Richard recalled. "That fall, tens of thousands of fish died in the Yellowstone River from DDT poisoning." Richard recounts a chain reaction that reverberated from one kind of poisoned animal to another over years and even decades after that one DDT spray.

A few years later, after Richard returned from a tour of duty in Vietnam, his father died, and Richard took over the operation of Parks Fly Shop. This naturally gave him a lifelong concern with water quality (he refers to the fish in the Yellowstone River as his "business partners."). But water quality isn't his only concern. Richard sees how environmental issues are often tied with boom/bust cycles in communities, and how his interests as a fishing guide so often mesh with the interests of farmers and cattle ranchers who live downstream from him.

....

George Nickas works in Missoula, Montana, for an environmental organization called Wilderness Watch. George got started in this work in the 1970s when a wild place where he often went to hunt, camp, hike, and simply recover from day-to-day life was ruined by an energy development project. He told me that it wasn't just the physical damage to the area, but the lack of respect that the developer displayed. When he looked around, he saw that other public lands all over the West were under the same kind of pressure. That led him to devote himself to helping keep wild places wild.

....

Julia Page, who for many years ran a river rafting company in Gardiner, Montana, got involved in environmental work when the Church Universal and Triumphant – which some regard as a cult – began buying up land near her community just outside Yellowstone National Park, and building extensive facilities there. Erecting large buildings without adequate sewage treatment and installing 35 large fuel tanks (some of which leaked 19,000 gallons of diesel and gasoline into the soil), CUT created major environmental issues along the upper part of the Yellowstone River. Julia felt the CUT officials just weren't being straightforward with the people who lived in her town.

Julia later became a leader in the Northern Plains Resource Council, and worked as hard to protect the distant rivers of the Montana plains as she did to protect the Upper Yellowstone that flowed through Gardiner.

She didn't much care for public speaking, but she learned how to do it anyway. She didn't much care for fundraising, but she learned how to help raise money for our work.

A state official bent on intimidation actually sued Julia when she criticized his job performance. The suit was thrown out of court. He had no idea of this woman's tenacity in working for the things she believed in.

As a business owner, Julia reflected that "We can have both a strong economy and protect clean air and water at the same time. Actually," she added, "I believe we have to protect clean air and water in order to prosper as a society."

....

When Wally McRae was a boy in Rosebud County, Montana, his mother expressed concerns when the ranch used poisons to control grasshoppers. She didn't really have a scientific reason for her concerns, but simply worried that the poisons might have unintended consequences to the land. Later, when Wally went to college, he learned about "ecological balance" and about unintended consequences.

Wally is well-known in Montana for his positions on stewardship of the land, dating back to the advent of large-scale coal strip mining in Montana in the early 1970s. Strip mining directly threatened his ranch and other ranches along Rosebud Creek. When coal companies began eyeing his neighborhood, he had three concerns: social costs, long-term economic costs, and environmental consequences. "The first two concerns were hard to sell and there were no handy parameters to address them," he told me, "but it was possible to place numeric and logical standards on some environmental aspects. So, although I was never considered an economist or a social engineer, I was categorized as one of those 'damn environmentalists.'"

....

Nick Golder, raises cattle a few miles from Wally's place. Nick says, "I am the environmentalist who believes that the land should be in at least as good shape when I get done with it as when I started with it." Nick's family began ranching in 1939, when he was five years old. He first got involved with an environmental organization when coal strip mining and power plant construction, and their associated impacts to surface and ground water and to air quality, came to his neighborhood.

Nick told me, "If I have a dog, and take good care of him, it arouses no particular notice. Both my friends and myself like a friendly, healthy dog. But if I abuse the dog physically, or don't provide food and shelter for him, people will begin to notice. If it gets bad enough, someone is likely to take up the dog's cause... Some of the people who can cause years, or even centuries, of trauma to an ecosystem could be quite indignant about someone abusing a dog. But they can cry 'over-regulation' pretty quickly when someone points out that they are abusing the land."

Reflecting on his own ranch, Nick says, "Nature's effects on the land are immensely varied, intricately inter-related and interwoven, and complex enough that people can spend a lifetime getting really acquainted with the most significant functions of their particular bit of real estate."

Nick often wears a belt buckle that bears the Christian symbol of the fish. He sees environmental damage as contrary to God's plan for Creation, and a reckless pursuit of the "Almighty Dollar" as an insult to God.

....

Nick's point of view reminds me of a time many years ago when I was working in Sam Weller's Zion Book Store in Salt Lake City. An older employee, Wilf Clark, was hurrying by me as he often did on busy days. But this time he stopped and leaned over to me. He asked, "Do you know what the main problem in the world is?"

"What?" I asked. Wilf looked serious.

"Simple human greed." That said, Wilf hurried along on his way.

Paul's first epistle to Timothy (6:10) said the same thing a long time ago: "For the love of money is the root of all evil: which while some coveted after, they have erred from the faith, and pierced themselves through with many sorrows."

....

Retired geology professor Arnold Silverman taught at the University of Montana for many years, and eventually retired to Florida. Silverman was a co-author of the Montana coal reclamation law in the 1960s. What he had been shocked to learn was that the bill's language had been changed the night before its introduction by the Montana Bureau of Mines to make reclamation <u>voluntary</u>. He and others worked to improve the law in subsequent years, and it eventually became a model for the federal strip mine law that was enacted in 1977.

....

Kevin Williams of Montrose, Colorado, works for the Western Organization of Resource Councils, an organization that addresses environmental and family agriculture issues, but he told me he doesn't really consider himself an environmentalist. "I do consider myself to be someone who cares deeply about saving the world," he told me. "Saving the world gets at fundamental root causes, 'protecting the environment' deals with the symptoms... People are much more complicated than the labels that are applied to them, and being an 'environmentalist' is no exception."

....

Kathy Masis began her medical career as a nurse, then as a doctor, in Cleveland, Ohio. During three years of family practice residency on Cleveland's west side, she regularly treated steel workers (and former steel workers) whose work lives – and, in some cases, the location of their homes – exposed them to considerable air pollution. Many of them were dying from its effects. After she moved to Billings in the early 1990s, the sulfur dioxide pollution that was so heavy at the time recalled to her the way that air pollution can ruin lives and families. She has been active in Northern Plains and other organizations since then, and started a local chapter of the Citizens Climate Lobby because of her concerns about the disruption of the earth's climate.

....

Paul and Elli Hawks raise cattle near Melville, Montana. Paul grew up in southeastern Montana, and his first contact with environmental issues was when a ranch belonging to friends, the Charters, was threatened by coal strip mining in the early 1970s. He has been involved off and on ever since. In 1999-2000, Paul helped negotiate a legally binding agreement between citizen conservation groups and a large platinum / palladium mine. This agreement settled several issues for the parties involved, and has improved protections for two important watersheds downstream from where the company's mine operations are located. Sixteen years later, Paul is still volunteering lots of time and effort to keep the agreement working so that this huge mine doesn't wreck the mountains and watersheds where it operates.

. . ..

The late Les Skramstad lived in Libby, Montana, where he had once worked for the Zonolite Company, at an asbestos mining operation. Years later, when he was diagnosed with asbestosis, he filed suit against the W.R. Grace Corporation, the subsequent owner of the company. Les had never been involved in environmental issues until he got involved in efforts to hold the company accountable for the hundreds of asbestos-related deaths in Libby, and the many more premature deaths yet to come (including his own). "I'm not for stopping all logging and mining," he once told me, "I just think it should be done in the proper way without hurting our air and water." Les Skramstad's asbestosis killed him in 2007.

. . ..

This is no representative sample of environmentalists... these are just some people I've crossed paths with, people who got personally involved with environmental issues.

Just like most Americans, there's not really one quality that they all have in common. In fact, that's probably the single biggest point I can make to you – environmentalists, as a group, are like anyone else. I've met plenty of them over the years. Some are involved for their whole lives, some for just a while. Some are religious and some aren't. Some are wealthy and some struggle to get by. Some of them are the nicest people you could meet, and some are real pains in the neck. They're women and men; Democrats and Republicans; rich people and poor; Catholics, Lutherans, Baptists, Jews, atheists; Northern Cheyenne, African-Americans, and white people; New Englanders, Tennesseans, and Montanans; business people, school teachers, farmers, and politicians; old people and young people; urban and rural; vegetarians and cattle ranchers.

They want different things, and they have different ideas for how to get those things.

CHAPTER EIGHT

Environmentalists Are...

What gives me the right to claim that I'm an environmentalist?

....

A lot of people hear the word "environment" and they think it only means places far from where humans live, places that have no meaning in our day-to-day lives. That's not true.

The environment is my house, my town, my nation, my job. It's my family, my pet cat, the people on my block, the people I know at work, the checker who waits on me at the Good Earth Market. It's the other drivers on the streets I travel, and the police who patrol those streets. It's the kind of art they show around here, and the museums, and the churches. It's the farms and ranches that surround Billings, as well as the oil refineries, the sugar beet factory, and all the sulfur dioxide they put into Billings' airshed. It's the air I breathe and the water I drink. It's the time I live in, and the time that my daughter will live in after I am gone. It's the political climate, and the people who lead our nation. It's the food I eat, and the people who raise it, and the place where they raise it. It's the grass, the lilacs, and the garden in my back yard, as well as the birds and squirrels and insects that live there. It's the Yellowstone River that flows through Billings, the sandstone cliffs that run along the river. It's the mountain ranges upstream – the Beartooths, the Pryors, the Crazies, the Absarokas – and all the trout and mayflies and turtles in the river, the elk and badgers and coyotes and rattlesnakes and great blue herons. It's also the cold fronts that sweep down from Alberta in January, and the hot winds that move across the country in July. It's those glorious high-pressure systems that make the air so clear in September. It's the night sky, or what little of it I can see from town. It's the sound of the fans cheering at Dehler Park when the Mustangs score in the late innings.

"The environment" is all these things to me. It's also Yellowstone National Park, and the wolves and grizzlies that live there. It's the brilliant night sky above the South Dakota Badlands, it's the disappearing glaciers of Glacier National Park, it's the Delicate Arch in Utah, and West Ten Sleep Lake in the Bighorn Mountains.

And it doesn't stop with where I've personally been. Even though I've never been to Death Valley or the Everglades (or the Statue of Liberty or the Gettysburg battlefield), I'm glad these places are protected so all Americans forever will have the chance to take in the wonder that is our country. If we were to lose those places in my lifetime – even though I've never seen them – I would mourn the loss to our nation. The glaciers of Glacier National Park will be gone soon, possibly during my lifetime. If I'm still living, I will grieve at that loss. It was not necessary to America's future that we lose those magnificent glaciers.

Some people who dedicate large parts of their lives to protecting the environment don't call themselves "environmentalists" because it's such a loaded word. But I'm using the word in this book because it's part of the language. I haven't been able to think of a better word.

Realistically, though, it would be better if we described them as people who want to protect something important:

- People who want to protect our nation's wild places
- People who want to protect the health of their families
- People who want to protect family farming and ranching
- People who want to protect clean water
- People who want to protect the right of citizens to help steer our country
- People who want to protect the quality of the air they breathe
- People who want to protect the quality of their day-to-day lives.

What gives me the right to claim that I'm an environmentalist? If I go backpacking, does that make me an environmentalist? If I recycle, does that make me an environmentalist? If I drive a fuel-efficient car, does that make me an environmentalist? How about if I buy organic food or if I use efficient light bulbs throughout my house? Can I claim to be an environmentalist if I simply have a vague belief that it's good to conserve and protect natural resources?

- Some people who work to protect America's environment are very involved with politics. They believe in and work for political outcomes. They believe in the political process. Some of them even enjoy it.

- Some of them are people who believe deeply in the capacity of American citizens to change things for the better. They work with their neighbors or friends or family members toward a common goal. That goal may be to protect some local natural feature, or to protect their community from some destructive development. They may end up working in the political system, but a good number of them do it reluctantly.

- Some people care a great deal about the impact of their lifestyles on the world. They respond to their concern by changing their lifestyles so they generate less waste, less pollution, use less of the world's resources. Some of these people also work for change in other ways, while some are content with whatever it is they can do through personal lifestyle changes and shopping habits.

- Some people go into the outdoors for their recreation, and they often come to care a great deal about those places. Maybe they climb mountains or hunt elk. Maybe they go ice fishing. Maybe they ride horses or watch birds. Maybe they go rafting, maybe they even use motors in their recreation – a car or a motorcycle. Some of them go no further than try to protect their preferred kind of recreation, but some of them come to understand that protecting the places where they love to go also means protecting other kinds of places.

- For some people, being out in wild country is about much more than recreation. It's about the personal liberty and responsibility that are part of being an American. Spending time in wild America, responsible for their own actions, measuring themselves against the land while protecting it for others, is an exercise in patriotism. The wild landscapes of our country – the forests, the deserts, the few remaining wild rivers, the great mountains, undeveloped coastlines – and the wild animals that live there are part of our nation's heritage. Many American game animals have come back to thrive after generations of overhunting, due in part to the efforts of hunters who have stood up for wildlife conservation and protecting wildlife habitat.

- Some people are motivated by a concern for future generations. Perhaps it's a very specific motivation – for example, I think about the world my daughter will live in, more than she knows. But some people, myself included, think about all future Americans, and what kind of nation we will be passing on to them.

- Some people are attuned to what science tells us about the world, how we're affecting it, and how we'll affect it in the future. Some of these people – not all of them by any means – have a deep faith in science to solve problems. They believe people and governments will do the right thing when they come to understand what science reveals about pollution or other impacts to the environment, and how those impacts can affect us.

- Some people view the way we produce food as key to how we treat the environment. They use their dollars to purchase food that's raised closer to home, with fewer chemical inputs and less processing, food that's healthier for them and their families. The also get involved in trying to change our food production system for the better.

- Some people are motivated by a sense of justice. They regard pollution as someone dumping garbage or even poisons onto someone else – into their water, into their lungs, into their neighborhoods. They see fighting pollution as fighting injustice.

- Some people feel connected with animals, but in a different way than hunters do. Many people are instructed by the story of Noah's Ark that animals are mankind's companions on earth, and that we need to behave respectfully toward them. Maybe their beliefs lead them to become vegetarians. Or maybe they express their concern through their relationship with their pets. Or maybe they work to protect wildlife habitat or species of animals whose very existence is in danger.

- And, speaking of Noah's Ark, some people are motivated by how they conceive of man's relationship to God – that how we treat Creation reflects how we feel about God.

- Some people want to be part of nature. Maybe they're backpackers or backcountry survivalists, maybe they are hunters or fishermen, or maybe they're people who simply seek inspiration from nature. As Henry Thoreau said, "I went to the woods because I wished to live deliberately, to front only the essential facts of life, and see if I could not learn what it had to teach, and not, when I came to die, discover that I had not lived."[1]

I don't know how many other factors may motivate people's feelings about the environment. People are influenced by factors like geography, how they were raised by their parents, and how they may have been personally affected by some kind of environmental damage. In my experience, people who care about the environment are moved by more than one factor. I know I am. And all these people we call "environmentalists" can be very, very different from one another.

I asked several people to write down for me what they think an environmentalist is, and found it to be a trickier question than I would have guessed. My wife Candace and I had a lengthy conversation one evening, and we never did reach a conclusion. Is it merely a belief? Does it imply personal involvement at a certain level? Is it enough to adopt a lifestyle where you reduce waste and recycle what you can? Or does it imply being politically involved as well?

Defining who people are – this can be tricky when those people are identified by their beliefs or their actions rather than race or national origin or something else that's readily visible or documented. For example, how would you describe what a Christian is? Is a personal belief enough to call yourself a Christian? Do you have to go to church to call yourself a Christian? Do you have to dress a certain way? Vote a certain way? Some Christians ask themselves, "What would Jesus do?" I think that's a great question, because it implies that the way you actually live is part of what defines you as a Christian. (Would Jesus dump toxic wastes into someone's watershed?)

But back to environmentalists. I asked a few environmentalists about what it means to be one.

The late Anne Charter told me that "an environmentalist is one concerned with all of God's creation and the inter-relation of all its parts and with the inter-relation with the people who inhabit it." Anne's life, though, went beyond concern – she was a direct pain in the neck to coal company executives and some politicians, and a public advocate for energy efficient building practices.

Mark Trechock, who used to work as the staff director of a North Dakota conservation group, described an environmentalist as "someone actively working on environmental policy issues, either for pay or as a volunteer."

Coloradan Amy McBride described an environmentalist as "someone whose way of living is respectful of the earth...making the reduction of your footprint on the planet a central part of your thinking and way of life."

Fishing guide Richard Parks told me, "An environmentalist is a person who understands that, while the web of life which supports us is very tough and very complex, it doesn't think through the consequences to us of how it responds to human actions, and it therefore behooves us to do so."

Wilderness advocate George Nickas told me he believes an environmentalist is "someone whose concern for protecting the environment goes beyond rhetoric to action, who is willing to make personal sacrifice in order to protect the environment and does it routinely enough that it is no longer considered sacrifice. That sacrifice might be small or large, the key is that environmental protection is part of their way of living."

Jeanne-Marie Souvigney, a longtime conservation activist, defined an environmentalist as "someone who acts to maintain and improve the quality of our air, lands, landscapes, and wildlife."

Cattle rancher Paul Hawks told me, "An environmentalist is someone who knows that we have to sustain the earth if we are to sustain ourselves."

Ellen Pfister, another rancher, said she regards an environmentalist as "One who realizes that plans and actions can have unintended consequences, and that many more things may be related than people would like to think."

Tennesseean Boomer Winfrey told me he considers an environmentalist to be "someone who has enough concern for his/her fellow man to become actively involved in improving the place in which we live."

In this small sampling of opinions, religion is there and so is personal lifestyle. Working on public policy is included. Understanding the interconnectedness of things is also part of it. Concern for our fellow man is wrapped up in it.

You can see there's no single opinion on what makes an environmentalist. But among all the people I heard from, there's one opinion that <u>didn't</u> show up in anyone's definition: none of them think that joining an environmental organization makes you an environmentalist.

To most of the people I contacted, being an environmentalist implies taking action or getting involved with other people to take action. That can be a broad definition. For the people I spoke to, that means getting involved in the public debate over an issue. This is inherently political, and that's pretty distasteful for a lot of people.

For myself, I believe that one's personal lifestyle is part of it. And I know from experience that a personal lifestyle comes with compromises. I drive a car more than I should, and I don't buy as much organic food as I ought to. I try to make conscientious buying decisions, but I don't know as much as I should, and life's little compromises sometimes get in the way anyhow.

Knowledge is definitely part of it, too. In a democracy, all citizens should be as informed as possible... that's why the Founding Fathers placed such a high value on freedom of the press. But there's an awful lot of information out there, and some of it just isn't credible.

But for you and me and any other American, if we care and gain some knowledge, we <u>can</u> take action. Some people limit their actions to things that nobody would disagree with, like picking up trash along a highway. It's worthwhile, but it's not the kind of action that really changes anything. It doesn't challenge the mindset that put the trash along the highway.

Neither does cultivating an organic garden, heating water with solar collectors, recycling, driving a hybrid car, riding a bicycle, taking our kids into the woods, or helping build a nature center in our community. These are all good things, but – to me – they don't challenge the mindset (and the political policy that comes with the mindset) that has made it acceptable to dump pesticides, dry cleaning chemicals, soot, asbestos, heavy metals, carbon dioxide, garbage, and sewage into our surroundings. They don't challenge the mindset (and the political policy that comes with it) of irresponsible mining practices, animal factories, clearcut forests, depleted aquifers, and the failure of public agencies to enforce standards that are supposed to protect the air that Americans breathe, protect the water that we drink, protect our land, our health, and our children.

Taking action to challenge that mindset is political. And, for understandable reasons, a lot of people detest getting involved with this. Politics is slow and it's messy. It usually seems tilted toward whomever has the most money or is willing to fight the dirtiest. And it always means compromise and delay.

So a lot of people just sit it out. For one reason or another, some people who genuinely care about the environment simply can't stand to get involved with politics. Instead, they join an organization (which at least helps the cause in some way) but don't want to take a personal role in a political process. For some people, this is just a function of where they are in their lives (e.g., living far away, being busy raising kids, etc.).

Some people convince themselves that shopping decisions and lifestyle choices will protect America's environment. They won't, not by themselves.

Getting involved with politics is hard and it's frustrating, and everyone has their limits. But it's a huge part of how good things and bad things happen in our nation. And it's something every American can do to one degree or another.

It's not the only way, though, and those people who are narrowly focused on politics still need to look at the tangible changes they can make in their own lives.

Unlike politics, this side of environmentalism can be done privately and alone. Lifestyle changes and smart shopping are not enough, not nearly enough, but they are necessary. It's important that I use less gasoline, less hot water, less electricity. It's important that I recycle as much as I can.

And then there are people who want to play a visible role, but they just can't stand the messiness and the glacial pace of politics. So they do something like chain themselves to a tree. This kind of act can actually hurt the cause by making it appear that only people who would chain themselves to trees are concerned about the issue. Sometimes, though, it succeeds at drawing attention to a problem. This is legitimate, and sometimes necessary. But it also is not enough. Want to dress up like a turtle and march down the street, chanting? OK, but tomorrow put on a necktie and get involved in politics, if you really want to make a difference over the long haul.

It's easy to dismiss and ridicule a guy in a turtle costume. It's not so easy to dismiss people who work hard and long, who build citizen power, and who get laws passed, hold agencies accountable, and go to court if necessary. These are the people who can challenge powerful interests, and that's why they make those powerful interests so mad. (And that's why these people get demonized in some circles.)

If I were to ask Rush Limbaugh or Ann Coulter or Ron Arnold why they feel the way they do about environmentalists, I can't imagine they'd be all that upset that some people prefer to waste less or drive economy cars or buy organically-raised beef.

I could be wrong, but I think it's more likely they feel the way they do because some environmentalists have been successful at challenging political or economic interests that Limbaugh or Coulter support. To prevent environmentalists from succeeding in the future, the people I've quoted at the beginning of this book have implemented a strategy to generate outright hatred toward Americans who want to protect a part of our country's environment. Make people think that Helen Waller is some kind of extremist. Make people think that Nick Golder believes in a pagan God. Make people think that Wally McRae is a Green Nazi, or that Eileen Morris is trying to dismantle industrial civilization.

Am I saying there's no such thing as a "wacko environmentalist?" Of course not... there's wacko everything.

There are moms and dads who do crazy things, and Republicans, and wage-earners, and business people, and blood relatives, and even Lutherans. Certainly there are some wacko environmentalists, people who don't understand the political process or economics or science.

But are all environmentalists wacko? Are all Lutherans? All Republicans? All business people and wage-earners?

CHAPTER NINE

Nazi Environmentalists???

"Hitler sounded remarkably like contemporary environmentalists."

. . . .

Just how far would someone go to get you to hate environmentalists? Well, a few people – and I've quoted a couple of them – like to use language that characterizes environmentalists as Nazis or fascists or Marxists or terrorists.

Writer Alston Chase, (in his book *In a Dark Wood: The Fight Over Forests and the Rising Tyranny of Ecology*) detailed how a German scientist – Ernst Haeckel – was the first to give a name to the science of ecology in 1866. Chase went from there to insinuating (without actually saying so directly) that the Nazis were philosophically rooted in environmentalism. He wrote, "To anyone who cares about the earth, the Nazi-ecology connection is profoundly disturbing."

Haeckel was a leading scientist of the 19th century who built upon the work of Charles Darwin and others who worked before Darwin. He was also viewed by many as an anti-Semite and ardent German nationalist... that's still being debated by scholars. Such anti-Semitism and German nationalism was a philosophy which took a twisted path toward the National Socialism that – after a few generations – became Hitler's Nazi Party. In his book, Chase constructed a case much like Marc Antony's speech in Shakespeare's *Julius Caesar*, making careful caveats that environmentalism doesn't lead to Nazism, yet proceeding with arguments that seem – to me, anyway – intended to imply that very thing. He referred to the "checkered past" of environmental ideas.

Meanwhile, some of the scientists quoted by Chase weren't too happy about their work being used that way. Robert Jay Lifton remarked, "To equate a notion of biodiversity, or some biological balance, with the rabid, lethal biological determinism of the Nazis is outrageous. This completely misuses my work. It takes actual scholarship and distorts it."[1]

Chase painted a picture of a Nazi Germany committed to a pastoral rural life, organic agriculture, and the protection of wildlife. The Nazis, in his description, were against industrialization. He quoted the late historian Robert Pois in saying, "Hitler sounded remarkably like contemporary environmentalists," and that Hitler believed in "the sanctity of nature."

This doesn't sound much like pre-WWII Germany, does it? Somewhere along the way, Chase's description of the Nazis omitted the fact that the Nazis dramatically industrialized Germany in order to build up the biggest war machine the world had yet witnessed. And it wasn't just the military machine – it was ramped-up steel production and other heavy manufacturing, it was building new highways, motorizing the nation, and developing a synthetic gasoline program to fuel those motors through expanded coal production. The nature-loving Nazi Germany portrayed by Chase bears little resemblance to the real Nazi Germany that stopped at nothing to build and fuel a modern military juggernaut.

But perhaps the main fact that writers like Chase have ignored altogether is the fact that American environmentalism was well under way before Haeckel's ideas were ever published.

As early as the 1600s, British colonies in the New World began to regulate the harvest of certain natural resources such as timber and wildlife. The first forest management experiment in the United States began in 1828.[2]

American scientists (e.g., John Bartram, Thomas Jefferson in the 1700s), American artists (e.g., George Catlin and John James Audubon in the early 1800s), and American writers (e.g., William Cullen Bryant and James Fenimore Cooper in the early 1800s) had done much to bring our country's flora, fauna, and landscape to the public's attention.[3]

In May of 1832, artist George Catlin spent time at a fur company's fort on the current location of Ft. Pierre, South Dakota. When he wrote about his experience (published in 1844), Catlin proposed a "nation's Park," where the buffalo and the Plains Indians could continue to live as they had before the nation's growth began to threaten them.

Ralph Waldo Emerson's treatise, *Nature*, was published in 1835, and his second essay by that same title appeared in 1844. Henry David Thoreau was actively publishing his nature essays in the 1840s, and his classic *Walden* was printed in 1854. In 1855, Walt Whitman published the original edition of *Leaves of Grass*.

In 1864, George Perkins Marsh published his landmark book, *Man and Nature; or Physical Geography as Modified by Human Action*. Marsh detailed the destructive effects of deforestation, and how it had led to the decline of earlier societies.[4]

Also in 1864, Congress granted the Yosemite Valley to the state of California to be set aside for protection as a state park (Yellowstone, the world's first national park, would be created eight years later, and Yosemite would become a national park in 1890).[5]

By the time Ernst Haeckel introduced the term "ecology" to the scientific world in 1866, the American conservation movement had already sent its roots deep. It was already part of our nation's literary tradition. A parks movement was already in progress and America would soon establish the world's first national park. We had long since been regulating natural resource harvests. And John Muir had already begun the wanderings that would soon take him to California and later lead to the founding of the Sierra Club.

Before the Nazis appeared on the world scene, the United States had established a system of national forests and established the United States Forest Service to administer them. The national parks movement had grown, and the 1916 Organic Act systemized the national parks and created the National Park Service.

Does respecting the importance of nature and of conserving natural resources make you a Nazi?

The late Anne Charter told me once, "We have been blessed with a vast, wonderful country filled with many resources. It is our responsibility to take care of this tremendous gift." Does that make her a Nazi?

Montana wheat farmer Arlo Skari says that, "If we love this country, we must take care of it in all its aspects so the following generations can enjoy it in perpetuity." Does that make him a Nazi?

The late Les Scramsted, one of the asbestos victims in Libby, Montana, told me, "The country I love is 'America the Beautiful.' To protect what I love, I became an environmentalist with the concept of being a good steward of the land." Nazi thinking?

Janet Zimmerman from Pony, Montana, told me simply, "conservation of our natural resources is a true sign of a Patriot."

Boyd Charter fought to protect the environment. He even helped start an organization that still fights to protect the environment. So, was World War II veteran Boyd Charter really a Nazi at heart? When he fought to protect his Montana ranch from the coal companies, was he really trying to install some sort of green despotism in America?

CHAPTER TEN

American Liberty

Does someone who loves America have to let their farm be strip-mined?

. . . .

A merica is the greatest country in the world, and that didn't happen by itself.
It took work, courage, enterprise, loyalty, capacity to change, and belief in
the future among people who were born here and people who came here by
choice. Together, they defended our nation, grew our food, cleaned our hotel
rooms, built our homes, healed the sick, educated our children, and stood up for
what was right even when it was unpopular.

But all their work and all their progress could be undone. And the most likely
way this could happen is for money to become more important than liberty,
more important than justice, and more important than a healthy future for our
children.

When everything is measured in dollars, we will no longer be the nation that
the Founding Fathers conceived and that generations of Americans have faith-
fully tried to build ever since.

In the late 1990s, I attended a presentation by an environmental activist from
Azerbaijan (located on the Caspian Sea, it used to be part of the old Soviet Union). She explained that her organization had formed after the Soviet Union collapsed, when western oil companies began making plans to develop the oil
reserves there and build pipelines across neighboring countries.

As she described her organization's work, it became clear that they have an
enormously difficult time addressing environmental issues in a country that
doesn't have a democratic tradition. Although the Soviet-era government had
collapsed and her homeland was newly independent, there were no real avenues
for citizens to affect the policies that her government adopted.

Montana rancher and WWII veteran Boyd Charter probably wouldn't have lasted long in Azerbaijan.

But being an American, he did the American thing. In the early 1970s, he and his wife Anne talked with neighbors and friends who shared their concerns. Boyd and Anne and a few others co-founded a citizens group, the Northern Plains Resource Council. They did their homework. They organized. They sought better coal mine reclamation laws at the state and federal levels. They worked for laws to protect the land, air, and water upon which their ranch depended. They lobbied to improve the rights of landowners who live above federally-owned coal deposits. They challenged bureaucrats who were paid by the taxpayers but who, for all practical purposes, worked for the coal industry.

The Northern Plains Resource Council probably wouldn't have thrived in Azerbaijan, either. Neither would other American environmental organizations.

When you look around the world, where are environmental groups active? You don't see many of them in totalitarian societies. You see them primarily in countries that have a democratic tradition. Those who would protect the environment need a freedom-loving society.

It wasn't until South Africa got rid of apartheid that environmental organizations were allowed to operate there. The country is paying today for a century of ignoring the toxic pollution of gold mining. Taxpayers there will have to pay a lot of money eventually to clean up polluted water that ruins property and makes people sick.[1]

When farmer Helen Waller got involved in challenging strip mines being planned near her Circle, Montana, farm, she was able to play a part as a citizen largely because benchmark environmental laws like the National Environmental Policy Act (NEPA) established processes to guarantee that citizens have the right to take part in policy decisions. NEPA doesn't mandate any particular environmental outcome, it mandates that citizens in the United States have a right to participate. It was laws like NEPA, upholding the public's right to participate, that made it possible for Helen to protect her farm and her family. Laws like this don't exist in dictatorships. They exist in places like America, where citizens are valued, where the participation of citizens is welcomed.

But right here in America, laws like NEPA, the Clean Water Act, and numerous state laws that also foster citizen participation have been under heavy attack. At the state and national level, legislative attacks on environmentalists have often become attacks on the right of citizens to participate. Legislative attacks against the work of environmentalists often translate into attacks on democracy itself:

- making it easier for polluters and agencies to exclude citizens from meaningful public involvement;

- making it harder for citizens to get information about what government agencies are doing;

- making it harder for citizens to gain access to the courts to defend natural resource protections; and

- making it harder for citizens to take an issue directly to the voters.

It's getting a little more like Azerbaijan.

Democratic processes and the laws that guarantee them are what make the activities of environmentalists possible. Environmental advocates depend on the right to participate.

Fishing guide Richard Parks is a citizen in the fullest sense. He participates. He studies. He speaks up. He writes, he meets with fellow citizens, he lobbies those who enact laws in his state capital of Helena and in his nation's capital. He's never been paid for any of the environmental work he does. He depends on liberty in order to do what he does as an environmental activist. He depends on clean rivers to run his business.

Are environmentalists really Communists? Ron Arnold called them, "Watermelons - green on the outside, red on the inside."[2] Columnist George Will once described the environmental movement as "a green tree with red roots."[3]

People who work to protect the environment, myself included, have long been accused of having pro-Communist tendencies or being otherwise against personal freedom – an ironic claim because Communist countries always had the worst pollution and the weakest rights for citizens to fight it. From Eastern Europe, to the Soviet Union, to China, to North Korea, to Cuba, Communist countries had no historical concern with protecting the quality of the environment in which their people live.

Back in 1982, the East German council of ministers declared that all environmental data was a state secret. Five years later, the secret police raided and shut down an environmental library and underground magazine that had tried to make environmental information available to citizens. That's how citizens concerned about the heavy load of carbon and chemical pollution in East Germany had to operate... state suppression of public dialog on the environment was routine there.[4]

The Soviet nuclear plant program brushed aside all safety and environmental concerns, leading to the Chernobyl disaster. Philip R. Pryde of Republicans for Environmental Protection observed that: "...the average life expectancy of workers in some of the major coal mining regions of Russia is under 50. Many Russian rivers are so polluted that their waters cannot even be used beneficially by industry."[5]

Late in 2005, an industrial explosion killed several people and discharged toxic, carcinogenic solvents into China's Songhua River (which flows through Russia further downstream). The release of these solvents was initially met with a cover-up by the polluter and a range of government officials. Word got out, at which point the chagrinned government implemented measures to protect the millions of people along that river. At the end of the year, Chinese officials admitted that about 300 million people in China's countryside drink water that is tainted by chemicals and other contaminants.[6]

Since then, we have read and heard a steady stream of stories about pollution in China, about people being poisoned by industrial wastes, about air that is thick with God knows what poisons.

In Russia, in January 2010, plainclothes police officers raided the office of an environmental group called Baikal Wave. What the group had done was criticize the government's plan to re-open a large paper plant that had long polluted Lake Baikal, the world's largest body of fresh water. The government's objective in carrying out the raid, it quickly became clear, was to seize the group's computers and the information stored on them.

Russian security officials have carried out dozens of similar raids in recent years, confiscating the computers of citizen groups using fabricated charges of software piracy, even drawing in the help of the Microsoft Corporation to help silence the advocacy organizations.[7]

Why would an environmentalist want America to be like that? Dictatorships of all kinds are inconsistent with environmentalism.

Novelist and historian Wallace Stegner wrote in 1960 that, "Something will have gone out of us as a people if we ever let the remaining wilderness be destroyed... We need wilderness preserved – as much of it as is still left, and as many kinds – because it was the challenge against which our character as a people was formed."[8]

Author Edward Abbey didn't have many kind words to say about national environmental organizations, but he was a fiery defender of wild spaces in the West. Abbey made a lot of deliberately outrageous overstatements in his life, intended to poke fun at crooked politicians, moralistic environmentalists, and greedy developers. However, he got serious when he spoke of what wild nature means to freedom-loving people, and this theme resonated through his essays and his novels. He talked about how the discovery of America loosed the feudal bonds of Europe, and seemed to promise a "new age of freedom." [9]

Theodore Roosevelt felt that, "Conservation is a great moral issue, for it involves the patriotic duty of ensuring the safety and continuance of the nation."[10]

Ninety years later, Republican environmental activist Philip Pryde said, "People cannot be truly patriotic if they fly the flag on the Fourth of July and pollute a productive American river on the fifth."[11]

Sometimes we Americans talk about energy independence as a point of patriotism.

But our nation has depended on oil – mostly foreign oil – for well over a century. To secure sources for that oil, we've had to ally ourselves with the anti-democratic governments that sit atop much of the world's oil reserves.

Arlie and David Hochschild wrote in the months following the September 11, 2001, attacks that "...perhaps the most meaningful and lasting contribution Americans can make to the anti-terrorism efforts is to break the oil habit."[12]

Just over 2% of the world's proven oil reserves are in the U.S.[13], yet we consume over 20% of the world's oil production.

America took a few steps toward making better use of energy from the sun and wind more than three decades ago. But we backtracked. We decided instead to drill our own lands more than we already had and, for a generation, we increased – not decreased – our dependence on foreign oil and on the governments that control that oil. David Morris of the Institute for Local Self-Reliance in Minnesota called this approach the "exhaust America first" plan.

Today, we're drilling more than ever in the U.S., and we have finally made what is likely a short-term dent in the percentage of our oil consumption that's imported. But it's coming at a price that includes farmland converted to oil waste pits, soils polluted by pipeline breaks and saltwater spills, rural communities no longer livable or affordable, and aquifers depleted to provide water for hydraulic fracturing. Most of that water leaves the hydrologic cycle forever, sequestered deep underground and polluted with a stew of toxic chemicals.

A great deal of that oil and gas being produced today will be exported. Sometimes oil companies like to talk about energy independence if it means they get to do more drilling. But when it comes to transporting and selling that oil and gas, suddenly energy independence isn't quite as important to them.

Even if the oil and gas boom were a net gain for America, it remains a finite energy source that, when burned, will put more greenhouse gases into our atmosphere.

The fact remains that oil and gas and coal all share those same flaws – they will run out, and they will disrupt the earth's climate. Year after year after year, every year worse than the year before.

America needs energy that will never run out, like the sun and the wind. America needs energy that doesn't excrete greenhouse gases and other pollution into the air we breathe.

The nuclear power industry (the people who once promised electricity "too cheap to meter") tells us – and a number of environmentalists have bought into this – that nuclear-generated electricity is a viable alternative to fossil fuels because it produces no greenhouse gases. That's another debate, because the nuclear option involves a whole new set of environmental problems and other societal costs, from the mining of precious aquifers, disposal of radioactive mine tailings, the mishap-ridden record of the reactors themselves, the increased production of material that could be used in nuclear weapons, and the end problem of how to dispose of reactor waste that stays dangerously radioactive for tens of thousands of years.

Such an imagined tradeoff also stands in contradiction to our actual experience... during the dramatic expansion of nuclear power in the U.S., we did not use less coal. To the contrary, our extraction and burning of coal increased at the same time. What the nuclear expansion did accomplish was to delay America's ability and will to wean ourselves from energy sources that will eventually run out. Nuclear power doesn't guarantee independence from foreign energy sources. And it's not renewable.

Meanwhile, developing sun and wind power on a large scale is going to take time. We've already squandered decades by walking away from renewables in the early 1980s. By continuing to put off a serious commitment to renewable power, we continue to make our nation dependent on – and vulnerable to – foreign energy sources and energy corporations that have little loyalty to us and our democratic traditions. We continue to destroy our own land and watersheds and the air our children breathe to extract energy from the ground. Is this an act of patriotism?

And energy conservation? The return on investment is quick, so it saves money. It creates jobs, and not just in a few places.

I came across a 1942 issue of *House Beautiful* magazine – in an article titled "The Patriotism of Insulation," the magazine explained the value of energy conservation to American homeowners and to our nation during wartime.[14] It was a far cry from what our national leadership told us in 2002 – as we prepared for war in Iraq – when they offered tax breaks for buying gas-guzzling SUVs.[15]

As a nation, we can get serious about making our buildings and our vehicles more efficient. We can gather solar power – for heat or for electricity – on our nation's rooftops. Along the way, we can create jobs, save energy, and save money.

We can end this dependence on dictators – foreign or corporate – and on dirty energy. We can secure our energy future, strengthen our economy, reduce the pollution we inflict on ourselves and our children, and renew our commitment to democracy by building a foundation under solar and wind energy today.

If our democratic processes are to take us in this direction, it will be due – in large part – to the persistent work of freedom-loving citizens doing something characteristically American: organizing with other citizens, petitioning their government, taking part in public hearings, testifying on legislation, lobbying their elected representatives, sometimes even asserting their rights in court.

No doubt, some people will once again call them "Nazis" or "environmental al-Qaida." But the time is here to ask ourselves, is it patriotic to destroy watersheds? Does someone who loves America have to let their farm be strip-mined? Does a good American have to go along with poisoning our people? Our rivers? Our parks? And is restricting public participation a tool for greater democracy?

Many Americans don't think so. Many Americans see that our liberty will be more secure when we no longer link our nation's future to the prosperity of dictators or corporations that have no national loyalty whatsoever, unless it can be made to pay.

In the end, Boyd Charter was about freedom. Wild places are about freedom. Citizen activists are about freedom. The solar transition is about freedom.

O, beautiful for spacious skies,
For amber waves of grain,
For purple mountain majesties,
Above the fruited plain!

Katherine Lee Bates, America the Beautiful, 1913

CHAPTER ELEVEN

How I Came to Be an Environmentalist

If you find environmentalists inconvenient, then I guess it helps to have a caricature of them.

....

I was a lot luckier than some of the other environmentalists I talked to. Nobody was dumping poison into my water or threatening to strip-mine my family's property. (Not that we had any property.) More than anything, I grew into the role, and discovered how things are connected.

When I was a boy in Sioux Falls, South Dakota, my father bought a camera for our household. It was a little Kodak Brownie, and I was allowed to use it on my own once in a while (black and white film mostly, because color film was expensive). Among the earliest snapshots I remember taking were a pair of photos showing marks left by a bird that had briefly settled on the snow. I liked the design of the feathers in the snow, but I also liked how those marks showed a little something of nature at work.

Although this was the cheapest possible camera, it helped open a door for me, taught me how to look a little more carefully at nature—at what was going on, what had happened, what was going to happen. More than anything, using a camera helped sharpen my eyes for what was happening at my feet, on the horizon, in the sky. It helped me understand how I am connected to all those goings-on.

Like many children, I enjoyed picking up rocks. Sioux Falls is situated on glaciated prairie, in the middle of rich farm country. The soil is the most important geological feature there, and the rocks at the surface of the ground are almost all rounded beyond recognition from being transported by ancient glaciers. Still, I liked to bring home rocks.

I think one appeal that rocks have for many children is that they are so real. The world of a child is filled with imitations of things. Those imitations might be made out of metal or plastic or wood, but a child figures out before too long that they are mere imitations of real objects. Rocks are as real as things get. They are hard. They are ancient. They often hold mysteries. I still enjoy rocks. I still have boxes of them in my basement, and a few displayed in my living room.

My dad and I lived in an apartment complex in Sioux Falls. Just down the hill from the lower parking lot was an undeveloped area my friends and I simply called "the woods." We spent a lot of time chasing around in the woods, imagining bigger woods and longer chases.

One autumn day, I captured a big striped caterpillar and brought it home in a jar. The next day I took it to school and, to everyone's surprise, by the end of the day it had attached itself to the inside of the jar lid and begun to make a cocoon. We looked it up in a reference book and discovered this caterpillar would become a monarch butterfly.

I left it in the classroom, sure that it was going to be a great learning experience for all of us in my class. But accidents happen… someone bumped the jar a few weeks later and the cocoon broke loose and fell to the bottom. The cocoon eventually turned black and we realized that the life inside it had most likely ended. We held on to it through the winter and spring, but it never opened. A disappointment, but monarch butterflies have been special to me ever since. Years later, when scientists discovered that monarchs migrate thousands of miles to winter in a small area in Mexico, it underscored to me how sturdy these little creatures are, and yet how vulnerable, since they depend for their survival on the health of a small patch of trees in a small part of a faraway place. And the survival of each generation depends on milkweed, a common plant that is rapidly disappearing due to expanded use of pesticides and the increasing scarcity of undeveloped lands where it grows.

I enjoyed "Westerns" and other television and movie dramas in which the outdoors was a prominent part of the story. I admired characters who were comfortable in nature and were able to "read" it. I felt such characters were more independent, and were rarely motivated by greed.

Remember what 1 Timothy 6:10 and my old co-worker Wilf Clark said about simple human greed? The reason I remember it is that, in many stories I've come across from an early age – whether a fictional story in a book or movie or in a play, or a true account of actual events – I learned that greed is at the heart of many of mankind's moral failures. And as an adult, I learned that simple human greed is at the heart of many environmental conflicts. We humans always seem to want more than we have. And we have pierced ourselves through with many sorrows.

It wasn't that I thought wealth was bad. After all, I liked watching TV's Cartwrights – Ben, Adam, Hoss, and Little Joe – with their sprawling Ponderosa ranch and their big house and their Chinese cook, Hop Sing. Their wealth was readily apparent, but they took stands against villains who were exploiting other people or despoiling the land and water. I admired that. Wealth and greed aren't the same.

Dad and I moved to Rapid City, South Dakota, when I was ten. He had been out of work for a time, and Rapid City was a growing town where housepainters would have better prospects. Dad had lived in Rapid City when he was younger, and always had a fondness for the nearby Black Hills.

But our spare time in the Hills mainly consisted of Sunday drives. I remember enjoying a particular outing to Roughlock Falls, a popular stop adjoining Spearfish Canyon. Dad told me it was OK to drink the water from the creek... I had never done that before. My cousin Carol and I waded up the creek to the base of the falls and Dad took our picture.

During a couple summers, I spent a week at a church camp, a place called Outlaw Ranch. We hiked, rode horses, sang camp songs, and met people from other towns. It wasn't exactly a communion with nature, but the surrounding hills and forests made it a great place for communion with other people.

Dad and I attended a Lutheran Church in Rapid City. One of the hymns we often sang (by Reginald Heber in 1826) had a line in it that went...

Holy, holy, holy, Lord God Almighty,
All thy works shall praise thy name in earth and sky and sea!

It made sense to me that, if God created the universe and the universe is full of praise for God, then I shouldn't behave in ways that destroy God's creation. It made sense to me that if God takes pleasure in His creation *("...and God saw that it was good"),* then it's probably OK if I also take pleasure in it. What it all comes down to is this – the God of the stars is the God of the soil; the Lord of the universe is the Lord of the chickadee.

As a young man, several books I read complemented what I had been learning in church. They were written by American writers with American ideas about the American land.

I can still remember that little book *On the Loose,* by Terry and Renny Russell. It was a very personal collection of thoughts by two young men, just a little older than I was at the time. One of these brothers died in a rafting accident shortly before the book was published.

I'm pretty sure *On the Loose* is no longer in print. It's not a conventional book at all, with hand-lettered text, a passionately-produced combination of the Russells' thoughts and quotes of others. The text was illuminated by photographs which were, in the authors' own words: "the lowest fidelity obtainable. They are as far from the photographer's vision as cheap cameras, mediocre film, and drugstore processing could make them."

On the Loose was more passion than intellect, but it was honest, and it helped me to get a better grasp on what I was feeling in my own heart and mind. There is a passage in the book where the Russell brothers wrote:

We must look funny to Someone,

Tumbling through the universe locked in a death grip with our tiny ball Earth and ripping her busily to pieces, trailing a stinking film of gas and pieces of satellites and mushroom and dust clouds.

Think of her new.

An unspoiled country lying open to the sun.

Think of oceans of beauty instead of scattered puddles, muddy and drying up.

The book asks, *Was I just born too late?*

And the answer:

No.

My salvation is that I was not born into the adolescence of my race.
Its beautiful childhood may be gone, but its manhood is now.

While *On the Loose* was about the love of beauty and not about politics, this line reminded me that it's not enough to love the beauty of the earth. I must also work to protect it.

When I was old enough to go out on my own, my friends and I spent many days and nights exploring the Black Hills. This small range of hills is built upon varied geology arranged in concentric rings, starting with a sandstone hogback and ending in the south-center with granite spires. Black Hills weather also varies a great deal from north to south and east to west, and all this variation shapes the plants and animals that live there.

About half the area of the Black Hills is made up of public land, mostly national forest, so we were free to follow paths through the pine forests, or to leave the paths and find our own way over hills and across streams. Together, my friends and I discovered many places new to us, and we value them still. Though I haven't lived there for more than 20 years, I still carry this landscape in my heart.

When certain development schemes arose that threatened this special landscape, that's when I finally got involved with other people to protect it. The first one I remember was a proposal by a Colorado company to build a tourist tramway up Harney Peak, the highest point in the Black Hills. For many years, commercial Jeep rides for tourists had ripped up the trails on Harney Peak. Those rides had since been discontinued, and now someone was planning to cut a permanent scar onto Harney Peak's slopes to transport tourists up the mountain by tramway, turning it into a busy motorized destination and pocketing a lot of money.

Let me tell you a little bit about Harney Peak. It is small by Rocky Mountain standards, but at 7,242 feet, it is nevertheless a mountain – the highest point east of the Rockies. Its top is a prominent outcrop of pegmatite granite, surrounded by ponderosa pine forest. It is not a primeval scene; for a few decades, fire lookouts manned a tower on the summit, built from the same granite the mountain is made of. Just a few yards away, a narrow mountaintop canyon contains a small dam that captured rainwater for the lookout personnel. Just below the summit was a log cabin, where the lookouts lived during fire season. The cabin is gone now, and the fire lookout has not been manned since the 1960s.

Mountain goats frequent its highest places, and the wind is almost always blowing there. From the top, you can see Terry Peak, at the northern end of the Black Hills. You can see the back of Mt. Rushmore. You can see the granite landmarks of the Needles, the Cathedral Spires, and Little Devil's Tower.

You can also see highways and mining scars. In the summer, tourist helicopters violate the quiet with their low-altitude flights. So does the tourist train in Hill City, where the sound of its steam whistle travels for miles. On summer days, quite a few people make the hike from nearby Sylvan Lake. Some of them are respectful of the place, some of them are loud and litter-prone.

The place is magnificent, but there's a sense that its magnificence is unraveling.

In the book *Black Elk Speaks* by John Neihardt, the aged medicine man Black Elk refers to Harney Peak as "the tall rock mountain at the center of the world." The Black Hills are sacred land to the Lakota (Sioux), who reigned on the surrounding plains for a century or so. Harney Peak stands at the heart of that land. The Black Hills are also a sacred place to me and some of my friends.

I was 21 when Dad died. I didn't inherit any land. I didn't inherit a house or a car. There was no life insurance, no savings account. When Dad died, I inherited his clothes, his fishing rod and tackle box, and an old desk. We had some dishes and pans and, because Dad was a smoker, I inherited a couple ash trays. And there was our photo album. It had a picture of me holding a northern pike I had caught, and the photo he took of me and my cousin Carol standing in the creek just below Roughlock Falls. Of course, Dad gave me more than those material things.

The only reason I even mention the lack of personal property in our household is because I've heard environmentalists like me characterized as idle, wealthy people who don't need to earn a living, people who want to keep nature as sort of a pristine playground for themselves.

It was after Sam Clauson's collection agency contacted me about my late father's debts, after he and I talked about the tramway someone wanted to build up Harney Peak – that was when I joined an environmental group for the first time.

Sam grew up in eastern South Dakota and recalls how his mother taught her seven children that "we share this planet with thousands of species of plants, birds, fish, and animals."

After a stint in the Army, Sam moved to Rapid City, where he bought into a local collection agency, collecting on bad debts for local businesses. Sam's collection agency had been contracted to collect an unpaid medical bill of my father's. When I told him that Dad had died, and that there was no estate except for his clothes and household belongings, Sam wrote off the debt.

I had previously heard of Sam's involvement in trying to save Harney Peak from the proposed tourist tramway. We visited for a while in his office… he was a leader in the local Sierra Club group that had recently formed, and told me a bit about what that its members were doing. Not long afterward, I sent in a membership check.

Sam had become a local leader of the public opinion that was overwhelmingly against the tramway proposal. He had two young daughters at the time, but he took on this issue, forming that local Sierra Club group in the process. It was a small organization with a real dedication to saving what was left of the Black Hills and keeping it from falling to pieces.

The tramway proposal eventually faded away.

The Sierra Club group that Sam helped form began to organize outings into the Black Hills and Badlands. They also challenged some of the U.S. Forest Service's practices involving logging and roadbuilding on the public lands in the Hills, especially on theretofore undeveloped lands.

The group's officers came from varied work backgrounds, their politics were different, and their priorities weren't all the same, but they all agreed that some places in western South Dakota should be protected under the Wilderness Act. Its members advocated for wilderness protection of a few undeveloped areas of the Black Hills National Forest, Badlands National Park, and Buffalo Gap National Grasslands.

We were able to make a strong enough showing of public support to convince Republican Congressman James Abdnor, normally no ally of environmental protection, to introduce a bill to protect the Harney Peak area as an officially designated wilderness area in 1979. Established by Congress in 1980, that wilderness area is comparatively small, just over 13,000 acres, but it was the first – and so far the only – wilderness area established in the Black Hills. Its acreage amounts to just over one-half of one percent of the Black Hills, just over one percent of the national forest land in the Hills. To some vocal advocates of motorized recreation, protecting even that much American wilderness is too much.

Rep. Abdnor had originally intended to name it the "Harney Peak Wilderness," but he went along with suggestions to name it after Black Elk, the Lakota holy man.

Mining is just one threat facing the Black Hills. These ancient hills contain many kinds of rock, some of them heavily mineralized. For a century and a quarter, the Homestake Mining Company operated a gold mine that was, for many of those years, the largest in America. The Homestake Mine destroyed Whitewood Creek, making it one of the nation's most thoroughly polluted waterways, and one that was eventually cleaned up because determined regulators forced innovation that would have been unlikely to develop on its own.

In some places, the historic gold mining in the Black Hills was accomplished by small-scale placer mining and, in some places, with terribly destructive dredges that left behind creek bottoms still scarred today. More modern gold mining was undertaken with the cyanide heap-leach process, which processes the ore using cyanide in open-air piles, and which have a habit of losing that cyanide, along with metals and acidic water, into watersheds and groundwater. This modern type of mining is capable of economically recovering gold from very low-grade ores, meaning that such a mine will sometimes blow apart entire mountaintops to recover tiny amounts of gold. (There was a mine in Montana that operated in the 1980s and 1990s which mined 66 *tons* of ore for every *ounce* of gold recovered! Just think of how much mountain has to be torn away for that gold, the vast majority of which would be used in jewelry.) Pegmatite minerals in the southern Black Hills have found many uses, though not as much today as in the mid-twentieth century. Pink limestone is quarried in numerous locations. With a lot of federal government encouragement, uranium was mined from the early 1950s, to the early 70s, and may be mined again.

Though ponderosa pines are not exceptionally large trees, the Black Hills are one of the most heavily logged national forests in the West, about 25,000 acres annually.[1] That's about twice the acreage of the Black Elk Wilderness – every year – and your tax dollars subsidize it. The national forest contains about three and a half miles of roads for every square mile of the forest, among the most heavily roaded of the national forests. To many people who care about the Hills, those roads are the worst impact of logging because, after the timber harvest, they provide easy access for more motorized vehicles to go deeper into the forest. This steadily shrinks the areas where there is quiet, where wildlife is undisturbed. It means more litter. It means deeper ruts in the roads, and thus more erosion, and thus more silt in small mountain streams.

Like other areas across the nation, the Black Hills face ever-increasing pressure from subdivision development. Rural subdivisions take away wildlife habitat, bring yet more people into the forest, more wells drawing on the aquifers, more septic tanks, more lawn chemicals, more noise, and more loose dogs harassing wildlife.

The Black Hills have long attracted tourists. Even before the carving of Mount Rushmore was completed in 1941, tourists used to visit the Black Hills for scenery, for the cool nights in summer. Of course, the presence of tourists leads to tourist attractions, which lead to wider highways, more motels, more gas stations, more stores, more restaurants, and untold numbers of gaudy billboards. Billboards are a big deal in South Dakota, for there is a deeply held mythology that billboards are what keep a tourist place in business.

It's not that I was ever against all mining, logging, homebuilding, or tourism – it's that the Black Hills are a comparatively little range of hills and mountains, and they can't absorb everything that people want to do to them. I believed as a young man that, out of the two million acres in the Black Hills, at least some decent measure of these lands should be protected from the impacts of mining and logging and industrial tourism and subdivision development. How about 5 percent? Was that so unreasonable? 50 percent of the Black Hills belongs to the people of the United States. Can't we as a people make a decision that five percent of this little range of hills and mountains should remain how God created it? Doesn't quiet have some value for us humans? Doesn't space for wild animals and wild streams have some value?

I was never asking for the Black Hills to be de-populated. I never asked for the entire West to be returned to its primeval state. I've never asked people to live in tipis and travel by horseback.

What I asked as a young man was that a decent remnant of this land to be allowed to exist in its natural state. Many years later, some people in the Black Hills still make this request of politicians and federal land management agencies. Whenever they do, extractive industries and motorized recreationists shout "NO!" They add, "Any protected land is too much! Logging and mining companies must be allowed to cut trees and build roads on every square mile of the forest, four-wheelers must be able to ride over every square inch of the forest. Access to 95 percent of this forest isn't enough… we must have 100 percent!"

Living in Montana now, I don't see these conflicts up close anymore. But the Black Hills are a special landscape in my heart, and the times I spent climbing their rocky slopes, soaking my feet in their cool streams, or sleeping on beds of kinnikinnick– these times are a big part of why I became an environmentalist. And I've seen how the issues that play out in this little range of hills and mountains are played out in many other places.

That little book *On the Loose* was just one of many that guided me toward a life of involvement with environmental issues. Here are just a few.

Walden, by Henry David Thoreau, helped me stop and take notice of what was around me. I used to know people who would go on a hike and it was all about how far they went, or how fast, or how exotic the location. Thoreau helped me to slow down and absorb the loveliness, the roughness, the interconnectedness of my surroundings.

If the day and the night are such that you greet them with joy, and life emits a fragrance like flowers and sweet-scented herbs, is more elastic, more starry, more immortal,

-- that is your success. All nature is your congratulation, and you have cause momentarily to bless yourself. The greatest gains and values are farthest from being appreciated. We easily come to doubt if they exist. We soon forget them. They are the highest reality. Perhaps the facts most astounding and most real are never communicated by man to man. The true harvest of my daily life is somewhat as intangible as the tints of morning or evening. It is a little star-dust caught, a segment of the rainbow which I have clutched.

Aldo Leopold's 1949 book, *Sand County Almanac,* called on us to expand our sense of ethics to include the land and the creatures that live on the land.

One basic weakness in a conservation system based wholly on economic motives is that most members of the land community have no economic value. Wildflowers and songbirds are examples. Of the 22,000 higher plants and animals native to Wisconsin, it is doubtful whether more than 5 per cent can be sold, fed, eaten, or otherwise put to economic use. Yet these creatures are members of the biotic community, and if (as I believe) its stability depends on its integrity, they are entitled to continuance.

Historian and novelist Wallace Stegner wrote a letter in 1960 to comment on a state commission report on outdoor recreation in California. His letter took on the subject broadly, and he observed how important wilderness is to the character of Americans, how it is "part of the geography of hope."

...the wilderness as opportunity and as idea, the thing that has helped to make an American different from and, until we forget it in the roar of our industrial cities, more fortunate than other men. For an American, insofar as he is new and different at all, is a civilized man who has renewed himself in the wild.

Wendell Berry reminded me of the importance of my personal actions, not just as an activist, but as a human being. In an essay called "The Nature Consumers" (in his book *The Long-Legged House),* he wrote:

Nature has never permitted freedom from responsibility.

In another essay, "Think Little," in his book *A Continuous Harmony,* Berry told me again that activism alone isn't everything, warning me against:

...too little personal involvement, and too much involvement in organizations that were insisting that other *organizations should do what was right.*

He went on to say:

We need better government, no doubt about it. But we also need better minds, better friendships, better marriages, better communities.

Written during the Vietnam War, "Think Little" reminded me that the environmental movement is bigger and more important than a lot of environmentalists realize:

The mentality that exploits and abuses the natural environment is the same that abuses racial and economic minorities, that imposes on young men the tyranny of the military draft, that makes war against peasants and women and children with the indifference of technology. The mentality that destroys a watershed and then panics at the threat of flood is the same mentality that gives institutional insult to black people and then panics at the thought of race riots. It is the same mentality that can mount deliberate warfare against a civilian population and then express moral shock at the logical consequence of such warfare at My Lai. We would be fools to believe that we could solve any one of these problems without solving the others.

My friend Sandy Weiss got involved in environmental issues when the water beneath her home was poisoned; for Arlo Skari, it was seeing a distant river on fire; for the late Anne Charter, it was when a coal company wanted to turn her ranch into a coal mine. For me, it was gradually picking up ideas about what people's relationship with nature ought to be. It was a slow process of learning – taking pictures with my Kodak Brownie camera, seeing how greed affected people, singing hymns in church, developing a relationship with a piece of the earth, taking in ideas from American conservation writers. And, finally, it was coming to a realization that I have a responsibility, that I must work to protect the land and the water and the clear skies that I regard so highly. If I indeed have dominion over the earth, then this is how I must exercise that dominion… protecting God's Creation.

In all, I regard my environmental activism as an act of service – to my family, to my nation, and to my God.

I've seen many people who love the outdoors and spend a great deal of time enjoying it, and yet who won't lift a finger to protect it. Won't write a check, won't stuff an envelope, won't make a phone call, won't attend a meeting, won't speak up. Some of them call themselves environmentalists. They may love cross country skiing or rock climbing, they may even love a certain place. But if they aren't involved, it's hard for me to regard them as environmentalists.

Still, as Wendell Berry reminds me, politics isn't everything, and we have to change what we can with our own hands, in the way that we live, make purchases, obtain food, raise children, and participate as citizens.

So, in my growing up, I developed a love of one little piece of creation, and I became an environmentalist to help protect it. This fits the picture that many people have about environmentalists, but some carry that image to an absurd and silly extreme in order to come up with the Narrative about environmentalists – a caricature of someone who wants to turn the whole country into a wilderness area, who wants to stop all logging, all mining, all real estate development, who wants everyone to be a vegetarian, pagan, anti-capitalist, anti-freedom, commie peace queer, bent on destroying America.

If you find environmentalists inconvenient, then I guess it helps to have a caricature of them. Caricatures worked well for those who wanted to keep down the Irish, or African-Americans, or Italians, or Latinos, or those women who wanted the right to vote. A caricature and a narrative helped us round up Japanese Americans and put them in prison camps during World War II. If we have a caricature – a Narrative – in our minds, we can convince ourselves of pretty much anything we find it convenient to believe.

Eventually, most (not all) people come to realize that caricatures aren't reality. It happens gradually with most people, and never with some others.

And, who knows, maybe there are some environmentalists out there who fit that caricature… the Narrative. They could exist, though I've never met any.

I've learned, however, that there is much more to environmentalism than the desire to protect beauty. By saying this, I don't mean to trivialize that desire, because it often comes from a person's deepest beliefs about the nature of God, Creation, and our place in Creation as human beings. With a basis like that, it's no wonder that the destruction of American places can draw deeply-held responses from people who love our country.

As I've grown older, I've learned more and more about what it means to protect the environment, how what we call "the environment" connects with people, how it connects to other issues. I believe strongly in protecting wild places, but I also believe in working landscapes – family-scale farms and ranches – and in the participation of citizens in a free nation, and in doing as much as we can to limit the damage we cause when we extract minerals from the earth.

CHAPTER TWELVE

Stouthearted Citizens

None of us had ever been involved with such an endeavor and would probably not have done it if we had realized how much work it was and how much the deck is stacked against citizens who challenge powerful corporations.

..….….…..…..…..…..…..…..…..…..…..…..

When I was still involved with the Sierra Club, I received a phone call one Saturday morning from a rancher named Lawrence Perry. I had met him before through a common friend, but never knew him well. Lawrence invited me to join him for breakfast; there was something he wanted to talk over with me. He took me to a Job's Daughters pancake breakfast where his niece was one of the girls serving pancakes.

It was the late 1970s, and renewed interest was building for mining uranium in the southern Black Hills. Uranium had been mined there from 1952 through the early 1970s.[1]

For a time, uranium prices were high. The Tennessee Valley Authority and commercial uranium companies were seeking out new sources of fuel. (By that time, the U.S. had already become a net importer of uranium.) One uranium company had laid out plans to develop a mine in Craven Canyon, in the far southern part of the Black Hills.

Lawrence was very fond of remote Craven Canyon, the site of ancient Indian pictographs. He wondered if it might be possible to watchdog uranium activity and perhaps keep it from destroying this and other special places.

In the weeks following that pancake breakfast, Lawrence and I, along with several others, revived a group that had met a few times the year before but hadn't yet developed a structure, the Black Hills Energy Coalition. The more we learned about uranium mining, the more we realized that it raised issues about water. Most uranium mining would require the dewatering of aquifers, something that's always a concern, especially west of the 100th Meridian.

We read about contaminated wells in Colorado.[2]

We read about dropping water levels in wells.[3] The Tennessee Valley Authority planned to remove 675 gallons per minute from one of its mines in the Black Hills.[4]

We read about aquifers in Wyoming and Texas contaminated by in situ mining, a process in which acid is injected into a uranium-bearing rock strata – often an aquifer – and is then pumped to the surface containing the dissolved uranium. We knew that reversing the damage to an aquifer was difficult – if not impossible.[5]

We read about uranium tailings polluting rivers in Colorado and New Mexico.[6]

We read about livestock suffering from molybdenosis in Texas and North Dakota, a disease caused by trace amounts of molybdenum found with uranium.[7]

And the more we learned about nuclear power, the more we felt it was not a path toward energy independence for America. Although the nuclear industry portrayed itself as a way to get out from under the thumbs of oil-rich dictators, nuclear energy was only a way to generate electricity... it could not in those days power our cars or airplanes. Also, much of our uranium supply came from foreign countries. It was expensive, and it required heavy subsidies from American taxpayers (including insurance, because it was too risky for private insurers). Past uranium mining had left many scars across the lands of the American West, and polluted waterways as well. And then there's the problem – one that's still unresolved – of what to do with the radioactive waste. You can bet your billfold that the taxpayer will pick up that tab, too.

In the process, it would destroy more land, more aquifers, and would further put off the investment that we really needed to make (and still need to make) – renewable power that will secure America's future and make us more independent of foreign dictators.

While the Energy Coalition focused on uranium mining and how to deal with it, we also published information on other issues – for example, there was a company that wanted to pump huge volumes of ground water out of the Madison Formation in South Dakota and use it to slurry Wyoming coal to Arkansas. We stood opposed to that plan. We also considered very seriously the role of citizens in government, and the government's too-often collusion with corporate interests against citizens.

The people I knew best from the Black Hills Energy Coalition came from all walks of life. There was Jean Jantz, Lawrence's cousin from Rapid City who simply loved the Black Hills. There was Linda Hasselstrom, whose family operated a ranch near Hermosa. There was Linda's neighbor Margaret Brazell, a young ranch wife and mother who looked forward to spring mostly because she loved working in her garden. There was Dave Strom, the Chicago native and sheet metal worker who had moved his family to the Black Hills. There was Sandy O'Donnell, an office manager for a local construction company. There was John Sanderford, a bright young man who didn't know it yet, but who would be off to law school eventually.

We added members from across the state – farmers from Hutchinson County, working people from Sioux Falls, business people from Pierre. There were a number of members from Dell Rapids, where my dad grew up, because the rich farmland there was being explored for possible uranium mining. Membership was often a family affair that spanned generations.

All these people taught me a lot. Lawrence was probably the best natural community organizer I ever met. He talked to everyone he knew about our issue. He also kept meticulous records on index cards and in notebooks, working on a card table in his living room.

As a rancher, Lawrence's single biggest concern was water: He told a reporter, "Where I'm coming from is protecting my property rights and my water."[8]

Linda was a skilled writer and editor. She would do whatever needed to be done, and she was a true warrior with a fighting spirit that inspired all of us. Linda was the editor and chief writer of our newsletter, which we had christened *The Shaft.*

Dave brought a determination and tenacity that he shared with all of us.

John's command of information and his debating skills were extraordinary, and he wasn't intimidated by anyone. There was a PR man from Union Carbide Corporation who actually offered John a job, thinking that maybe he could buy off this troublesome young man. He couldn't.

Early on, our members approached county governments and the South Dakota legislature to find ways to minimize uranium mining's impacts, but with little success. Uranium exploration spread to other parts of western and eastern South Dakota, and more South Dakota residents were becoming concerned about the potential impacts of uranium extraction.

For a time, many people thought the exploration was just taking place in one county at the southern end of the Black Hills. It was impossible to find out from the state what areas were under exploration – the state employed a policy of keeping exploration permits secret "to protect proprietary information" of the mining companies. This kept the general public in the dark, it also kept landowners in the dark who stood to be directly affected by mining activities.

Twenty companies were exploring for uranium in South Dakota, including Union Carbide Corporation, Kerr-McGee, Phillips Uranium, Anaconda (then a subsidiary of Atlantic-Richfield), and the Tennessee Valley Authority.[9]

The local Sierra Club group shed some light on the extent of uranium exploration by hiring one of its members to go from county to county, looking up individual records that were maintained in county courthouses. That seven-county courthouse search discovered that uranium exploration permits had been issued covering about 40% of the Black Hills region.[10]

But the issue was much more widespread than that. It became known that farm country in eastern South Dakota was also being explored for uranium, and those people weren't so accommodating to an industry that threatened their land, their water, and their communities. Residents of Bon Homme County in eastern South Dakota voted by a 5 to 1 margin to ban uranium exploration there.[11]

The state of South Dakota was not well-prepared to deal with all the attention it was getting from uranium companies. The state Conservation Commission – which had, in fact, been chartered to encourage mining development – lacked the manpower to handle permit inspections.[12] Each state inspector was responsible for covering 250,000 acres per month, and legislative direction was vague as to the extent of inspections prior to issuing exploration permits. In 1979, a state inspector testified in a permit hearing that he had inspected a Kerr-McGee site when, in fact, he hadn't.[13]

Frustrating for many was the piecemeal approach that state regulators had taken toward uranium development. Each permit was considered individually, and citizens had little access to information that would shine a light on the big picture – what would be the cumulative effect of all this development on agricultural land, on water resources, on the budgets of small communities having to deal with rapid growth?

Because it was becoming clearer that uranium mining had the potential to do a lot of damage, because the state legislature and the county commissions we contacted had been unresponsive, and because the state was unprepared to handle a rush of uranium exploration and mining, we decided to undertake a ballot initiative. California is widely known for its many ballot measures – initiated by citizen groups and by corporations – but South Dakota was the first state that made it possible for citizens to directly initiate legislation. None of us had ever been involved with such an endeavor and would probably not have done it if we had realized how much work it was and how much the deck is stacked against citizens who challenge powerful corporations.

It was July 1979. First, we created a campaign committee. We had to gather thousands of signatures of registered voters in just a few months. This meant we had to recruit volunteers all across the state and train them to gather signatures in a way that would pass legal scrutiny. We stood on street corners and outside businesses and churches. We knocked on doors. We worked booths at fairs and other events.

A Rapid City attorney who had close connections with the mining industry issued a public threat to challenge every signature on our petitions, so we knew we had to make our signature-gathering process as clean as possible, and we also knew we had to gather plenty of extra signatures to withstand the threatened challenges.

Keeping our petition clean meant that every volunteer who gathered signatures (and all of the signature gatherers were volunteers) needed to understand that only registered voters could sign. The printed name that accompanied each signature needed to be legible. Those of us at the center of this petition drive reviewed every petition; we crossed out some names that wouldn't pass muster and actually threw out a couple of completed petitions (75 names apiece). Somebody had signed for other people on one petition – every signature was in the same handwriting. There was a big Native American fellow who signed my petition in front of a grocery store. As he walked away, I looked down at my clipboard and saw he had signed his name as "Frampton Comes Alive" (the best-selling record album of 1976). Very funny. I had to cross out that signature, too.

Of course, the petition itself was simply the very first step we had to take in order to place our proposal before the voters. We knew that most people wouldn't feel they had enough expertise to decide on the issue itself – after all, it hadn't really been debated at all in the public arena. But we hoped that people's sense of fairness would incline them to give us the chance to get the issue debated by placing it on the ballot. And a lot of people felt that way.

But a lot of people we asked to sign just didn't want to become involved.

I was surprised by the number of women who declined to sign our petition because they needed to ask their husbands.

I was more surprised by people who assumed that the government at some level is taking care of everything. These citizens – I don't remember how many I encountered – believed that there must already be government regulations to take care of everything that would harm us.

But what really shocked me was the number of people who believed that our state legislators were the experts, and we should leave such important decisions to them.

During that year's legislative session, I spent a few days trying to raise lawmakers' awareness of what problems uranium mining was likely to bring, and to propose some solutions. And I saw the same thing that many citizens witness (citizens from rural states, anyway) when they spend time in their state legislatures – most legislators have no special qualifications, no particular expertise, and no experiences of note. Some legislators will absolutely not listen to an everyday citizen. Citizens are strangers in the legislature; it's the lobbyists who are paid to be there every day that legislators come to know on a first-name basis. Some legislators become unabashedly loyal to those lobbyists and the firms they represent. Some legislators – even in a state like South Dakota – come to think of themselves as big shots. Some legislators think God speaks through them. Some legislators are vindictive. And some just aren't very smart.

Some of them are smart, of course. Some of them are responsible and responsive to citizens. Some of them are capable people who understand that being a state legislator doesn't make you a big-shot. Those legislators are asked to vote on hundreds of bills during a session that begins in January and ends in March, and they would acknowledge that they are not experts.

As the deadline loomed nearer, we were short on signatures. But we made a final push, gathering signatures as fast as we could at every opportunity. We also discovered that a lot of people had been out there gathering signatures the whole time, and we received many petitions in the mail just before the deadline.

In the end, we managed to gather about fifty percent more signatures than the law required. We reviewed them all, counted up the signatures, drove our petitions to the state capitol in a small convoy, and delivered them to Secretary of State Alice Kundert. Her staff immediately set about verifying the signatures and, in a few days, she announced that we had not only qualified our initiative for the ballot, but that the petition contained unusually few errors of the kind that disqualify signatures. She said, "It's one of the cleanest ones I've come across."[14] That combination of facts dissuaded would-be challenges and we were on the ballot! We held a small party at Sandy's office, complete with a bottle of champagne.

But the work had really just begun.

By this time, we had built a statewide organization. First, we set about raising money. There was a food booth we ran at the Wilson Park Festival in Rapid City. We held a statewide raffle of art pieces, all donated by the artists who created them.

There was the bluegrass festival at the Ox Yoke Ranch near the tiny village of Nemo. The promoters hired us to serve as the parking crew for the weekend, getting drivers – many of whom had been drinking before they arrived – to park in straight rows on a rolling pasture. We got the job done, and earned a $1,020 donation.

We raised money with letters and by face-to-face requests. Most of it came in amounts of $5 to $10.

We did everything we could to educate the public about our ballot measure. What we sought in our proposed law was to give South Dakota citizens the right to approve or disapprove nuclear facilities in the state. It probably wasn't the most elegant solution, but we knew – to have a chance – that our proposal must be simple. A complex set of regulations and procedures wouldn't stand a chance in the election.

We hired a young man, Arlen Crane, who grew up on a farm near Artesian, South Dakota, to be our campaign director. I'll bet he was the most poorly-paid campaign director for any statewide issue anywhere; he lived and breathed the uranium initiative for months, making practically no money for his work.

We had mailing parties, gathering together to stuff and address envelopes. We arranged speaking engagements to public groups. We printed flyers and handed them out wherever we could. We made appearances on local and even national news broadcasts.

John Sanderford told the crowd at a public meeting moderated by Sen. George McGovern that, "The decisions we make in this coming decade we'll have to live with for many years to come. Conservation and renewable energy is how we look to the future for our future needs. We don't intend to stand here and say we oppose all energy sources, but we do intend to stand here and say it's necessary to make a serious commitment to renewable energy."[15]

Almost forty years later, all of us in America are still waiting for the United States government to make a serious commitment to power from the sun and the wind, and to energy efficiency. In the meantime, it has committed many billions of taxpayer dollars to help the oil and gas and coal and nuclear industries.

Our most active opponent in the uranium initiative was the Union Carbide Corporation, a company with an annual budget which exceeded that of the State of South Dakota (and the company that would kill thousands of people at Bhopal, India, a few years later). But Union Carbide had plenty of financial help against our initiative; all these companies contributed[16]:

Gulf Oil Corp.

Anaconda Copper Co.

Chevron Oil

Westinghouse Electric

Chicago Bridge & Iron Co.

Baltimore Gas & Electric Co.

Commonwealth Edison (Chicago)

Carolina Power & Light Co.

Public Service Electric & Gas (Newark)

Detroit Edison

Consumers Power Co. (Jackson, MI)

Southern California Edison Co.

Pacific Gas & Electric Co.

Old Ben Coal Co. (Chicago)

Conoco

Kerr-McGee

Western Nuclear (Lakewood, CO)

Phillips Uranium

Sunedco (Dallas)

Corporate contributions amounted to all but $500 of the campaign spending against us.[17] We were outspent 22 to 1.

This cast of characters organized a campaign committee against our initiative and called it "Citizens Against the Ban," even though their membership included no citizens and the initiative itself was not a ban.

Our initiative was debated intensely through the summer and fall of 1980; it was endorsed by the South Dakota Education Association and South Dakota Farmers Union.

When a television station in Rapid City (South Dakota's second-largest city) decided to host a televised debate on the ballot measure, they were inexplicably confused about whom to invite to speak on the initiative's behalf.

Instead of contacting the organization whose name and address were all over the initiative's campaign materials, instead of calling one of the several people who had been covered in the local newspaper for the past year and a half, that TV station invited another organization in the area, a visibly countercultural group called the Black Hills Alliance, to provide a spokesman for the ballot measure in the TV debate. This group had not even endorsed the ballot measure at that time. Nevertheless, they accepted the invitation, and the station began airing promotional announcements for the debate.

Members of the initiative's campaign committee confronted that station's news director about the station's decision to invite someone to speak for the ballot measure who was not part of the campaign and who had not yet even endorsed it. We asked them not to broadcast this debate. But the debate had already been recorded, and the station had invested heavily in promoting it. They refused to pull the original debate, agreeing instead to hastily arrange and broadcast a second debate that wasn't nearly as heavily promoted. The original debate, unfortunately, became THE debate for most viewers.

Thus the televised spokesman for our initiative was a man with a ponytail, a noticeable New York accent, and a shallow grasp of the issues surrounding the initiative (shallow, because he had not been debating and discussing the issue for a year, as had the members of the Energy Coalition and our campaign committee). Watching that debate was painful for those in the Energy Coalition who had worked so hard for a year and a half.

On Election Day, the ballot measure failed to pass by 51.6% to 48.4%. It won handily in many parts of South Dakota, including the farm country east of the Missouri River, but failed decisively in those parts of the state where that TV debate was broadcast.

My wife Candace and I left for Utah the following year to attend graduate school, so I missed out on the Black Hills Energy Coalition's activities for its last few years. While I was away at Utah State, the Energy Coalition collaborated with another group on a 1984 ballot measure to give South Dakota voters the right to decide whether South Dakota should host a low-level radioactive waste site or join a multi-state radioactive waste disposal compact. Voters passed this measure by 62% to 38%.

The Black Hills Energy Coalition had a short life, but an active one. The whole experience drew me into contact with all kinds of people who cared about South Dakota's environment for a whole rainbow of reasons.

It also taught me how people can organize to effect change. It taught me how poorly the press sometimes does its job of informing citizens. It taught me how disparate people often have more in common than they might have expected. It taught me how the most unassuming people sometimes have a deep reservoir of courage.

In the end, the new uranium mines planned by Union Carbide and the Tennessee Valley Authority never came to be. The collapse of the nuclear industry – which had begun even before the Three Mile Island reactor incident in 1979 – led to a collapse in uranium prices, and that removed the incentive for more uranium mining. But, years later, new uranium mining is again being promoted in the southern Black Hills and a new public relations push is being made for a new wave of nuclear reactor construction in the United States. And, as with most forms of energy, the great majority of Americans will be somewhat aware of the pollution that comes out of the power plants, but won't seriously consider the impacts of extracting that energy from the ground, nor of dealing with its waste products. And you and I will heavily subsidize new nuclear power plants with our tax dollars.

CHAPTER THIRTEEN

Beauty

There was a turkey vulture in the Badlands that showed a very definite interest in me, and I'm pretty sure I know why.

.. ..

I want to put in a word for beauty. Some environmentalists work hard to protect beauty, and I think we need to appreciate that protecting beauty has a value to all of us. You know as well as I do that life without beauty would be a lesser life.

When I say "value," I don't mean money, of course. The marketplace does sometimes give a monetary value to beauty – human beauty, a beautiful home, a beautiful site for a beautiful home, and the paintings of Van Gogh (after he died). But it doesn't end with the marketplace. Real estate for sale isn't the only real estate that matters. Art that sells for lots of money isn't the only art that matters. (Van Gogh would have told you that.)

So let me raise a toast to the night sky. It has utterly no financial value to me. I can't possess it; every other human being has as much access to it as I ever will. But it is one of the great blessings of being alive on this planet we call "home."

Here in Montana, we call our state "Big Sky Country." The phrase came from the title of a book, *The Big Sky*, by Montana author A.B. Guthrie. And that title came from a note Guthrie had written down as a boy, something his father had said on his first day in Montana: "Standing under the big sky I feel free."[1]

Even that old Massachusetts minister Ralph Waldo Emerson spoke of how it feels to be under the open sky: "The health of the eye seems to demand a horizon. We are never tired so long as we can see far enough." And he had never come anywhere near the Great Plains.

In one of his beautifully illustrated books, my friend Paul Goble wrote of the "Great Race," the legendary race around the Black Hills between the four-leggeds and the two-leggeds. The race continued for days, with animals of all kinds taking part, as well as a Lakota brave. The many racers stirred up a great deal of dust that floated into the heavens and became the river of stars we know as the Milky Way. That's the legend, anyway.

Sadly, the increasing glow of artificial lights is gradually taking away our ability to enjoy the Milky Way and many other things the night sky has to offer. Street lights, illuminated billboards, parking lot lights – our lights are getting brighter and more numerous. And, ironically, they make it harder for us to see at night.

Oh, and the coal burning which generates much of the electricity for those artificial lights is itself dirtying our skies with gases and particulates.

We are losing something beautiful every year. We are losing more every year than the year before.

I know that Emerson enjoyed the night sky. "If the stars should appear one night in a thousand years," he wrote, "how would men believe and adore; and preserve for many generations the remembrance of the city of God which had been shown! But every night come out these envoys of beauty, and light the universe with their admonishing smile."[2]

The stars are really something, when you think about it, and the Great Plains is a great place to see them. My friend Steve Parker is a serious amateur astronomer, and he has guided me on trips to the moon and stars on dark nights. For many years, Parker took care of a small observatory for the Black Hills Astronomical Society in South Dakota, but he didn't always need that telescope to enjoy what the night sky has to offer.

One August, Parker and his friend Louie and I drove down to Conata Basin to spend the night watching the Perseids. The Perseids are remnant particles in the orbit of the Swift-Tuttle comet, and the earth passes through that orbit every year around August 9-13. Some of those dust particles collide with the earth's atmosphere and burn up as meteors, mostly coming out of the northeast sky from the direction of the constellation Perseus.

Conata Basin is a large, dry flat on the southern edge of the South Dakota Badlands. The sky there would be big, dark, and dry. We wanted to get there before dark, so we left Rapid City in early evening. We took the Scenic route; that is, we drove state highway 44 through the town of Scenic. It was a good drive – pronghorns, jackrabbits, and a pair of young golden eagles just off the road. We found a dirt road that pretty much led to nowhere and chose a spot at the end of that road to park and set up our lawn chairs and a couple telescopes.

Telescopes are next to useless for watching meteors because those bits of cosmic debris are so fleeting and random. But astronomers don't like to waste a dark, moonless night. There's a lot to see out there – planets, glowing celestial dust, ancient light from stars that may not even exist anymore.

With his degree in mathematics, you might expect Parker to emphasize the hard facts about celestial bodies. He can, if you want him to. But he wasn't in Conata Basin that night to chart the meteors, their speed, direction, and brightness. He was there just to look at them.

A few of the Perseids are bright. Some are so faint and quick that they are gone before you're really sure you saw them. (After all, these little bits of dust or rock are traveling around 130,000 miles per hour!) The darker the sky, the more you can see.

True night isn't as long as a person might think. Long after the twilight is gone, there are still faint rays of dust illuminated by the sun from far below the horizon. The rays come back before dawn. In between, you have true night sky.

Even on a moonless night, there was still some light out there. To the south, in Nebraska, a robust lightning storm was stirring things up. To the north, we could see just a bit of faint red aurora borealis.

I tried to catch a few meteors with my camera. It would only be able to catch the brightest ones and, yes, some bright, beautiful meteors burned across the sky that night. But my lens missed every one of them, never aimed in the right direction at the right time.

Parker, on the other hand, always catches something. He spent an overcast night in the Badlands several years ago and came home with a shot of a meteor coming down through the clouds.

"Oooh!" says Louie as Parker and I are looking in another direction. We wheel and look, knowing that the burning streak Louie saw is probably gone already. The three of us repeat this dance many times in the night.

Sometimes we are all looking in the same direction. All three of us saw one bright Perseid skip across the upper atmosphere, tracing a succession of fiery lines across the stars.

We saw the Summer Triangle and, later on, the Great Square. With Parker's telescope, we saw the Ring Nebula, the Andromeda Galaxy, Saturn. Very late, the winter constellation Auriga comes above the horizon. "Ah, Capella," Parker sings out, unaccompanied.

A while later, the first hints of dawn begin to appear. We decide to call it a night, and we retire in our lawn chairs.

....

My daughter Emily was born around 3:00 in the morning. The next night, after visiting Candace and Emily in the hospital, I came home around 11:00 pm. We lived a few miles in the country at the time, not a particularly dark place, but much darker than town. When I got out of my car, I looked up and saw a clear sky aflame with aurora. It was mainly a bright green glow from the north but, before long, tongues of light began to flash toward a spot slightly to the south of overhead.

I had seen those flashing tongues of light before – they resemble bits of flame. They flowed in repeating patterns from the northern horizon to a point high above, and they cover that distance in an eyeblink. I ran over to my neighbor Tom's house. He was still up, and so I told him what was going on outside, and he joined me for a while. I also called my mother-in-law, Mary Margaret. I knew that a night owl like her would still be up, and she could see a fair amount of sky from her house.

I went back outside and watched the big show. I knew the leaping banners of light wouldn't continue all night. After a time, they began to fade, and the green glow in the north was all that remained. I was about to go inside, but then I saw more activity toward the west. In a few minutes, a river of green and pink light was flowing across the sky. This was a form I hadn't before seen in aurora light. It lasted for maybe half an hour; then it, too, began to diminish.

When I went to bed, the green light was still shining in the northern sky. I couldn't help but wonder how all this was connected to the birth of my daughter. But, then, how many other babies had been born that night? How many people died that night? How many couples fell in love that night?

Emerson was right. What happens in the night sky is a blessing conferred on us always, whether we see it or not, whether we appreciate it or not. Those blessings circle through the sky – Cygnus the Swan every summer, Orion and the Pleiades every winter. There is our beautiful and ever-changing moon. There are fellow planets in the night, auroras, galaxies, comets, meteors.

When Emily was just about three years old, she and my wife Candace and I, along with a couple of friends, had spent a lovely day in Custer State Park in the Black Hills. We decided to walk to the top of a small hill and watch the evening come. Sitting among yuccas and grass and small sandstone outcrops, we looked to the west as the sun settled behind the pine forest skyline. We stayed and talked a while, and then we all fell silent, just watching it get dark. We saw the last dull streak of red slowly disappear and the stars slowly begin to emerge. A group of coyotes yipped and howled, and then fell silent. As evening transitioned into night, we could hear some large hoofed animal – elk? bison? – moving about in the dark valley below. We heard hooting from an owl, and a nighthawk buzzed near us. We heard crickets. We heard the breeze through the ponderosa pines.

For a long time after that, Emily would talk about "listening to the sunset."

··

While I'm on the subject of beauty, I'd like to say a few words about our feathered friends. That Lakota story of the Great Race wasn't a light-hearted tale – the race would decide whether people would eat buffalo or buffalo would eat people. It was a race pitting a buffalo and all the other four-legged creatures against a Lakota man and all the other two-legged creatures – the birds. And, in the end, it was a slow-flying magpie that won the race for the humans.

I'm not a "birder." I'm not one of those people who knows all the bird songs, or who can identify a raptor soaring high against a bright sky.

Still, I appreciate the birds as a different kind of beauty than the night sky. They are more immediate. Our actions have more direct impact on them, and they react to what we do. Some of them have direct economic value to us. They breathe the same air we do, and they drink the same water. The live pretty much everywhere.

I was out for a walk on a service road along U.S. Highway 16 many years ago, just south of Rapid City. I began to notice a bird that was following me. There being some distance between us, I never could identify what kind of bird it was. But I walked along and the bird would accompany me, following along in short, intermittent flights and landing on a power line. I would walk a little further, the bird would wait a moment and then fly up behind me and land on the power line. I would walk on, the bird would catch up and land on the power line.

I don't know what the bird may have had on its mind, but it followed me for nearly half an hour. I always figured it was just bored and followed me for amusement. It kept a safe distance, but it was definitely interested in me. I can't say I've ever known a bird to be interested in me before.

A few years later, though, there was a turkey vulture in the Badlands that showed a very definite interest in me, and I'm pretty sure I know why. Some friends and I were camping on Hay Butte and I walked over to the end of the butte just to watch the shadows lengthen before sundown. Looking out over the basin and up at the fair-weather clouds, I noticed a lone turkey vulture sailing along, and realized it was coming in my direction.

Not many people would tell you that a turkey vulture is beautiful. But look at them fly, and you appreciate that turkey vultures are among the best and most graceful gliders in the world. This vulture sailed effortlessly, and it gradually came nearer. I wondered if it had seen me, it was coming in so close and low. And then I realized that it had indeed seen me and that I was the reason it was coming in for a close look. I held my position, not moving, just watching as it gradually descended. It came closer and closer. I could see its featherless red head turning and looking me over. It came within 30 feet before something about me told the vulture I was not dead or near-dead, and there would be no easy snack there that day. When it turned its wings slightly to change direction, I could hear the breeze in its feathers – it was that close.

I didn't think too much about being mistaken for dead. Turkey vultures do us all the favor of cleaning up carcasses on the land, getting rid of disease in the process. But to watch them fly – their skill at using invisible pockets of warm air to stay airborne for hours with scarcely a wingflap has always amazed me.

Cliff swallows are a completely different kind of flyer. They aren't built for sailing like the vultures, but they build speed and do a different kind of gliding, cutting speedy arcs through the air. Swallows of all kinds benefit us by eating insects, lots of insects. Cliff swallows earn a living in the Badlands and other open country, building nests out of mud in the overhangs of cliff faces. And they are beautiful flyers.

People notice meadowlarks for their singing. They don't hide when they sing, they perch on a fencepost or the top of a yucca or any high spot on the open plains where their song will carry great distances. I know that I'm not the one for whom they sing, but the song of the western meadowlark is one of the many little pleasures of living on our little blue planet. A world without their song would be less of a world for me.

Parker and I were hiking one early April morning through the Badlands. It was quiet and we began to notice the calls of sandhill cranes overhead. They were migrating north and, as they came above us, they encountered strong thermals, columns of heated air rising from the bare ground of the Badlands. We saw seven flocks that morning. Each flock of cranes, when they came to the thermals, began a slow spiraled ascent, gaining hundreds of feet in altitude without having to flap their wings – a most valuable conservation of energy for birds migrating thousands of miles under their own power.

They made several spirals, becoming almost too small to see, and then they emerged from the thermals and continued north. Seven times we watched this strategy for gaining altitude without effort. Seven times the sandhill cranes became so small we could barely see them. Seven times their calls went from loud to faint as they climbed above the Badlands and headed north.

"Angels we have heard on high, sweetly singing o'er the plains."

Wherever we live, we have birds, the ones that live near us, and the ones that migrate above us. They sing into the air around us, they bring color into our surroundings. Many of them bring us direct benefits that make our lives better. Some of them are amazingly intelligent, like the magpie and the crow. Some are startlingly beautiful and graceful. Some are just fascinating to watch, as they make a living on the ground and in the trees, exposed to the weather, mating and raising babies, making long, desperate migrations twice a year, or else staying and surviving conditions that change constantly with the seasons, all with animals and people preying on them. Oh, and they can fly! My wife Candace believes this single ability is what people find most appealing about birds.

Whatever it is we find appealing, we're blessed to live in a world that has birds. We're fortunate to live in a world that has a lovely, changing moon revolving around it. When the moon is full, I like to leave my curtains open to let that soft light into my house.

Beauty isn't everything. But it also isn't nothing. And we do not want a world without it.

We're not so poor that we and our children are fated to see beauty slip through our fingers without being able to do anything about it.

CHAPTER FOURTEEN

We Will Rejoice and Be Glad In It

This is the day which the LORD hath made; we will rejoice and be glad in it.

Psalms 118:24

....

In his 2015 Encyclical, Pope Francis wrote "The entire material universe speaks of God's love, his boundless affection for us. Soil, water, mountains: everything is, as it were, a caress of God."[1]

296 years earlier, in his hymn *Joy to the World* (1719), Isaac Watts wrote about how nature itself praises God with phrases like "and heaven and nature sing" and, in the next verse, "While fields and floods, rocks, hills, and plains repeat the sounding joy!"

In 1907, Henry van Dyke wrote a hymn to the tune of Beethoven's "Hymn to Joy." The second verse goes like this:

All your works with joy surround you, earth and heaven reflect your rays,
Stars and angels sing around you, center of unbroken praise.
Field and forest, vale and mountain, flowery meadow, flashing sea,
Chanting bird and flowing fountain, teach us what our praise should be.

The Bible tells us over and over – the world belongs to God, and is precious to God. The world is full of God's glory; the world itself is the voice of praise and rejoicing. This is one of the things I learned in church as a boy.

Let the heavens rejoice, and let the earth be glad; let the sea roar, and the fulness thereof.
Let the field be joyful, and all that is therein: then shall all the trees of the wood rejoice.

Psalms 96:11-12

And one cried unto another, and said, Holy, holy, holy, is the LORD of hosts: the whole earth is full of his glory.

Isaiah 6:3

The heavens declare the glory of God; and the firmament sheweth his handywork. Day unto day uttereth speech, and night unto night sheweth knowledge. There is no speech nor language, where their voice is not heard.

Psalms 19:1-3

Let the heavens be glad, and let the earth rejoice: and let men say among the nations, The LORD reigneth. Let the sea roar, and the fulness thereof: let the fields rejoice, and all that is therein. Then shall the trees of the wood sing out at the presence of the LORD, because he cometh to judge the earth. O give thanks unto the LORD; for he is good; for his mercy endureth for ever.

1 Chronicles 16:31-34

All thy works shall praise thee, O LORD; and thy saints shall bless thee: They shall speak of the glory of thy kingdom, and talk of thy power; To make known to the sons of men **his** *mighty acts, and the glorious majesty of his kingdom. Thy kingdom is an everlasting kingdom, and thy dominion endureth through all generations.*

Psalms 145:10-13

You are worthy, our Lord and God, to receive glory and honor and power, for you created all things, and by your will they were created and have their being.

Revelation 4:11

Praise ye the LORD. Praise ye the LORD from the heavens: praise him in the heights. Praise ye him, all his angels: praise ye him, all his hosts. Praise ye him, sun and moon: praise him, all ye stars of light. Praise him, ye heavens of heavens, and ye waters that be above the heavens. Let them praise the name of the LORD: for he commanded, and they were created. He hath also stablished them for ever and ever: he hath made a decree which shall not pass. Praise the LORD from the earth, ye dragons, and all deeps: Fire, and hail; snow, and vapours; stormy wind fulfilling his word: Mountains, and all hills; fruitful trees, and all cedars: Beasts, and all cattle; creeping things, and flying fowl: Kings of the earth, and all people; princes, and all judges of the earth: Both young men, and maidens;

old men, and children: Let them praise the name of the LORD: for his name alone is excellent; his glory is above the earth and heaven.

Psalms 148:1-13

Make a joyful noise unto the LORD, all the earth: make a loud noise, and rejoice, and sing praise. Sing unto the LORD with the harp; with the harp, and the voice of a psalm. With trumpets and sound of cornet make a joyful noise before the LORD, the King. Let the sea roar, and the fulness thereof; the world, and they that dwell therein. Let the floods clap their hands: let the hills be joyful together Before the LORD; for he cometh to judge the earth: with righteousness shall he judge the world, and the people with equity.

Psalm 98:4-9

The glory of the LORD shall endure for ever: the LORD shall rejoice in his works.

Psalms 104:31

And the LORD God took the man, and put him into the garden of Eden to dress it and to keep it.

Genesis 2:15

Thus saith the LORD, The heaven is my throne, and the earth is my footstool: where is the house that ye build unto me? and where is the place of my rest? For all those things hath mine hand made, and all those things have been, saith the LORD.

Isaiah 66:1-2

But as truly as I live, all the earth shall be filled with the glory of the LORD.

Numbers 14:21

The land shall not be sold for ever: for the land is mine, for ye are strangers and sojourners with me.

Leviticus 25:23

Thou, even thou, art LORD alone; thou hast made heaven, the heaven of heavens, with all their host, the earth, and all things that are therein, the seas, and all that is therein, and thou preservest them all; and the host of heaven worshippeth thee.

Nehemiah 9:6

He hath made every thing beautiful in his time: also he hath set the world in their heart, so that no man can find out the work that God maketh from the beginning to the end.

Ecclesiastes 3:11

That he who blesseth himself in the earth shall bless himself in the God of truth; and he that sweareth in the earth shall swear by the God of truth; because the former troubles are forgotten, and because they are hid from mine eyes. For, behold, I create new heavens and a new earth: and the former shall not be remembered, nor come into mind. But be ye glad and rejoice for ever in that which I create: for, behold, I create Jerusalem a rejoicing, and her people a joy.

Isaiah 65:16-18

The trees of the LORD are full of sap; the cedars of Lebanon, which he hath planted; Where the birds make their nests: as for the stork, the fir trees are her house. The high hills are a refuge for the wild goats; and the rocks for the conies. He appointed the moon for seasons: the sun knoweth his going down. Thou makest darkness, and it is night: wherein all the beasts of the forest do creep forth. The young lions roar after their prey, and seek their meat from God.

Psalms 104:16-21

He hath made the earth by his power, he hath established the world by his wisdom, and hath stretched out the heavens by his discretion. When he uttereth his voice, there is a multitude of waters in the heavens, and he causeth the vapours to ascend from the ends of the earth; he maketh lightnings with rain, and bringeth forth the wind out of his treasures.

Jeremiah 10: 12-13

Hearken unto this, O Job: stand still, and consider the wondrous works of God. Dost thou know when God disposed them, and caused the light of his cloud to shine? Dost thou know the balancings of the clouds, the wondrous works of him which is perfect in knowledge? How thy garments are warm, when he quieteth the earth by the south wind? Hast thou with him spread out the sky, which is strong, and as a molten looking glass?

Job 37:14-18

Behold, the heaven and the heaven of heavens is the LORD's thy God, the earth also, with all that therein is.

Deuteronomy 10:14

There was another hymn Isaac Watts composed, this one in 1715:

I sing the mighty power of God that made the mountains rise,
That spread the flowing seas abroad, and built the lofty skies.
I sing the wisdom that ordained the sun to rule the day;
The moon shines full at God's command, and all the stars obey.

I sing the goodness of our God that filled the earth with food;
God formed the creatures with a word, and then pronounced them good.
Oh, how your wonders are displayed, where'er I turn my eye:
If I survey the ground I tread, or gaze upon the sky!

On earth there's not a plant or flower but makes your glory known.
The clouds arise and spread their showers by order from your throne.
All life is but a gift from you and ever in your care;
Wherever people gather, you, O God, are present there.

Stop here for a few seconds before you read the next verse...

But ask now the beasts, and they shall teach thee; and the fowls of the air, and they shall
tell thee: Or speak to the earth, and it shall teach thee: and the fishes of the sea shall declare
unto thee. Who knoweth not in all these that the hand of the LORD hath wrought this?
In whose hand is the soul of every living thing, and the breath of all mankind.

Job 12: 7-10

All this leaves me with three lessons:
- I was created from the earth.
- The earth is the loving work of God's hands.
- Setting aside and protecting a wilderness is a lot like building a church.

But among all this praise and rejoicing, there's this word of caution:

And I brought you into a plentiful country, to eat the fruit thereof and the goodness
thereof; but when ye entered, ye defiled my land, and made mine heritage an abomina-
tion.

Jeremiah 2:7

CHAPTER FIFTEEN

Wacko Environmentalist Song

Oh, give me a home where the buffalo roam,
Where the deer and the antelope play;
Where seldom is heard a discouraging word
And the skies are not cloudy all day.

Home, home on the range,
Where the deer and the antelope play;
Where seldom is heard a discouraging word
And the skies are not cloudy all day.

Where the air is so pure, the zephyrs so free,
The breezes so balmy and light,
That I would not exchange my home on the range
For all of the cities so bright.

The red man was pressed from this part of the West,
He's likely no more to return
To the banks of Red River where seldom if ever
Their flickering camp-fires burn.

How often at night when the heavens are bright
With the light from the glittering stars,
Have I stood there amazed and asked as I gazed
If their glory exceeds that of ours.

Oh, I love these wild flowers in this dear land of ours,
The curlew I love to hear scream,
And I love the white rocks and the antelope flocks
That graze on the mountain-tops green.

Oh, give me a land where the bright diamond sand
Flows leisurely down the stream;
There the graceful, white swan goes gliding along
Like a maid in a heavenly dream.

Then I would not exchange my home on the range,
Where the deer and the antelope play;
Where seldom is heard a discouraging word
And the skies are not cloudy all day.

Home, home on the range
Where the deer and the antelope play
Where seldom is heard a discouraging word
And the skies are not cloudy all day.

Based on a poem by Brewster M. Higley, 1873
Lyrics published by John A. Lomax
Cowboy Songs and Other Frontier Ballads, 1911

CHAPTER SIXTEEN

Justice

It's a scenario that should offend any American's sense of justice.

. . . .

There's a particular and widely discussed injustice that happens when pollution and other environmental costs are specifically pushed onto the most vulnerable in society, onto those who don't have the money or the political clout to fight back. Sometimes this means poor neighborhoods in large cities, sometimes it means Indian reservations, sometimes it means struggling rural communities desperate for economic development because the surrounding farms and ranches have been driven to the brink by policies that favor corporate domination of our food supply.

But it goes beyond that. When you speak of a free market, you speak of a market in which – among other things – the costs involved in the transaction are borne by those who are parties in the transaction. When those costs are shifted onto someone who's not a party to the transaction, the costs are being "externalized." This is a market failure and, to the extent that costs have been externalized, the market is dysfunctional; it is no longer a truly free market.

One way of externalizing costs is releasing pollution into the environment instead of paying the cost of treating or capturing or preventing it. In my life, I've seen many kinds of developers fight determinedly to externalize costs onto the public. Keeping pollution out of the environment is too expensive, they say. It will cost jobs, it will prevent needed economic development, and it will reduce tax revenues.

So legislatures and other public bodies go along with these market failures. They allow the pollution of water or air. They allow the public's wildlife to lose more and more habitat. They abandon their responsibility to protect the interests of the public. They make the decision – without actually stating it – that it's better for American society to let the taxpayer foot the bill for treating the polluted water, or to simply let the water be polluted. This latter choice means letting the public foot the bill in another way, in the form of water-borne illnesses, in the form of shortened life spans, in the form of higher medical bills, in the form of poisoned soil.

This is one simple scenario that has been played over and over in the United States. It's a scenario that should offend any American's sense of justice.

Justice – as well as a free market – would mean we don't allow developers to shove the costs of their projects onto the public.

Expecting people to pay a price, even a non-monetary one, when the person or company that caused the problem refuses to pay – this is unjust. Environmental issues almost always speak to me about justice. My old co-worker Wilf Clark at Zion Book Store in Salt Lake… he and the Apostle Paul were right: simple human greed is very often behind it all.

..…..…..…..…..…..…..…..…..…..…..…..…..

You may have seen a certain black and white photograph by W. Eugene Smith. It shows a Japanese mother, gazing lovingly upon her malformed child as she carries the child into a bath. It reminds many people of Michelangelo's sculpture, *Pieta*, in which Mary holds the lifeless body of her crucified son.

An American photo-journalist, Smith went to Minamata, a small Japanese factory town, in 1971 to work on a story about that city's struggle with mercury poisoning. That pollution centered on a Japanese company, Chisso Corporation, which originally manufactured fertilizer, but later made plastics, drugs, and perfumes. In doing that, they used a chemical called acetaldehyde, of which mercury is a key component.

Chisso had routinely dumped mercury-laden waste into Minamata Bay from 1932 to 1968. The fish in the bay were poisoned, thus poisoning the residents of Minamata, whose normal diet included those fish.

It was in the 1950s that local people began to notice a "strange disease." They developed numbness in their limbs and also in their lips, causing slurred speech. Some people developed vision problems, while some manifested more serious brain damage. Some were afflicted with involuntary muscle movements or began shouting uncontrollably, and some lost consciousness. Furthermore, people began noticing strange behavior in their pets. Eventually, birds fell from the sky for no readily apparent reason.

In 1956, Dr. Hajime Hosokawa from the company's hospital in Minamata publicly announced the appearance of an unknown disease of the central nervous system. The doctor felt that fish diets were a contributory factor, and it was no great leap of logic for some to begin wondering aloud if the Chisso Corporation's effluents might be connected. The company denied this, but moved their dumping site to the Minamata River. Within a few months, however, residents there began to show symptoms also.

The regional government was not about to challenge the Chisso Corporation, and so ordered local fishermen not to sell any fish they caught in Minamata Bay. Fisherman were still allowed to catch fish, they just weren't allowed to sell them. In this decree, the government felt it had dealt with the problem. But local fishermen were left with no way to earn a living.

In 1959, Kumamoto University researchers identified mercury poisoning as the cause of what had come to be known as "Minamata Disease." Chisso Corporation responded by denying any connection with its mercury wastes. Dr. Hosokawa performed secret demonstrations for company management, showing them the effects of acetaldehyde on cats in experiments. The company's response? They concealed the findings and forbade Dr. Hosokawa from conducting any further research. They then began to make secret financial deals with victims, offering these desperate people cash payments in exchange for the victims agreeing not to hold the company further responsible even if its actions were proven to be the cause of the illness. Some people protested, but they were easily intimidated by the company.

Chisso only ended its mercury pollution in 1968 when its manufacturing process became widely outdated. The cleanup of polluted sludge wasn't completed until 1990, and lawsuits for victims – ultimately their only recourse – continued into the 1990s.

During W. Eugene Smith's visit in 1971-72, victims of Chisso's poisoning were working to gain payments from the company to accomplish whatever restitution was possible. Smith was accompanying a group of them to a meeting with a Chisso company official, planning to photograph and record the meeting.

The Chisso official never showed up, but a gang of about 100 men did, crowding into the meeting room and attacking Smith. He later described the attack: "They grabbed me and kicked me in the crotch and snatched the cameras, then hit me in the stomach. Then they dragged me out and picked me up and slammed my head on the concrete." The attack left him with limited vision in one eye, but his photo essay was eventually published in the book *Minamata*.[1]

....

Late on a December night in 1984, something was happening at a Union Carbide pesticide plant in Bhopal, India. As the people in Bhopal slept, almost 40 tons of methyl isocyanate, a chemical used in the manufacture of the pesticides, leaked from a tank. Being slightly heavier than air, the methyl isocyanate gas stayed close to the ground as it crept through the town.

Nearly 4,000 people died that night. In the following days, thousands more people died. Still more people – estimates range from 15,000 to 20,000 – died in the next 20 years from the effects of the poison.[2] Many, many more thousands did not die, but have suffered ever since with lingering disabilities to their eyes, their lungs, and their nervous systems. In the months that followed, many pregnancies ended with spontaneous abortions, stillbirths, and birth defects. Cattle, pets, and wild animals were also killed. Trees lost their leaves.

Union Carbide had a nearly identical plant located in Institute, West Virginia. Nearly identical, except that the company had dropped the safety standards at its Bhopal facility well below those it maintained in West Virginia. The West Virginia plant had a computerized monitoring and warning system, while the Bhopal plant had to rely on manual gauges and human senses to detect leaks. Unlike the West Virginia plant, the facility in Bhopal had no emergency evacuation plans.[2]

The Indian government, in the opinion of many observers, did not do what it could to hold Union Carbide accountable for the disaster. Instead, the company made an out-of-court settlement, which avoided any damaging legal precedent or liability. The Indian Supreme Court ordered that all civil or criminal charges against the company or its officers be dismissed, and also gave them immunity from future prosecutions. Through its unwillingness to pursue the case aggressively, the Indian government was also attempting to maintain a favorable investment climate.[3]

....

In 1920, the land along a partially completed canal project near the city of Niagara, New York, was sold at auction. A man named William T. Love had been the one who originally attempted to build the canal, and it was known locally as the "Love Canal." For the next 33 years, that land would be used as a dump site by the Hooker Chemical Corporation (chemical waste), the city of Niagara (garbage), and the U.S. Army (unknown materials). In 1953, Hooker Chemical sold the land to the Board of Education at Niagara. The deed transfer included a warning about chemical wastes buried on the property, and a clause absolving Hooker Chemical from any future liability.

The following year, the school board began construction of a new elementary school on the site, which opened in 1955. Home sites were also being sold in the 1950s, and homes constructed. Those new homeowners never received any warning that the property was the site of a chemical waste dump with 20,000 tons of toxic wastes buried beneath it.

By the late 1970s, some 800 homes and 240 low-income apartments had been built on that land. People often complained of odors, or sometimes unknown substances coming up through the soil. In 1976, the city and county commissioned a scientific study of the area.

The study didn't just happen by itself; it happened because families with sick children demanded it after conducting their own study which revealed astoundingly high rates of birth defects among families living near the site.

The study found toxic chemical residues in the air, and also in sump pumps in numerous homes. The study found buried metal drums just beneath the ground surface, and also found the neighborhood storm sewers contained high levels of PCBs. The city's response was to place window fans in a few homes that had been found to contain high levels of chemical residues.

In 1978, the New York Department of Health began a study of air and soil, and also of the health of 239 families that lived in the most immediate proximity of the old canal. That summer, an organization of area residents formed to ensure that the people who were most directly affected would have a voice in what happened. One of those residents, a diminutive homemaker named Lois Gibbs, became a citizen leader. Her young son attended the elementary school on the site, and his health had been poor. Ms. Gibbs took notes from two physicians to the school board, recommending that her child be transferred to another school. But the Board refused the transfer. If the school was unsafe for her son, they reasoned, then it would be unsafe for all the children who attended it. They were not about to close the school because of one sickly child. Ms. Gibbs' response was to talk with the other residents and, in doing so, she discovered that health problems were widespread.

By early August 1978, the Department of Health issued an order recommending that the elementary school be closed, that pregnant women be evacuated from the neighborhood, along with children younger than two years old, that neighborhood residents not eat vegetables from their home gardens, and that residents limit the amount of time they spend in their basements. Within a short time, the state agreed to purchase the 239 homes closest to the canal. This decision to purchase some of the affected homes, and not the others, was a reflection of the state's lack of knowledge of how the chemicals were spreading underground.

Local residents knew from their own neighborhood survey that health problems affected families who lived outside the area of those original 239 homes. They knew that their homes now had little or no market value, and that their children were being affected by whatever was buried in the ground. They received support from a scientific survey of neighborhood residents, and the results were not encouraging to families who were raising children there, and who knew they would have little chance of selling their homes and moving elsewhere. Numerous health problems were confirmed:

- increases were noted in miscarriages, stillbirths, crib deaths, nervous breakdowns, hyperactivity, epilepsy, and urinary tract disorders;

- miscarriages were found to have increased 300% in women who had had previous pregnancies while living in other locations;

- there were almost three times as many birth defects. During the 5-year period from 1974 to 1978, 56% of the children in the Love Canal neighborhood were born with a birth defect (9 birth defects among 16 children born) that included three ears, double row of teeth, and mental retardation;

- out of 22 pregnancies occurring among from January 1979 to February 1980, only four normal babies were born. The rest of the pregnancies ended in a miscarriage, stillbirth, or a birth-defected child;

- an increase of almost 300% in urinary tract disorders;

- epilepsy, liver abnormality, headaches, and rectal bleeding.

The state health department issued a partial evacuation order in 1979, and President Carter evacuated the rest of the neighborhood in 1980, with an offer by the federal government to purchase their homes for fair market value.

In the end, it wasn't the scientific data that carried the day. It was persistent political pressure by the people who lived in the neighborhood. They demonstrated in the streets of their city, they wrote to their governor and the President. They marched on Mother's Day, they carried coffins to the state capitol, they held prayer vigils.[4]

....

The world was horrified in 1952 when the Great London Smog killed 4,000 people in a few days, and an estimated 8,000 more people died prematurely because of that pollution catastrophe. All told, about 0.15% of the city's 8.3 million people died from the Great London Smog.

The death rate from a pollution catastrophe in the small town of Libby, Montana, has killed more than *85 times* the proportion of that city's population as were killed by the Great London Smog. More than 13% of the town's people – at least 400 human beings – have died prematurely, and more are still dying.

In addition to those 400 people who have died in Libby, another 1,750 local residents have been sickened by asbestos dust.

And in the case of Libby, the source of the deadly pollution is known very precisely. It came from a vermiculite mine located a few miles outside of town, a mine that poisoned the people there with asbestos fibers for decades. A mine that poisoned the miners, their wives, and their children.

Gold miners had discovered vermiculite near Libby in 1881. Edgar Alley owned the mountain and, in 1919, he discovered that the rock, when heated, would expand to 15 times its normal size, was fireproof, and was exceedingly absorbent. He named the product "Zonolite" and began selling it as an insulation material and a soil conditioner. Zonolite was distributed to 60 processing plants across the U.S., starting its journey by being trucked into Libby, where it was dropped off for rail shipment.

W.R. Grace and Company bought the mine in 1963 and operated it until 1990.

At the height of operations, the mine alone generated five tons of dust daily (dismissed as "nuisance dust"). In 1969, tests showed that an additional twelve tons – 24,000 pounds – came out of the dry mill stack every day. And there were other stacks at the mine's operation also. Why was mere dust a concern?

The mine's vermiculite ore, when processed, released tremolite, the deadliest, most carcinogenic, form of asbestos. The tremolite's microscopic fibers can hang suspended in the air for long periods in the dust, and exposure to the fibers came most frequently from inhaling the dust. When inhaled, the fibers embed themselves into lung tissue, and cannot be expelled by coughing. It can take anywhere from 10 to 40 years for asbestos-related diseases to manifest themselves.

The State of Montana knew about the dust problem back in the 1940s. As was all too common at the time, the company operating the mine was notified beforehand when inspections would occur.

At the time that W.R. Grace purchased the facility in 1963, there had already been a whole series of reports, starting in at least 1956 from the Division for Disease Control of the State Board of Health, that the dust that was being generated at this facility contained asbestos that was of considerable toxicity to the men.

Roger Sullivan

Kalispell, Montana, attorney who represents clients in Libby

A Montana Division of Disease Control report dated January 12, 1956, described 77 "major offenders in either the production of dust or in sacrifice of exhaust capacity which permitted dust to be generated at points that should have been controlled as designed." The report was stamped *"CONFIDENTIAL: This report is confidential and is not for distribution except to the management of the Zonolite Company of Libby, Montana."*

Two and a half years later, the Board of Health followed up to see if improvements had been made, and repeated their earlier warning: "Inhalation of asbestos dust must be expected sooner or later to produce pulmonary fibrosis... pulmonary asbestosis [pulmonary fibrosis with asbestos present], once established, is a progressive disease with a bad prognosis."

The first known asbestosis case associated with Libby was diagnosed in 1959.

Earl Lovick worked at the mine for 29 years, including several years as its manager. On December 19, 1996, Lovick – at that time retired and in poor health – gave a legal deposition regarding what was known about working conditions at the mine...

Q: So, as of 1956, the company knew there was asbestos in the dust, correct?

A: Yes, sir.

Q: And the company also knew that asbestosis is from inhaling asbestos dust, correct?

A: Yes, sir.

Q: And the company also knew that there were workers at Zonolite who were inhaling asbestos dust, correct?

A: Yes, sir.

A 1959 company report, based on chest X-rays of workers, showed more than one in three workers at the mine (48 out of 130) had developed lung abnormalities. However, the company never informed workers of those X-ray results.

In all, more than a dozen Montana Health Department reports and the U.S. Bureau of Mines had warned of the asbestos-laden dust before W.R. Grace bought the mine in 1963. All the state inspection reports had the same "CONFIDENTIAL" stamp that only allowed the company management to see the information inside. At the time, this promise of confidentiality was the only way state officials were allowed access to sites they were inspecting.

Federal regulatory officials faced similar obstacles. Former inspectors of the now-dismantled U.S. Bureau of Mines told the *Seattle Post-Intelligencer* that taking forceful action against a mine in the West was almost impossible because of the mining industry's historic political clout. One former inspector said, "You would have to have bodies stacked up like cordwood and the public screaming for someone's head before we could get the government's lawyers to do anything."

A deputy U.S. attorney who owned a cabin near Libby reported to the Public Health Service in 1969 that "there is a dust problem at Libby... affecting workers and the community." But still, no federal action ever followed.

Also in 1969, W.R. Grace received a warning from its insurance company: *When an X-ray picture shows a change for the worse, that person must be told and that person must be gotten out of the environment which is aggravating his condition. Failure to do so is not humane and is in direct violation of federal law.*

Even before the insurance company's warning, though, W.R. Grace was already looking at ways to reduce potential liability for workers' health problems. The company's safety chief, Peter Kostic, wrote an internal memo marked "personal and confidential" in which he suggested reassigning 32 employees whose X-rays showed lung disease to other jobs at the operation, jobs where dust was less an issue. Kostic wrote, "If we minimize their exposure to dust... chances are we may be able to keep them on the job until they retire, thus precluding the high cost of total disability."

An internal W.R. Grace report that same year warned company president Peter Grace that "tremolite is definitely a health hazard."

X-rays conducted in 1969 revealed a heavy presence of lung disease among employees – of employees who had worked at the mine for 21-25 years, 92% of them had a lung disease.

An internal memo by another company executive in1969 warned that, "We should also be concerned with the obligations to our employees; namely, permitting them to perform their services under working conditions which we have good reason to believe are hazardous."

But W.R. Grace never significantly improved their working conditions. They never told the workers how dangerous the material they were handling really was. The state never told the workers. The federal government never told the workers.

In 1973, the U.S. Bureau of Mines told W.R. Grace that it needed to install showers for employees so they wouldn't be carrying the dust home on their clothing, spreading the dust to their homes and their families. Two years later, Grace installed two shower stalls – for shifts of 60 men each. Three years after that, Grace promised more showers, but they never built them.

A Grace internal memo dated May 24, 1977, discussed and rejected the notion of placing warning labels on their product:

There is a risk that Grace will attract adverse publicity from national media concerning the presence of asbestos in vermiculate (sic).

We believe that a decision to affix warning labels to our products would result in substantial sales losses.

The EPA documented in 1982 that air samples in the town of Libby (over six miles from the mine) had captured significant levels of asbestos fibers, five times the current air quality standards.

An EPA study from the mid-1980s projected a death rate of "almost 100 percent" for W.R. Grace mine workers.

They come up to us one time – and you were totally covered with dust all the time – and they told us, "Whatever you do, don't use the air hose to blow the dust off you."

We said, "Why?"

And they said, "You'll embed it in your skin."

"Embed what?"

"Well, the dust. Just the dust."

They never told us – you know – what it was, that it was toxic. They knew about it; they never said a word to us.

Butch Hurlbert

former mine worker, diagnosed with asbestosis

However, the company wanted to show it was a good corporate neighbor. Grace donated land in front of one of its bagging plants for two Little League fields in Libby. Waste from the mine was used in the soil at the fields, along the dugouts and backstops, at the base of the grandstands. A local resident said it was "as common as gravel." There were large piles of the dirt near the baseball fields – those piles were never fenced off, and there was never a sign cautioning people against playing on them. Those Little League fields were used until 1997.

Contaminated soil was also found at the high school track, the middle school track, and an area near an elementary school. It was also brought home and spaded into gardens and around foundations in town.

Grace closed the mine in 1990 due to lagging sales and mounting lawsuits by former employees and their families. As more workers got sick, and also their family members, more of them began to file lawsuits against W.R. Grace, though some workers died before their cases came to trial.

It wasn't just workers who were poisoned. Wives of miners were poisoned. Children of miners were poisoned. People whose only connection to the mine was playing at the Little League field were poisoned.

Libby resident Gayla Benefield lost both her parents to the disease. In all, 42 members of her family had been diagnosed by 2005.

Benefield had never considered herself an environmentalist. In fact, she used to speak out against what she perceived as environmentalists' efforts to dictate to her community how to deal with their environment. In the summer of 1999, however, she drove up Rainey Creek Canyon, where W.R. Grace had operated its mine.

I had not been up there for nearly 30 years and was amazed to see for myself what industry and the government's perception of reclamation was! The area looked like a moonscape... at that time, I didn't know how contaminated it actually was. All I knew was that the mine site had used a process to separate the ore that involved chemicals. At the base of the mountain of tailings was Rainey Creek. That creek ran into the Kootenai River which in turn runs by my home.

As Benefield's mother Margaret Vatland lay dying of asbestosis, she told her daughter, "Get the bastards. Don't let them get away with it."

By 1999, when a series of articles in the *Seattle Post-Intelligencer* broke the story about what was happening in the town, Libby residents had filed 140 lawsuits. The company had long denied in court that it knew asbestos was dangerous, and they claimed they did everything they could to protect their workers.

Three days after the *Seattle Post-Intelligencer* began reporting on Libby, the EPA sent staffers to Libby to investigate the scope of the contamination and the necessary cleanup.

Starting late in 1999, an attempt was made by some in Congress, including then-Senator John Ashcroft and two Montana Republicans – Sen. Conrad Burns and Rep. Rick Hill – to pass legislation that would have limited Grace's liability to lawsuits.

Montana's then-Governor Judy Martz had the authority, as do other governors, to request the EPA to "fast track" a site for Superfund designation, which would quickly put federal dollars into the cleanup process. In 2001, Martz rejected using her "fast track" authority to designate Libby for federal Superfund attention. Under heavy pressure, she reversed herself a couple months later.

W.R. Grace filed for Chapter 11 bankruptcy in 2001. In an effort to insulate itself from legal judgments, the company shrunk itself from $6.3 billion in assets in 1995 to less than $90 million in 1998 through creating subsidiaries and spinning off assets.

A lawsuit by Libby residents against the state of Montana resulted in a $43 million settlement in 2011. Grace contributed to a medical program in Libby in 2000 (after the story broke) and put in around $20 million over the next decade. Early in 2012, W.R. Grace indicated it was ready to enter a $19.6 million settlement for the medical program.

Money is only worth so much, though. Former Libby resident Mike Nelson, an asbestosis patient, had signed up for the state of Montana settlement when the case was in progress. After the settlement was announced, though, he told a reporter that it meant little to him. His own medical condition was getting worse, and "I've lost my father, my mother, my stepmother and my father-in-law... They're all dead. All from asbestos."

The company and seven of its executives were indicted in 2005 on charges that they knowingly exposed their workers and the general public to asbestos. Those company officials were charged with various crimes that involved concealing the hazards of tremolite from its workers, as well as obstructing justice. But charges against some were dismissed and the federal trial ended in 2009 with the rest of the defendants being acquitted. The statute of limitations was a problem; so was the amount of evidence that the judge excluded from the trial; so was the fact that the judge denounced a key prosecution witness – a former W.R. Grace employee – in open court and put strict limitations on the jury's ability to consider the testimony of that witness.

A former miner, the late Les Scramstad was poisoned by the asbestos. So were his wife and two of his children. Before his death, Scramstad spoke of his dream of a long row of gallows at the mine site, He said, "On those gallows I'd see swinging all the bodies of all the company bosses who knew they were killing us, who knew they were killing our wives and children, who knew they were killing this town and other towns where their poisoned ore was handled. They knew it and they hid it."

"I hope I live long enough to see them swing," he added But Les Scramstad died in 2007. Nobody has ever been convicted of a crime.

In 2009, some Grace executives were charged with breaking environmental law, along with conspiracy and obstruction of justice, but were acquitted by a federal jury.

Although more than 400 people were killed in Libby (so far), no one has been charged with their deaths. It's doubtful anyone will spend a day in jail for those deaths, nor for the premature deaths yet to come.

It's possible that many more Americans outside Libby have been or will be affected, because Zonolite insulation was used in somewhere between 15 and 35 million homes in the U.S. (and many in Canada as well), and the vermiculite from which it came was used in wallboard, gardening products, and cat litter.[5]

Stories like these are about the environment, of course. But look at what else they're about. In these four communities, simple human greed led to people being hurt – even killed – so that a company could make more money. In each of them, people faced dangers that were not merely unknown to them, but that were hidden from them. In each of these communities, the governments that should have acted in the interest of the public instead acted to protect the interest of the polluter that had poisoned the people.

The victims in Libby suffered a slow death. And the miners there, once they learned the truth, had to live with the knowledge that they had brought the killing tremolite fibers into their homes, where those fibers would also sicken, and in some cases kill, their loved ones. Many victims in Bhopal died overnight. Survivors suffered stillbirths and birth defects, as well as damage to their eyes, lungs, and nervous systems.

Residents of Love Canal suffered mysterious damages to the health of their families – miscarriages and stillbirths, nervous system disorders, birth defects – as well as their homes being rendered worthless. And the residents of Minamata suffered through nerve damage, brain damage, vision problems, slurred speech, loss of muscular control, and the loss of their livelihoods.

A terrible injustice was committed against these people – you don't need me to tell you that.

How angry would you be if you found out you had a fatal disease because you were being poisoned at work, and your employer knew it all the time? How would you feel if you had bought a house where dangerous chemicals were buried in the soil and nobody told you?

If your children were getting mysteriously ill, would you become an activist and demand answers? If your child was born with a birth defect because of exposure to buried chemicals, would you demand that the people responsible actually take responsibility? Does a free market give license for companies and governments to allow families to be poisoned? Is it OK for families to be saddled with worthless homes and chronic health problems so that a corporation can have a bigger profit margin?

Some people hear the word "environment" and they forget that it refers to us humans. The environment isn't just natural areas, it's our communities, it's our homes, it's where we work.

Some environmentalists forget this. And a lot of the people who really, really hate environmentalists forget this.

Do you hear of air pollution and think it's just an environmental issue – simply a matter of not being able to see as far over the Grand Canyon? What about the cost of that air pollution to millions of people for increased medical costs they will have to pay? What about the cost to businesses for the missed work and reduced productivity those medical problems create? What about the damage to buildings and bridges and other property because of the chemicals in the pollution? What about the people who die prematurely because polluting industries avoided the expense of treating their pollution? Some of these are issues of public health, all of them are issues of justice.

But we also have to remind ourselves, as in the story of Noah's ark, that we and the natural world – we're all in this together. Birds fell out of the sky at Minamata and, of course, fish were still alive but carried poison in their bodies. At Bhopal, pets were killed, so were livestock and wildlife and trees. I haven't come across information about animals at Love Canal and Libby, but it's not a real stretch to conclude that they likely suffered along with their human companions. Our pets and livestock and wildlife breathe the same air that we do. Our pets, at least, drink the same water. Poison sometimes doesn't kill until it passes a few links up the food chain.

We don't generally think about justice in terms of animals, do we? Perhaps we should. But we'd better think about it for ourselves, at the very least.

We'd better think about it when the most important determinants in deciding where to site polluting facilities are the race and economic status of the people who live there.[6] And we'd better think about it when citizens who raise questions about the effects of pollution are targeted with hate speech.

CHAPTER SEVENTEEN

Big Green

An environmentalist says something like, "We have to stop dumping toxic chemicals in our water, because it's poisoning children." Then someone... counters that you have no right to speak up, because he saw you use a paper napkin, which is made out of trees and will be thrown in the garbage.

From watching the news on TV, or listening to the radio, or reading the newspaper, or browsing the Internet, you might get the impression that environmentalists are one big, monolithic group. You've no doubt seen how often news stories referring to an environmental organization simply identify them as "environmentalists." The group being quoted may have a unique perspective or membership that sets them apart from other environmentalists, but this fact makes little difference to most news outlets – too many news organizations simply fail to distinguish one group of organized citizens from another. Whether it's a group that advocates for wilderness, or national parks, or renewable energy, or family-scale farms, or clean water, many reporters and news outlets are satisfied with simply calling them all "environmentalists."

Outside the context of news reports, sometimes you'll hear citizens working to protect America's environment being referred to as "Big Green," implying that environmentalists are unified and powerful, all working under the same banner.

This has not been my experience.

There are thousands of organizations in the United States that address environmental issues. Some have been around for more than a hundred years, while some form only to take on one localized issue and then go out of existence. Some groups have a nationwide membership, some exist only in one small town. Some environmentalists care most deeply about protecting America's natural heritage

– the beauty of her forests and mountains and deserts and rivers. Others care primarily about what kind of future we are building through our energy policy, or the way we use our farmland, or how our cities grow. Some want to save animals, all animals. Some want to conserve animals with the intention of preserving Americans' ability to go hunting and fishing. Some environmentalists have a very direct interest, trying to protect themselves and their families from direct harm due to the pollution of land, the depletion of water resources, or the poisoning of the air they breathe. Other environmentalists act out of more philosophical or maybe even altruistic motives, not being immediately affected by the outcome of the issue, but working for what they believe is right.

It's important to remember that different people have different personal histories. Have they or a loved one been sickened by pollutants? Have their land and livelihood been threatened by a coal company? Is their outlook something they learned from their parents? Is it based in a love of a place? Is it based on scientific knowledge? Religious belief? Many kinds of experiences motivate people to protect the environment, and those diverse experiences make them different from one another from the get-go.

I work for a Montana organization that has a certain perspective about how to best take on its issues, whether those issues are environmental, agricultural, or simple justice for citizens. We have members, people who write annual (or sometimes monthly) checks for membership dues. Some of our members have formed affiliate groups in their local communities. Those affiliates elect representatives to the organization's board of directors. The full membership elects at-large board representatives and also elects the officers. Members run the meetings. Members, or the board of directors they elect, vote on policy resolutions. Members represent the organization to the press. Members testify to policymakers.

Not every organization shares this grassroots philosophy, and that's OK. Different approaches work better in different circumstances and with different people. Some organizations have more of a top-down style, involving members only as donors, not real decision-makers. Some organizations are very confrontational, and some are very inclined toward negotiation and toward getting along with politicians.

Not only are environmental groups very different from one another, but those individual people we call environmentalists sometimes have deep differences with one another. They disagree about the best organizational model, the best strategy, the most important issues. They sometimes have turf battles, they compete to get recognition for their accomplishments, and their leaders sometimes have simple personality conflicts.

Some environmentalists can be very judgmental of other environmentalists.

For the sake of illustration, I invite you to walk through a small portion of a written debate that took place several years ago on the website of *Grist*, an online environmental magazine.

Matthew Prescott, a spokesman for PETA – People for the Ethical Treatment of Animals – said in 2007 that, "you just cannot be a meat-eating environmentalist." His provocative statement didn't just reflect PETA's longstanding desire to protect animals. It also made a case that meat production activities are a major contributor to global warming.

In order to draw publicity to this position, PETA announced plans to send a person touring the country in a Hummer while wearing a chicken suit. PETA also planned to advertise on billboards with a cartoon mocking Al Gore, showing him eating a drumstick, and captioned with the words "Too Chicken to Go Vegetarian? Meat is the No. 1 Cause of Global Warming."

These remarks and this plan drew a critical response in an op-ed on *Grist* from Alex Roth, a self-described environmentalist[1]:

By saying that "you just cannot be a meat-eating environmentalist," Prescott is recycling one of the oldest and stupidest retorts in the history of the environmental movement. I like to call it "the paper napkin defense." It works like this: An environmentalist says something like, "We have to stop dumping toxic chemicals in our water, because it's poisoning children." Then someone who thinks he's very smart counters that you have no right to speak up, because he saw you use a paper napkin, which is made out of trees and will be thrown in the garbage. As illogical and irrelevant as such a response is, haven't you heard it a thousand times?

And now you've heard it again, because PETA's new campaign is exactly in this vein. Environmentalists say we have to stop burning so much coal and gasoline, because fossil-fuel emissions threaten the future of our planet. And Matt Prescott, the Meatless Genius, wants to shout you down because – admit it – you ate a chicken Caesar salad last Wednesday.

Of course, most of us carnivorous environmentalists do sometimes eat factory-farmed meat, just as vegans sometimes eat products made from industrial soybeans. In a nation where more than 85 percent of soybeans are genetically modified, while none of them are labeled as such, it's hard to avoid. Likewise, most environmentalists drive cars from time to time, even though we know driving is bad for the environment. This doesn't mean we're not environmentalists -- it means we live in the real world.

These days, climate change is known to be exacerbated by most human activities, from stir-frying tofu to watching videos of endangered baby harp seals. To me, being an environmentalist simply means supporting policies and practices that promote a healthy environment.

Roth went on to say:

Unfortunately, many people mistakenly believe that being an environmentalist means being a shrill, opinionated extremist who tells others how to live their lives. Many associate environmentalism with exaggerated factual claims and an insufferable holier-than-thou attitude. Prescott, whom I admit is an environmentalist, is only perpetuating such insidious stereotypes.

It is these stereotypes that, for the better part of the last decade, have encouraged the public to ignore environmentalists' well-founded warnings about climate change.

Roth's op-ed brought in 72 pages of comments over the following three days, along with many passages from articles and links to other reading material. I am quoting only a few of those comments here, in the hope that it will help demonstrate how far afield opinions can range on only one subject, and how deep the disagreements can be. People who call themselves environmentalists have very diverse views on what that means, and what is the best way of changing the world for the better. Because these are blog entries, please excuse the spelling and punctuation errors that accompany the commenters' speedy typing.

One reader observed that:

A huge portion of the earth's surface is not suitable for cropping, but is great for growing permenant (sic) grass and pasture. That green stuff can very nicely be converted to usable protein for humans by ruminant animals (cows, sheep, goats etc.). Eating grass fed beef, lamb, and so forth is not a bad option.

....

Another defended PETA and their tactics:

Obviously, PETA is using hyperbole to make a point. Duh. Any activist group worth its salt does that. And the reason they do it is because it works. Look at how PETA managed to get global warming and animal agriculture's impact on it covered by the New York Times. Seems like they must be doing something right.

....

This reader looked toward bringing about change in small steps:

There's a big logical leap from "Factory farming is bad" to "People who eat any meat don't care about the environment (and probably kick kittens too.)" What about eating local and organic meat? What about catching it yourself? What if you eat factory-farmed meat, but you've worked tirelessly to protect large swathes of land? Some perspective, please.

This strain of self-righteous veganism is really counter-productive. If you want people to stop eating meat, stop talking down to them and start being helpful. Bust out the delicious meat-free recipes and take baby steps.

Encourage people to buy local, organic meat in the meantime. You're not going to stop industrial farming overnight. But the people whose dollars actually drive factory farming can be persuaded to put those dollars towards more sustainable practices. That's a step in the right direction.

....

This reader agreed, with a closing nod to Homer Simpson:

If you think for one second that you are going to convince Americans to stop eating meat you have lost your mind. Yes we should all eat less meat, but when you force this down their throat, no progress will be made. Most likely they will say, look at the wacka-doo hippie environmentalists, they are sooo silly. Its hard enough to get normal people to make good decisions about the environment without the "YOUR (sic) GOING TO HELL" complex turning the general public against the movement. Promote eating less meat. Calling the typical meat eating American the devil, you will get no positive results. What reaction are you trying to get? What good are you truly doing but beating your chest, look at me I am meat free!! Burning bridges with the meat eaters will only make it harder for us to do the right thing. Maybe just say a chicken nugget has X carbon emission while a Tofu nugget has this. Make your statement positive. This statement from peta makes me wanna go eat a burger. WITH CHEESE!! mmmm cheese.

....

This reader argued that alternative farming methods are just as bad as factory farms:

It is no more environment-friendly to eat these kinds of cattle than factory-farmed cattle. This kind of farming still damages the environment in the same way the factory farms do: it takes up land, creates huge amounts of waste, emits methane gas, and kills animals. As much as you try to escape the fact, eating meat= harming the environment.

....

And this reader disagreed:

It is entirely possible to eat meat and be an environmentalist, if one supports sustainable, humane farming; consumes reasonable (small) quantities; and speaks out against Factory Farming methods. In fact, it is probably the meat eaters who have the biggest clout in changing the horrendous methods under which most meat is produced! Unfortunately, most of them are uninformed about what really goes on, and most of the rest don't care.

....

A plea for reasonableness from this reader:

As I chomp down on my chicken cesar (sic) salad I wonder if we have lost our collective minds in America. Just like with religion there are those who will question how righteous others are in their beliefs. Are we going to start witch hunts next to determine who is "truly" green and who isn't? If eating meat is the new litmus test then check my name off the green list.

....

This reader differentiated the message from the messenger:

People love to hate PETA, including me. They're the reason I can't tell most people that I'm vegan. But no matter who the messenger is, or how it's delivered, it's true. The earth is warming, and we caused it to happen. What are you going to say to your grandchildren in 2050 when they ask you what you personally did to prevent global climate change?

....

Another reader expounded on the values of changing farming methods:

It is clear that consuming factory farmed animal products is one of the more destructive environmental acts we take part in. It needs to be made clear however that it is the industrial agriculture methods of livestock management that are the problem not meat and animal products themselves.

I also understand though that eating pasture raised, locally produced animal products (especially beef) can be one of the most positive environmental actions we can take. As I understand it, such livestock practices actually can contribute positively to energy systems, top soils and stream ecosystems. Small scale livestock farming is also a much more viable form of small scale farming economically (it is less labor intensive, more profitable and more appealing to young farmers) than production for a vegetarian diet...

...By this logic, dollars spent towards supporting this kind of animal husbandry can perhaps make a larger positive environmental impact than spending on a vegetarian diet, while directly challenging the very destructive practice of factory farming...

... The inputs for industrial agriculture to support even a vegetarian diet are highly energy intensive, on top of the extra travel involved with the seasonal and climatic demands of a vegetarian diet. Many of our organic carrots come from Israel, our apples come from New Zealnd (sic) and China, etc.

I also just read that row cropping soy destroys acres of habitat for wildlife, kills the soils and pollutes water systems, not to mention it promotes the development of GMOs...

...But again, it's the industrialized monoculture model that is the problem, not the plants themselves.

....

But this reader disagreed that the focus should be on "animal factories":

I love all this talk about supporting "sustainable," "family" farms. Does anyone who says this have any idea how many animals are killed every year to "sustain" America's meat habit? It's something like 25 billion, if you include the billions of fish vacummed (sic) out of the ocean (but not including the millions of dolphins, turtles, birds, and other sea animals killed as "by-catch.") 25 billion! That's, what, 4 times the human population of the entire planet?

....

This reader criticized PETA's sense of ideological purity:

...I've worked in the corporate-responsibility and grassroots environmental movements for a good while now, and from that I've come to see the worth of many ideologically purist groups within the movement. I'll never live in a purely green designed, zero waste commune, but from communities such as those new ideas and new technologies are born. But those groups don't attack potential friends all the time, and PETA does... It's not the same work, environmentalism is about saving ecosystems and species, not all individual animals, but it is work almost any animal rights supporter can and does get behind.

....

Same thing, different reader:

PETA's "if you like to eat hamburgers, you must like clubbing baby seals" rhetoric is counterproductive.

....

But another PETA defender stepped in:

Many people replying to this article seem to be attacking PETA on the basis of their so-called "radical" means of protest. To these people, I ask:

Does history remember best those who fought for justice, or the people who sat and did nothing?

Like the quote says: "All my heroes have FBI files."

....

This reader looked at people's personal moral choices:

I do believe I make moral choices everyday....I can attempt to be as humane as possible by purchasing grain fed and cage free chickens and eggs. I can also petition my representatives to pass humane killing laws for animal farms and producers. I can support organizations that help animals in need. These are things we can do that can minimize animal suffering.

⋯⋯⋯⋯⋯⋯⋯⋯⋯⋯⋯⋯⋯⋯⋯⋯⋯⋯⋯⋯

Another reader on the value of making small changes:

I know so many people who don't really get on board with the whole "green" thing, because they are afraid that they'll have to give up meat, wear hemp shoes and never use paper towels again. It's not the way to motivate people into action. Instead, the message should be "one change makes a difference - by all means go on eating you (sic) *filet mignon but why not make sure it's grass-fed" or "by all means, wear your fancy non-organic clothes, but have you thought about perhaps buying one organic t-shirt?" People are open to making small changes and should be encouraged to do so if we want the green movement to go mainstream.*

⋯⋯⋯⋯⋯⋯⋯⋯⋯⋯⋯⋯⋯⋯⋯⋯⋯⋯⋯⋯

This reader disliked PETA, but liked the message:

I don't like PETA as they misrepresent animal rights, but they are correct on this issue.

If you live in civilization, you cannot call yourself an environmentalist if you eat animal flesh.

⋯⋯⋯⋯⋯⋯⋯⋯⋯⋯⋯⋯⋯⋯⋯⋯⋯⋯⋯⋯

Commenting on survival of species:

Everything on this planet is energy. All species from bacteria to animals consume energy to survive. Thought, self awareness and morals play no part in basic survival. Your philosophy is interesting but not realistic. Living in civilization has no impact in my self definition. Here is the definition of environmentalist that I use: "any person who advocates or works to protect the air, water, animals, plants, and other natural resources from pollution or its effects". I will call myself that and I eat flesh.

⋯⋯⋯⋯⋯⋯⋯⋯⋯⋯⋯⋯⋯⋯⋯⋯⋯⋯⋯⋯

This reader defended vegetarianism for its humaneness, but went further:

Caring for animals, is to me, the basic point of empathy, but if you need more convincing look no further than how it affects ourselves.

"Environmentalism" though, typically means someone cares about more than just humans, more than even animals. They care about protecting tiny little plants and flora

and even microorganisms. I've heard environmentalists say they even empathize with water itself.

So "Environmentalism" is a step BEYOND vegetarianism, since you can be a vegetarian and not an "environmentalist". Someone can still earn the title of "vegetarian" by refusing to eat meat, even if that person doesn't typically get behind "environmental" issues or candidates.

....

Another PETA defender weighed in:

Even in the post factory farm happy cow in the field happy chicken in the barn smiling pig in the meadow world. they still use a minimum of twice the resources that plant based alternatives do ....and you cannot eat beef without cutting down rainforest it takes almost 25 acres of land per cow not to mention the vast resources of water to raise each cow...

...I think the real issue now is that the western diet if extended to the entire population of the planet so all 6.7 billion of us ate 100 kilos of meat per years we would need about 9.7 earths to do so if the same number of people just ate plant based food well we can all have children and restore about 50% of our farm land to wildlife.

....

A reader on the importance of overpopulation:

The real problem isn't that people eat too much, or that they eat the wrong things (both of which are true). The biggest problem is that we are over populated. Soon it won't matter how efficient we are with producing our food or green we try to be, we simply can not healthily support a population our size for any extended period of time.

....

This reader wrote about the value of incremental change:

I don't own a car. But I don't preach about it to other people. As much as I'd like to see a world without cars it doesn't help to tell people to stop driving cars. You can be much more effective if you are indirect. If you get people to think about environmental problems and what choices they have that's half the battle. Being holier-than-thou is always counterproductive.

....

A reader commented on the value of criticism from the outside:

To give a parallel example of PETA's stance: I personally am deeply puzzled by those many professed Christians who support pre-emptive war abroad and the death penalty here in the US. It would seem very clear to me that these forms of socialized murder are directly at odds with such fundamental Christian teachings as "Thou shalt not kill" and "Love thy neighbor as thyself". If I am not a part of that faith community am I therefore to be excluded from expressing this critique? To me it's a very reasonable call at this moment in our history to suggest that non-carnivory may indeed be fundamental to practical environmentalism. And whether that call comes from card-carrying "environmentalists" or not is actually quite irrelevant. You know, sometimes we need a comment from the outside to help us question those many comfortable self-justifications and self-satisfactions that we as a species seem so amply capable of.

....

A former vegan on a spiritual and philosophical quest:

Once I'd read those books, I could no longer convince myself that it was any more "wrong" for humans to eat cows or pigs or monkeys than for lions to eat antelopes, or rattlesnakes to eat rodents, or black widow spiders to eat insects, or orcas to eat seals, or...well, you get the idea. Feeding and being fed upon is central to life, the primary driving force in evolution, and humans are a part of the living world. We evolved not as herbivores nor as carnivores but as omnivores—we're biologically prepared to eat an enormous range of foods, including animal foods...

...Yes, it's true that the Standard American Diet--SAD—isn't healthy for people, either, but that's not because it contains animal foods. No, it's due to the fact that most of the animal foods Americans are eating have been produced in animal factories, resulting in higher total and saturated fat and lower essential fatty acids plus contamination with a variety of harmful substances including antibiotics and other drugs and, in cattle, growth hormones. Foods from animals that, in the case of ruminants such as cows and bison, are entirely grassfed have healthy nutritional profiles, as do foods from chickens and pigs that are pastured...

....

Another reader on the importance of baby steps:

Recently I read an article that encouraged everyone to take baby steps (re: climate change) and not be discouraged by those that call you a hypocrite because you aren't doing everything all the time. The theory is a light blub (sic) today and hybrid tomorrow – one small step precipitates another and the snowball effect takes over. PETA might consider this before making statements about meat-eating monsters.

A meat-loving, SUV-driving, soccer-mom probably does care about the environment and is concerned about climate change. But she is also over-worked, under appreciated and just plain tried. She'd probably be interested in making some earth-friendly changes, but needs to feel empowered to do so AND not overwhelmed with too much. I would envite (sic) her to visit her local farmer's market to buy locally grown foods. I'd say "Thanks for taking an interest and trying. Here's another easy thing to do ..." Before you know it she might be working with the PTA to get the school board to include locally grown food in the lunch menu.

Doesn't that seem more productive?

....

Back to discussing the value of in-your-face tactics:

To those who feel that Peta's in-your-face approach will lose them allies: I really don't think they are trying to win any popularity contests or get you to join their jolly club. Or to get others to join your jolly club for that matter. If just a few more Grist readers have started making the connection between their eating habits and their environmental aspirations as a result of discussions like this then I would guess they'd think they've succeeded.

....

And another reader on the other side:

Yes PETA's campaigns get people talking, but much of what they say is "wow those PETA people are a freak show, and I won't listen [to] any environmentalists anymore, they're all crackpots". PETA is an extremist animal-rights group whose actions are hurting the chances of reaching the broad-based political consensus needed to stop global warming.

These comments represent just a small portion of the reader comments in response to the PETA story and responding op-ed. As you can see, many people just plain dislike PETA. Most of the commenters did not regard it as an environmental organization.

And you can see as well that many people think deeply about what it means to be an environmentalist.

But more than anything, you can see how deeply and passionately divided environmentalists can be over this one, single issue, from strategy, to philosophy, to morality, to the facts of the issue, and more.

In 2006, the United Nations Food and Agriculture Organization said that meat production is responsible for 18% of worldwide greenhouse gas emissions, substantially more than motorized modes of transportation.[2] This and other similar analyses have contributed to the online debate above, but they have caused many to wonder what really contributes to greenhouse gas emissions by livestock.

Nicolette Hahn Niman, a California rancher and attorney, responded by distinguishing between meat that comes through the factory farm system and meat which is raised in more traditional ways, like pasturing outdoors instead of feeding crops like soybeans, minimizing the use of machinery, and avoiding synthetic fertilizers.[3] She cited research in Sweden showing that differences in how food is produced can cause carbon dioxide emissions to vary by a factor of 10.[4]

Kevin Boyer of the Schmidt Foundation's 11th Hour Project reiterated this, and also argued that healthy grasslands are important to sequestering atmospheric carbon. "When we understand carbon sequestration," says Boyer, "we see why cattle need not be the climate disaster they are often touted as."[5]

I'm not a vegetarian myself (though I was for a few years when I was younger). However, I try to buy my meat from sources that are not part of the "animal factory" system. Most of the meat I eat is produced by the Charter ranch north of Billings.

When I see stories like the 2007-2008 incident involving Westland / Hallmark Meats of California pushing "downer" cows into their packing plant, I get a little queasy. I would hope that anyone would get queasy (or angry, or horrified, or something) from that. And I'm not a bit surprised when some people swear off meat altogether after seeing sick and weak cows being pushed by a forklift as they lie on the ground, too weak to even get to their feet. It sure makes me think about my own morality if I take part in that transaction.

I sometimes think of a bumper sticker I once saw: *When we buy meat, we are paying for the suffering and death of the earth's most defenseless beings.* Some Native Americans speak of a tradition of paying homage to the spirit of the animal they killed for food, and exercising a responsibility to use that animal's life to the fullest, and not to waste it.

Jeanie Alderson, whose family raises cattle in Montana's Tongue River Valley, told an audience in 2013,

There is an inherent violence to our life that is raising animals for slaughter and for food. I understand how hard it must be for people who don't live this life to grasp the immense love that is a part of raising animals and caring for land. It is hard to put into words the ancient covenants we have with our surroundings. I know that words like grace, honor, dignity, gratitude and beauty are not what many think of when they bite into a hamburger or even when they eschew the eating of meat... for most of us in this line of work, the care and welfare of our animals is an ancient and sacred trust.[6]

The PETA discussion above is just a small portion of *one* online debate covering *one* issue over three days. Think of the many issues that could be discussed, and how much disagreement those issues could incite from environmentalists. Pundits and reporters who talk about environmentalists as if they are all the same – those pundits and reporters clearly don't know what they're talking about.

Some environmentalists don't understand this, either. I've met plenty of people who've joined environmental groups, thinking that everyone in the group would have the same thinking about all issues. Such people eventually come to a point of decision. They will realize that people who agree on some things don't necessarily agree on other things. Or they will angrily pull away, disappointed that the organization falls short of where they think it should be.

The Black Hills Energy Coalition in South Dakota went through a schism early in its development. Some early members wanted to address Native American issues along with uranium mining, while others wanted to stay focused on uranium mining and to seek solutions within the political system.

The group that split off called their new organization the Black Hills Alliance, and its direction was decidedly different from the original group. While the Black

Hills Energy Coalition kept its middle-of-the-road stance and its focus on the political process, the Black Hills Alliance eschewed politics and became perceived widely as more of a counterculture organization. While the Black Hills Energy Coalition focused on its statewide ballot measure to give South Dakotans the power to approve or disapprove nuclear energy projects, the Black Hills Alliance sponsored widely-publicized events like the Black Hills International Survival Gathering, which attracted countercultural folks from across the country and beyond, as well as stars from the entertainment industry. The Alliance even had chapters in Chicago and San Francisco.[7]

Sad to say, from the original group that drew together people with shared concerns about the impacts of uranium mining, there emerged two disparate groups that, to be honest, had a certain hostility and suspicion toward one another.

The Black Hills Alliance did manage to get some dedicated young attorneys who made successful courtroom challenges to uranium developers and inept (some would say corrupt) state regulators who simply didn't follow the law. For example, those attorneys discovered that Union Carbide had been drilling in Craven Canyon without a permit. It turned out that a state official with the South Dakota Conservation Commission had told Union Carbide to go ahead with its drilling. Black Hills Alliance attorneys urged the attorney general's office to prosecute, and that office did, but they also asked the judge to go easy on fining Union Carbide.[8]

Those of us in the Black Hills Energy Coalition appreciated the Black Hills Alliance's legal work, but there were so many other differences in strategy and in world-view that the two groups were never able to collaborate. Yes, the Alliance was interested in uranium mining and its impacts. But it was also interested in causes like releasing Leonard Peltier, convicted of murdering two FBI agents, from prison. As Energy Coalition member Lawrence Perry remarked, "If you don't gain the support of the ranchers, farmers, and businessmen, you can't get much accomplished. This is a conservative state."[9]

Those with a different outlook on the world saw all this through a different lens. I came across an excerpt from a doctoral dissertation at the University of

Wisconsin in which the doctoral candidate asserted that the Black Hills Energy Coalition "refused to associate with Native Americans because they feared alienating potential white followers."[10]

This assertion is false. But it does reflect the misunderstanding and suspicion that I'm talking about.

The group's countercultural approach alienated many South Dakotans. Being better-funded and more noticeable, the Alliance conveyed the impression to many people that those who challenged the plans of uranium companies, and environmentalists in general, were radicals – "hippies" – and not like most people who live in South Dakota. Union Carbide Corporation's representative in South Dakota capitalized on this, referring only to the Black Hills Alliance when he spoke, ignoring all the mainstream groups that had endorsed and worked for the uranium mining initiative in South Dakota.

All this served to confuse many local residents about the difference between the two groups. Some news outlets were beyond confused, and were utterly ignorant of the differences. Our experience with a Rapid City television station inviting the wrong group to debate for the uranium initiative in 1980 is a good example.

I think the main frustration that Energy Coalition members had with the Black Hills Alliance – beyond the Alliance's acceptance of that TV station's misguided invitation to speak for the uranium initiative – was that the Black Hills Alliance's success with out-of-state fundraising gave it wider visibility on uranium mining issues.

Obviously, I am not an impartial observer. But one thing I took away from this experience was the degree to which groups addressing environmental issues – as well as individuals – can be very, very different from one another.

I needed to learn that lesson, and so do other environmentalists, every day. So does the news media. So do politicians, and so does the general public.

The organization I work for today – the Northern Plains Resource Council in Montana – was founded by cattle ranchers like Boyd and Anne Charter, Ellen Pfister, and Bob Tully. To be truthful, Northern Plains is as much an agricultural group as it is an environmental group because of its long history of protecting farms and ranches from the impacts of energy development, protecting the rights of landowners facing such development, and working to restore competition to the meatpacking industry. With its deep agricultural roots, Northern Plains has a core belief that family-based farms and ranches are better for Montana's environment, economy, and communities than corporate agriculture or converting productive ag land to sprawling subdivisions.

The members I've met and worked with over the years are very different from one another. Some are lifelong Democrats, some are rock-ribbed Republicans. Some live in town, some live on farms and ranches. Some are wage-earners, some operate businesses. Some are prosperous, some struggle financially.

Those differences are among the things I value most about the organization. When varied perspectives are involved in debating an issue and making a decision, it's been my experience that it makes for a stronger decision-making process. Groups that only allow one perspective – whether an environmental group, a religious group, or a political group – are groups that have little room for the rest of America.

CHAPTER EIGHTEEN

17 Reasons Why Environmental Issues Are So Hard to Resolve

With environmentalists disagreeing among themselves – so often and so passionately – is it any wonder that the general public has trouble agreeing on the best resolutions for environmental problems?

Environmental issues are hard for a reason. Actually, a lot of reasons. For example:

1. Environmental issues are <u>scientifically complex</u>. There are many, many variables. There are trade-offs. We become heavily dependent on scientific experts, and most of us are limited in our scientific knowledge. There is a lot of junk science out there (some of it generated by polluting companies).

2. Our <u>knowledge is imperfect</u>. There's just a lot we just don't know. We want certainty, but it simply doesn't exist very often.

3. One big reason our knowledge is imperfect is that many environmental debates are about <u>the future</u>. We're trying to prevent a disaster instead of cleaning up after one, and that means we're trying to foresee something that hasn't happened yet. Sometimes we are trying to see far into the future.

4. Environmental <u>problems are sometimes intertwined</u>, and they interact with each other. Some environmental problems exist on a global scale – just imagine all the variables that figure in to trying to analyze such large-scale problems.

5. The effects of environmental pollution can be <u>cumulative</u> – cumulative over time, cumulative within a geographical area.

6. Environmental pollution – from bad water to cigarette smoke – doesn't affect everybody the same way.

7. The real impacts of environmental pollution may take years to manifest themselves, making it very difficult to draw a precise line from cause to effect. Consider how hard it would be to show for certain that a case of lung cancer resulted from that person's cigarette smoking (or cigarette smoking by someone in that person's home).

8. Pollution isn't always easy to see. A lot of pollutants are colorless, odorless, tasteless. Some of these invisible pollutants cause serious damage to people's bodies.

9. The responses we choose in addressing environmental problems are sometimes irreversible. If we allow industrial development in a wilderness, odds are it will never be wilderness again. If we allow a species of plant or animal to go extinct, it is gone for all time. In the words of the late Rep. George Darrow, the original sponsor of the Montana Environmental Policy Act, "Actions such as revenue collection and allocation, facility design, and management strategies can be revised or reversed with minimal disruption. However, a river valley and stream channel, however reshaped to accommodate a railroad or an interstate highway, are essentially changed for all time. The farmland stripped of its topsoil and paved over for a shopping center will not grow crops again. Ore bodies and oil fields depleted for present uses are not available to our descendants to meet their needs. Wildlife and fish habitats converted to other uses cannot readily be restored to their original productivity."[1]

10. Government regulation is an imperfect tool. Agency decision-making is often colored by political pressure and lack of resources. And most people just don't like the idea of their behavior being regulated.

11. Politics has a way of corrupting a debate and encouraging Americans who disagree to demonize one another. Politics favors the wealthy. Politics seeks quick solutions that don't really change things. Politics seeks

solutions that politicians will support – instead of seeking the best solution or the right solution.

12. <u>Corporations</u> have excessive and increasing influence over who gets elected to office, who has access to those officeholders, and how those officeholders behave every day.

13. <u>Externalizing the costs of pollution</u> can enlarge the profit margin of a polluter, and such polluters will do whatever they can to avoid being held accountable for the impacts (that is, the costs) of the pollution they create. And those who benefit financially – stockholders, employees, or the politicians beholden to polluters for campaign contributions – may feel threatened if the polluter is held accountable for the costs of its pollution.

14. Externalized costs can be <u>difficult to identify and quantify</u>. And those who pay those costs are often dispersed, don't know each other, and are therefore hard to organize into a political force.

15. Those who pollute are <u>viewed by some as immoral</u>, and views of morality are deeply held.

16. Those who pollute are <u>viewed by some as unpatriotic</u>, because their pollution hurts America.

17. Environmentalists are viewed by many as… well, just as those quotes at the beginning of this book describe them. <u>If you think someone delivering a pro-environment message is somehow anti-American, you're not likely to take what they say very seriously.</u> In fact, there's a good chance you may come to think of protecting the environment itself as anti-American.

A lot of people believe environmental problems can be resolved if we just have the right information, or if people just understand what's really at stake. But it's a lot more complicated than that. That's why few environmental issues are resolved easily or quickly, no matter how obvious the solution may appear to some of us. And many "solutions" are sadly temporary.

I've met quite a few environmentalists who dive into an issue, thinking it can be resolved in a year or two, and then they can go back to their everyday lives. Some of them give up when they see how long and hard it can be to change anything. And some of them learn that – whether they are personally affected, whether they're working for the sake of their country, or for the sake of their children – striving for a better environment is the work of a lifetime.

CHAPTER NINETEEN

Our Only Companions

...large numbers of fish living in polluted waters have liver cancer, while the same kind of fish living in clean water do not suffer from this disease.

···

L ate in 2009, I saw fascinating film footage of an octopus selecting a coconut shell from the sea floor, emptying it of its contents, and then carrying it away to use as part of a shelter it was building. Just in my lifetime, we have learned more about the capacity of animals for using tools and making plans than we ever used to imagine possible. It seems we are just beginning to learn their secrets.

In an opinion piece in the *New York Times*[1], biologist Olivia Judson described the recent discovery of deep-sea worms that expel balls of green fluorescent fluid when attacked. She told of the discovery of more than 400 new species of mammals between 1993 and 2009. And not just little mouse-like critters from the jungle floor; the discoveries included an antelope, a sloth, a forest-dwelling ox, monkeys, and many more.

All these creatures, and all this diversity! It makes me think of Ecclesiastes again:

He hath made every thing beautiful in his time: also he hath set the world in their heart, so that no man can find out the work that God maketh from the beginning to the end.

And of Isaiah:

Holy, holy, holy, is the LORD of hosts: the whole earth is full of his glory.

And yet songbirds are declining everywhere, and we know a lot of that is due to pesticides.[2]

As biologist Sandra Steingraber tells us, beluga whales in the St. Lawrence River are getting cancer. Fish and shellfish are getting cancer. A five-year study of ocean-going sperm whales reported high levels of cadmium, lead, and other toxic metals. The whales were sampled all over the globe, from the tropics to polar areas.[4]

Phytoplankton, the beginning step in the ocean's food chains, is on the decline. In addition to supporting animal life in the oceans, phytoplankton is an algae that captures carbon from the air and turns it into oxygen.[5]

....

The debate over eating meat versus vegetarianism does raise the issue of how we treat animals. Humans have always eaten animals for food, just as some animals eat other animals for food. Does that make us, or them, cruel?

Yes, some environmentalists are vegetarians, a great many refuse to wear furs, and protecting wildlife is a big part of what many environmental organizations work for.

But does that make those people anti-human?

Why would it? For thousands of years, how we treat animals has been part of what makes us human, and also part of how we regard our fellow humans. Just look at the public response to professional football player Michael Vick's involvement in dog-fighting.

Still, some people look at the story of the Garden of Eden and assume that God's grant of "dominion" to us means that we can do anything we want to any part of nature.

If we really felt that way, it would justify driving animals to extinction, and it would justify cruelty to animals. But few of us would teach our children that cruelty to animals is okay. Few of us really want to see the polar bear driven to extinction by melting ice caps.

Wendell Berry reminds us:

So long as we live, we are going to be living with skylarks, nightingales, daffodils, waterfowl, streams, forests, mountains, and all the other creatures that romantic poets and artists have yearned toward. And by the way we live we will determine whether or not those creatures will live.[6]

Paul Shepard referred to animals as "our only companions."[7]

In the story of the Great Flood in Genesis, God had made a decision to destroy life on earth because "the wickedness of man was great upon the earth." But he decided to spare the family of Noah, and instructed Noah to build a great boat to save his family from the flood that was to come.

But God wanted to save all the species of animals from the flood, too. He instructed Noah to gather male and female of "every beast after his kind, and all the cattle after their kind, and every creeping thing that creepeth upon the earth after his kind, and every fowl after his kind, every bird of every sort."

At the end of the Flood, God placed a rainbow in the sky as a covenant. The meaning of that covenant is made very clear in Genesis 9:8-16:

And God spake unto Noah, and to his sons with him, saying, And I, behold, I establish my covenant with you, and with your seed after you; And with every living creature that is with you, of the fowl, of the cattle, and of every beast of the earth with you; from all that go out of the ark, to every beast of the earth. And I will establish my covenant with you; neither shall all flesh be cut off any more by the waters of a flood; neither shall there any more be a flood to destroy the earth. And God said, this is the token of the covenant which I make between me and you and every living creature that is with you, for perpetual generations: I do set my bow in the cloud, and it shall be for a token of a covenant between me and the earth. And it shall come to pass, when I bring a cloud over the earth, that the bow shall be seen in the cloud: And I will remember my covenant, which is between me and you and every living creature of all flesh; and the waters shall no more become a flood to destroy all flesh. And the bow shall be in the cloud; and I will look upon it, that I may remember the everlasting covenant between God and every living creature of all flesh that is upon the earth.

The story of Noah gives man a lot of power over animals ("dominion"), but also gives us responsibility for them. God's position on driving species of animals to extinction is made very clear in this covenant.

I've heard people try to use the notion of dominion to justify behaving destructively toward God's creation, and toward our fellow creatures. But Pope Francis tells us "we must forcefully reject the notion that our being created in

God's image and given dominion over the earth justifies absolute domination over other creatures."[8]

I have dominion over my family's pet cat Frances. But does dominion give me the right to treat Frances with cruelty? If we are to take seriously God's covenant with Noah, then we have to think about our relationship with animals.

"Animal activists" are even more despised than "environmentalists" in certain circles, though many people just lump them all together. I don't lump them all together, and I disagree with some animal activists on some matters. At the same time, though, I believe there is a lot to agree on.

Maybe I don't agree with the PETA folks about vegetarianism (or effective strategy, or many other things). But I agree with them that cruelty to animals is wrong, and I'll bet you agree with me on that.

But what constitutes cruelty?

In 2005, two pedestrians were walking across a foot bridge in Missoula, Montana, when they heard the sound of a cat in distress. They looked over the bridge railing and saw, on the ice in the middle of the Clark Fork River, a cage containing a calico cat and a large rock.

The fire department was summoned and they managed to rescue the soaked cat. Someone had put it into a cage, along with a 16-pound rock, and tossed it off the bridge. Fortunately for the cat, the cage landed on the ice instead of in the water. Whoever it was that tossed the cat from the bridge had not been feeding it regularly, and it was very malnourished.

By the way, one of the firefighters involved in the rescue adopted the cat. He named it "Lucky."[9]

A man in Indiana was arrested in 2008 after forcing his seven year-old daughter to stab the family cat with a knife. According to the arrest affidavit, the man said he wanted his children to "learn how to kill." When he realized the cat was still alive after being stabbed, he stabbed the cat himself, then strangled it, and made his eleven year-old son throw the cat's body in the trash.[10]

I opened the newspaper a few days before Christmas in 2010 to see a photo of a male mallard duck with a 6-inch blowgun dart, a dart with a barbed tip, sticking through its head. A local citizen, Bill Pirami, took the picture at Riverfront Park in Billings, Montana, a city park on the banks of the Yellowstone River. Somehow the dart had failed to kill its victim, but Pirami observed the duck and saw that it wasn't eating. He contacted the local office of the Montana Fish, Wildlife and Parks, as well as the county sheriff.

A few days later, Pirami and a friend ventured out onto the thin December ice of Lake Josephine in the park and were able to catch the duck. They used wire snippers to cut and remove the dart, and Pirami felt optimistic about its prospects for survival. However, the next day, he spotted two more ducks waddling around at the park with darts sticking out of their bodies.

Someone had decided to practice blowing darts – which is not a lawful means of hunting in Montana, especially not within city limits – on the ducks which are accustomed to the presence of people at Riverfront Park.[11]

What's your opinion of someone who shoots a weapon at animals just for the hell of it?

In 2004, a PETA investigator shot a video inside a chicken processing plant operated by Pilgrim's Pride in Moorefield, West Virginia. The plant was a supplier for Kentucky Fried Chicken (KFC). The video showed chickens being kicked, stomped, and thrown against a wall by plant employees. The investigator "also obtained eyewitness testimony about employees 'ripping birds' beaks off, spray-painting their faces, twisting their heads off, spitting tobacco into their mouths and eyes, and breaking them in half – all while the birds are still alive.'"[12]

Cruelty? Not much doubt about that. I'm sure the PETA folks would say this is cruelty. I'm sure that a lot of people who don't like PETA or other animal activists would also think these incidents describe cruelty. This is what I mean when I say that there is a lot to agree on.

Recognizing cruelty and speaking out when we see it – this is part of what it means to be human. I'm glad that cat in Montana was rescued. I'm glad that S.O.B. in Indiana was arrested. I'm glad PETA helped us see what was going on inside that poultry plant.

PETA was also involved in getting a Japanese restaurant in Sacramento to quit serving a dish called "dancing shrimp." The shrimp were served to patrons while still alive, but what made them "dance" was diners squeezing lemon juice over the shrimps' exposed flesh so they would writhe as they were being eaten. This is considered a delicacy in Japan. In my neighborhood, this would be considered cruelty, even if it's a voiceless little creature like a shrimp.[13]

What is it that attracts some people to behaving cruelly toward animals?

Years ago, I worked at a zoo attraction in South Dakota that maintained a small pond near their front entrance during the summer. Several common local turtles – Western painted turtles and red-eared sliders – were kept in that pond during the summer and this display of very common animals was a favorite of visitors year after year. People enjoyed just watching the turtles as they swam, or as they sunned themselves on logs, or as they ate.

But the end of that pond came one night when some unknown persons took most of the turtles out of the water, spread them around on the parking lot, and proceeded to drive over them.

What the hell?

In 2012, a Clemson University student named Nathan Weaver ran a small study of people and cars and turtles. He placed realistic-looking plastic turtles in the middle of the lane on a busy road near the Clemson campus, then observed as seven drivers in the next hour swerved *in order to run over the turtles*. (He observed several other drivers who also swerved, but who missed the turtles.)[14]

Survival isn't enough of a challenge for a turtle in the modern world? Some of us have to deliberately kill them just for fun?

. . ..

In the 1970s, a few years before my wife and I met, she was a student at Art Center in Pasadena, California. In one class, the assignment called for using visual elements to elicit an emotion. One student laid out sheet of heavy black fiberboard on a table, then took a black goldfish out of an aquarium and placed it onto the black surface. Then he covered the gasping fish with white paint squeezed out of a tube.

As Candace watched the fish flopping around in the paint, desperately trying to get some oxygen through its gills, she couldn't believe that the student was just going to let this little fish die in agony just for the sake of an art project. She couldn't believe that the instructor just watched; she couldn't believe that all the other students just watched.

She grabbed up the goldfish, took it into a rest room, and ran water over the fish to wash off the paint and give it some water for its gills. Another student brought her a container to fill with water for the fish. She returned to the classroom to hear the instructor praise the student who brought the goldfish for his success at getting such a visceral response from a fellow student. That student told my wife she could keep the fish. "You're damn right, I can," she replied, and later found a good home for the rescued goldfish.

Candace knew cruelty when she saw it. Unfortunately, this college-level instructor and his students did not. She continued her education at another school.

....

Roger Muggli has another fish story. It's not about cruelty, but it's about our relationship with animals and the rest of nature. I know Roger because he became active in the Northern Plains Resource Council when coal bed methane development came to eastern Montana. Roger has a special concern for water because he runs the Tongue and Yellowstone Irrigation District, a private irrigation company near Miles City, Montana. The T&Y has been managed by Roger's family since the 1930s, first by his grandfather, then his father. Roger took over as manager in 1987.

Roger knows any threat to the water he provides his 470 customers is a problem. The salty-water discharges from the methane wells upstream could affect the quality of the water his customers use to irrigate their crops. In the early 2000s, he was pretty sure it had started to affect his alfalfa crops.

Roger's feelings about the river go deep, for it has been part of his life all along. As a boy, one of his farm chores was to help his father with irrigating. He noticed that fish from the river would sometimes get stranded in the fields as the irrigation water soaked in and receded. To him, it always seemed wasteful to let the fish die and rot in the fields, so he would carry with him a bucket of water, and save what fish he could by picking them up and dumping them into the river.

One day, he came across a good-sized smallmouth bass caught in the field. Instead of rescuing it, he decided to watch the bass and see how the process of dying in the field really worked. He watched as the suffocating fish flopped from puddle to puddle, trying to find enough water for its gills to work. It struggled harder and harder to breathe. Finally, Roger recalled years later, "the mud started to boil out of his gills. 'Whoa,' I thought, 'that's got to be some terrible way to die.'"

"I couldn't take it," he said. "I picked him up and threw him in a bucket of water." He returned the bass to the Yellowstone River.

Roger knows that irrigation takes a toll on the fish. The T&Y has a dam on the Tongue River that was built in 1885. Since its construction, the dam has blocked the migration of fish on the Tongue, preventing spawning of some species. When he took over as manager of the T&Y, Roger began a project that had been in the back of his mind for years, and that would take him another 20 years to make a reality.

His dream was a bypass that would allow fish on the Tongue River to migrate upstream for the first time in more than 120 years, and would help keep fish out of the irrigation canal. Roger sought out federal grants to help with the cost, and consulted with the Army Corps of Engineers and Bureau of Reclamation. Doing this required permits and environmental studies, and a ton of persistence to convince agency budget-writers to include his project. He helped keep costs under control by making the irrigation company the general contractor for the project. Finally, in 2007, his fish bypass was opened. It had been Roger's dream for 40 years, and he had been working on it for 20 years. All because he felt that he owed something to the fish and the river.[15]

Further downstream from the T&Y, the magnificent pallid sturgeon is on the brink. The wild Missouri River was a far different place than the dammed and channelized river that flows across the plains today. We keep producing more sturgeon in hatcheries, but the wild sturgeon – a very long-lived fish – have not been able to breed for a long time, some 60 years. Only about 125 wild pallid sturgeon are estimated to still be alive, and they could be extinct on the Upper Missouri and the Yellowstone by 2017. Scientists and engineers working for the state of Montana and the United States are working hard to save this ancient animal from extinction.[16]

....

In her book, *Living Downstream*, biologist Sandra Steingraber described what we are learning about the effects of the chemicals we dispose of into nature.[17] Much of the book is about cancer. While describing her own experience as a cancer survivor, she also described cancer among animals that live in the water.

Beluga whales, for instance. These comparatively small white whales live in waters off the Canada coast and also in the St. Lawrence River. The main difference between them appears to be that the belugas in the St. Lawrence, exposed as they are to chemical pollution, are full of DNA adducts, chemical attackers that often lead to cancer. The belugas that live in cleaner waters do not have these adducts.

She described the frequency of cancer among bottom feeding fish and mollusks, animals that are regularly exposed to whatever goes into our water – chemical pollution, toxic runoff from surrounding lands, boat exhaust, air pollution that mixes into the water. She described experiments in which healthy fish in clean water are exposed to extracts of these sediments, with many of those fish developing cancers.

She described how liver cancers in fish are rising, and how they correlate with the mushrooming production of synthetic organic chemicals since 1940. She told us how cancers in fish, like cancers in humans, have increased substantially in recent decades and tend to coincide with areas where the surrounding environment is polluted. She went through several examples of fresh and salt-water fish in which large numbers of them living in polluted waters have liver cancer, while the same kind of fish living in clean water do not suffer from this disease.

Of course, it's not just cancer that affects animals and humans. Infectious diseases, nerve disorders, reproductive disorders, and other ailments can follow chemical pollution. Steingraber described how turtles respond to hormone-disrupting chemicals in their surroundings. Brushing PCBs onto the eggs of red-eared sliders will turn males into females. Not a high concentration, mind you, but an amount that women in industrialized countries typically carry in their breast milk.

In 1984, a 39-foot sperm whale washed ashore in Italy. It had suffocated on 50 plastic bags that had lodged in its throat. Its body also showed that it had been shot, hit by a boat propeller, and had ingested large amounts of industrial waste.[18]

What have I learned – what have you learned – from watching news video of wild birds and other creatures doomed by the 2010 oil spill off the Louisiana coast?

For that which befalleth the sons of men befalleth beasts; even one thing befalleth them: as the one dieth, so dieth the other; yea, they have all one breath; so that a man hath no preeminence above a beast: for all is vanity.

Ecclesiastes 3:19

If there's nothing else to learn from the story of Noah's Ark, it's that people and animals… we're all, literally, in the same boat.

CHAPTER TWENTY

Free Enterprise

For years, the evangelists of no-rules economics pretended that external-
ized costs don't really matter. Now, trillions of dollars later, we all know
better.

. . . .

I love the word "enterprise." I love living in a country where somebody can
have an idea and get an honest shot at making it in the marketplace. I've
done it a couple times myself, and I managed a gift store at a tourist attraction
for several years.

The day-to-day nature of retailing can be a grind, and working on holidays
isn't much fun. But I enjoy the connection with people. Not just the face-to-face
part, but also the time spent figuring out merchandise purchases. That was a
good way to find out how well I understood who my customers were and what
they wanted.

When it comes to a marketplace, the "arm's length" transaction is what it's all
about. When I would conclude a sale, it meant I had arrived at an agreement with
my customer upon what was fair. We could each refuse to conclude the transaction. My customer could seek out another seller, I could try to attract another
buyer.

But what *is* fair? Would it be fair if I lied to my customer about the nature of
what he was buying? Would it be fair if I had monopoly power and my customer
was forced to deal with me? Would it be fair if I charged my customer less by
shoving off part of the cost of his purchase to other people who never had anything to do with the transaction? Would it be fair if I knew the product I sold
him was dangerous and hid that fact from him?

A lot of Americans today have been convinced that a free market means a marketplace without rules. In fact, a free market must have rules or it will cease to be free.

A free market must have competition, and be free of monopolies and near-monopolies. Buyers and sellers must have access to information about what's being bought and sold. The buyers and sellers must pay for all the costs of whatever they are buying and selling, and not shove those costs onto the general public. And along that same line, people outside the transaction should not be able to derive benefits for which they do not pay.

If we don't have these rules in our marketplace, then we don't have a free market. To me, it's a lot like having a rule book and umpires in baseball. Those rules are what define the game and keep it fair. It's the job of the umpires to enforce those rules for the sake of the game.

If we dispensed of the rule book in baseball, what would we have? Would it be fair? Would it be a true competition? Would it really reflect which team is the best? Of course not. The rulebook, enforced by umpires, is what makes the game fair. It's what makes the game baseball.

Without the rulebook and umpires, it's merely "jungle rules" out there.

··

All of us learned a hard lesson, beginning in 2008, about what can happen when you discard the rules, rules that had once protected businesses, investors, borrowers, and working people. But what, you may ask, does this have to do with environmentalists?

A trillion dollars were spent to revive key sectors of the economy following the 2008 collapse. A trillion dollars (and that was just the beginning)! That's money that you and I and my daughter and Americans who haven't even been born yet will have to pay back with our hard-earned money. Nearly eight-and-a-half million Americans lost their jobs in two years, starting in December 2007.[1] How many American families lost their homes, I don't know. These people gained nothing from the excesses of Wall Street, the overzealous lending and the schemes that can only be considered gambling. But they are all paying for those excesses, and for the absence of rules to prevent them.

This is what it means to externalize your costs, to manipulate the economic transaction so that your costs are shoved off onto somebody else. And external costs are what most environmental issues are all about. Whether it's mercury pollution in Minamata, Japan, or depleted aquifers from coal mining and coal bed methane drilling in Wyoming and Montana, these are externalized costs. The company or individual doing damage to the environment isn't paying the cost of that damage... but other people _are_ paying it. The costs may not be easily measurable in dollars; those costs may instead be shortened life spans or a ruined fishery. But they are real costs, just the same.

Externalizing costs isn't fair to those of us who have to live with the no-rules ideology that steered the world economy into an iceberg.

And it isn't fair that our children should have to breathe air that's polluted because a coal-fired power plant didn't pay the cost of cleaning its discharges. It isn't fair that a mountain watershed gets ruined by a gold mine dumping poisonous chemicals into the water rather than paying the costs of removing those chemicals or preventing the pollution in the first place.

For years, the evangelists of a no-rules marketplace pretended that externalized costs don't really matter. Now, trillions of dollars later, we all know better. Now, trillions of dollars later, we all see that externalizing costs is not consistent with a free market, nor with a decent sense of fairness.

Gernot Wagner, an economist at the Environmental Defense Fund, calls it "planetary socialism." We create costs (e.g., pollution, destroyed landscapes, making people sick) and then, instead of those costs being reflected (and paid for) in the transactions that created them, we socialize those costs onto the general public. Wagner says that "markets are truly free only when everyone pays the full price for his or her actions. Anything else is socialism."[2]

If a mine pollutes, the public pays for a ruined fishery and damaged groundwater. The public pays for any health effects on the people who live downstream. The public pays if the mining company walks away from its reclamation bond.

When a coal bed methane company pumps tremendous volumes of salt-laden water to the surface in the process of accessing the methane, and expects to be allowed to dump that salty water onto the soil or into rivers that people down-stream use to irrigate, that methane company is externalizing its costs. It's wrong. It's wrong in the same way that no-rules economics is wrong.

(I should mention that, here in Montana, lawsuits by citizens eventually forced the state Department of Environmental Quality to adopt rules outlawing the direct disposal of these salty waters into surface waters or onto the ground. Unfortunately, Wyoming has no such rules, and many of the small streams in northeast Wyoming flow northward into Montana's Tongue River.)

When free enterprise is working, it can reflect the true value of a transaction. It's capable of finding a fair point for buyer and seller. But when costs are externalized, when full information isn't available, or when there are monopolies, then the market isn't working as a market should. An honest-to-God free market wouldn't be externalizing its costs.

The marketplace can't do everything. It has a hard time preventing monopolies. It has a hard time valuing things like clean air and water, or public health, or museums, or animal life, or personal integrity. It doesn't even try to value things like the earth's atmosphere. The marketplace tends to have a short-term view of things, and to disregard long-term consequences. The marketplace rewards poachers who would drive an endangered rhinoceros to extinction just to make money by selling its horn for the manufacture of dagger handles in Yemen, or ornaments in China, or mythical cure-all medicines in much of East Asia.

Some people stereotype those who work for environmental protection as "uncomfortable with markets and capitalism."[3] Some probably are, but it's a pretty sweeping generalization from my perspective, a perspective which includes many farmers and ranchers and other business people. All of these people that I've known understand the importance of markets and private property rights. Many of them have seen those rights abused by polluters and by politicians and regulators who stand with those polluters.

Bottom line – pollution is an externalized cost, a market failure. Nobody who believes in a free marketplace should defend polluters, because polluters are doing the same thing to natural resources and public health that the Wall Street pirates did to the American economy and the American people.

Private Property

That day, she discovered that federally owned mineral deposits beneath three-quarters of the ranch had been leased to five different companies and individuals.

....

I'm a home owner, a property owner. The many farmers and ranchers I've worked with on environmental issues are property owners. Many, if not most, of the townspeople I have worked with are also property owners.

Some environmental laws indeed affect what property owners can do on their land. The laws I hear complained about the most are those intended to protect wetlands and endangered species. I've never had much direct exposure to the on-the-ground implementation of those laws, so I can't say much about them. I do believe they have a legitimate reason to exist – plants and animals span boundaries, and the spaces those plants and animals need to survive also span boundaries. We've decided as a society that protecting life on earth is in society's interest, sort of like God's decision in the story of Noah's Ark. Whether the solutions we've devised are the best solutions, I don't know. But, as a homeowner, I can appreciate how important a person's property can be.

The Great Depression was more than an economic calamity, it was also a major environmental disaster caused by the mistreatment of soil and water and forests. That environmental disaster wreaked havoc on many property owners.

During the depths of the Dust Bowl, poet Archibald MacLeish[1] wrote about people who lost their land during this disaster, and how important that land was to their sense of independence.

Now that the land's behind us we get wondering
We wonder if the liberty was the land and the
Land's gone: the liberty's back of us...

We can't say
We don't know
We wonder whether the proposition was self-evident
Because of a quarter section of free land
And the room as they used to say on the grass in Nebraska
To look any goddam sonofabitch in the eye
And tell him to head for hell at the next turn-off

Whether the proposition was self-evident
Because of the carpenter in the town in Wisconsin
Heckling the candidates: Lincoln telling him back –
"We will give you a farm.
Uncle Sam has a farm for every one of us."

And Uncle Sam has a farm for every one of us only they're
Gone now: the homesteads are narrower –

Whether the liberty we meant was standing
Easy and soft on the front stoop in our galluses
Giving the company lawyers directions for getting there

Whether the great American dream was the dream of
Standing alone on the front stoop in our galluses
Telling them soft and easy how to get there.

MacLeish went on to tell of the era of homesteading, the dark, rich soil, and the collapse of it all in the Dust Bowl, when farmers became tenant farmers, when tenant farmers were forced off the land and onto the open road.

...taking a good man's pride in a
Clean field well tilled: his children
Fed from furrows his own plow has made them

He continues:

We wonder whether the dream of American liberty
Wasn't the standing by the fence to tell them:

And we're not standing by the homestead fence
And telling any man where he can head for:

Not in these parts:
not with this wind blowing:
Not with this wind blowing and no rain

To tell the sonsofbitches where to head
You need your heel-hold on a country steady
You need a continent against your feet

Some people may say that the Homestead Act was socialism. Maybe it was. But all the private property that exists here in Montana is private because the U.S. government bought it from the French government, then took it – by force – from the people who lived here, then gave most of it away through mineral claims, homesteads, land grants to railroads, and other means. That's a good thing to remember.

There are other kinds of property rights besides ownership, like the right to use water.

Here in the West, water rights are a usufruct... rural water users may apply for a legally defined right to use the water, but they do not own it. They also need to meet certain criteria for how they can use that water. Though a stream may flow across someone's property, a landowner doesn't have the right to prevent the water from flowing to the downstream landowners, who have the legal right to use that water. As a society, we've decided that fair access to water is more important than an absolute property right over it by individuals. The system isn't perfect, but it does serve to conserve and allocate a limited and valuable resource. Yes, it limits property rights at the same time it protects them. Allowing an upstream landowner to deprive downstream neighbors of water would not work over the long haul. And it wouldn't be fair.

So private property owners are asked to help pay the costs of a public interest. Sometimes they are asked to do this for the sake of protecting endangered species, and for protecting the capacity of the land to fend off floods.

But it isn't only governments that mess with people's property rights. Property owners are also asked to assume many of the costs related to mining development and railroads and pipelines and power lines.

You don't hear as much about the impacts of mineral development and related projects on private property. For example, there's a railroad route that was first proposed in Montana in the late 1970s... its speculators said it would service a proposed coal strip mine near the Tongue River. When simple economics squelched that mine proposal, the railroad speculators expanded their plan, aiming to connect with another rail line to carry coal from Wyoming, down the Tongue River valley, and east to the Great Lakes. That plan also failed, but a new plan emerged in 2012 that resembled the original proposal – carrying coal down the Tongue River valley, but this time turning west instead of east, starting the coal on a long journey to China and other Asian nations. In 2016, that railroad and the coal mine it would have serviced both failed. But if it had been built, ranches along its route would have been cut in half. It would affected the day-to-day operations of those ranches, and would have lowered the value of all of them.

That proposed railroad was owned by a private company, but among the forms of government support it would have received was a grant of eminent domain. The company would have the legal right to condemn private property for its route, and would have had a tremendous impact on the property it cut apart. Weeds would have been transported in, fires would have been started, and pastures would have been cut off from their water sources.

Montana rancher Wally McRae, whose ranch was threatened by this railroad for nearly forty years, would have been profoundly injured if the project had been built. He wrote about the abuse of eminent domain in one of his poems.[2]

From the Highland Sod, with faith in God,
To this land, young and profane,
Grandad was drawn, long ere the dawn
Of Eminent Domain.

With no regrets he paid his debts,
Fought the elements to remain.

Each challenge met, long before the threat
Of Eminent Domain.

This land's been wet by my father's sweat.
His bones lie 'neath this plain.
But you'd rip in, with your dust and din,
And Eminent Domain.

My mother's tears and unspoken fears
That she always fought to restrain.
Did she somehow hear, and come to fear
Your Eminent Domain?

"Public need" we're advised to heed,
But it somehow comes out, "private gain."
You play the rune. Do we dance to the tune
Of Eminent Domain?

You praise to the skies, "Free Enterprise,"
Curse the government as your bane.
But you're quick to use, or even abuse,
Her Eminent Domain.

You pandering blights! Don't tell me of your rights.
Rights and obligations are twain.
Land's earned by sweat and love – not threat
Of Eminent Domain!

I'll not cower from lines of pipe and power
Or twin scythes of rail for your train.
Understand me full well. You can go to hell
With your Eminent Domain.

Sometimes the rights to property are a mixed "bundle" of rights. A lot of land-owners in the eastern part of Montana, as well as other places across the West, are split-estate landowners. They own the surface of their property, but not the mineral rights. These mineral rights may be owned by the federal government, or by a state, by a private party, or even by relatives. And those mineral rights may be exercised by their owners with little or no regard to the wishes of the surface owner.

....

One day several years ago, Jeanie Alderson called the U.S. Bureau of Land Management office in Miles City to ask about mineral leasing beneath her family's ranch in the Tongue River valley. That day, she discovered that federally owned mineral deposits (likely coal bed methane) beneath three-quarters of the ranch had been leased to five different companies and individuals. The BLM had never informed her family, who own and live on the land, about this lease.

Northern Plains, the organization I work for, has sought for a number of years to strengthen the rights of landowners who face condemnation by railroads and mines, or the occupation of their property by mining or drilling companies. We sought to give landowners more notice, more say about how their land is treated, and more assurances that mineral developers on their land wouldn't leave a mess behind. And our every effort to strengthen the rights of landowners was met with strong opposition from mining companies and drilling companies.

And the consistently pro-development groups that always say they believe in private property rights... where were they?

They sat it out. They never came to bat for the landowners who face condemnation, who face occupation of their land by mining and drilling companies. For years, groups like the chamber of commerce and others who say they support private property rights have sat on their hands while landowners facing intense intrusions on their property relied on environmentalists to stand up for them.

I'm a homeowner who lives in town. I know that my property rights aren't absolute, sometimes for legal reasons, sometimes for moral reasons. I know that, here on my quiet residential street, I can't turn my house into a hamburger stand or a tavern. I know that I shouldn't construct drainage fixtures that flood my neighbors. I know that I couldn't stage late-night rock concerts in my yard, nor open it up to short-track motorcycle races. This would not only be illegal in my town, it would also be wrong. It would ruin my neighbors' reasonable use and enjoyment of their property, just as it would wreck the value of their property. I just don't have the legal or moral right to do these things on my property.

But here in town, I also don't have to worry about a drilling company showing up at my door with a 20-day notice that my yard will become the site of a natural gas well for the next 20 years.

Here in town, I don't have to worry about a coal mine sludge pond failing upstream from my house and covering my home and property with hundreds of tons of molasses-thick toxic sludge – not like the thousands of people who live downstream from more than 200 such "ponds" (including the dozens of ponds listed as "high-risk"), and not like people along the Emory River in Tennessee, whose property was covered with a thick, black flood in December 2008, some losing their homes entirely.

No, property rights aren't absolute. But those who make the most noise about property rights are often strangely silent when protecting property rights would also mean fending off or exercising some control over a proposed mine or other development.

The 2005 U.S. Supreme Court decision, *Kelo v. City of New London*, caught a lot of people's attention because it gave a municipality the right to condemn private property for the simple reason that it would benefit a chosen economic interest, a developer whose interests the municipality wants to promote. This decision drew criticism from many points on the political spectrum. As an environmentalist, I thought it was an outrage. It's exactly the kind of tool that environmentally destructive developers want to have in their hands when they come up against a landowner who doesn't want to go along with their plans.

Justice Sandra Day O'Connor said in her dissent in the Kelo case:

Any property may now be taken for the benefit of another private party, but the fallout from this decision will not be random. The beneficiaries are likely to be those citizens with disproportionate influence and power in the political process, including large corporations and development firms. As for the victims, the government now has license to transfer property from those with fewer resources to those with more.

There is a place for eminent domain, but that place should be very limited, and used as little as possible. Landowners shouldn't have to stand by helplessly as mining companies, gas drillers, pipelines, or railroads move in to extract all the wealth they can from their property.

One of the biggest debates in the 2011 Montana legislature was over a bill designed to ensure that private companies – even foreign companies – could assert the power of eminent domain against landowners who stand in the way of development projects. House Bill 198 (sponsored by Ken Peterson, a Republican representative from Billings) would basically apply the principle of the *Kelo* decision to rural Montana landowners.

It all started when Larry Salois, representing his elderly mother who is a landowner in the path of a private power line, objected to the path which power line builders had insisted on. The route would cut through wetlands on her property that they wanted to protect, as well as tipi rings that they didn't want destroyed. They weren't objecting to the power line, they simply wanted a half-mile of the route slightly modified as it would cross their property.[3]

The company – Toronto-based Montana Alberta Tie Ltd. (MATL – a subsidiary of Toronto-based Tonbridge Power) – sued to condemn the property, but a state district judge ruled in favor of the Salois family, and said that the Canadian power line company did not have a legal right to condemn private property. The company's response was to get politicians to intercede on its behalf and change Montana's eminent domain law.

The company's position was sweetened because the power line in question would carry wind-generated electricity from Montana. Those who objected to its plans could be labeled as obstacles to economic development and to clean energy jobs. Without a law to override the court's ruling, some legislators said, this project would not be able to continue. It was a crisis.

Of course, the "crisis" that necessitated a legislative solution was a false choice from the beginning. The Salois family wasn't trying to stop the project. Rural landowners rarely stand in the way of projects that need to cross their land. A landowner in that power line's path recalled that someone told him he "should take one for the team." He responded that "his family – like many other rural families – has provided easements and property for county roads, electric cooperatives, rural water districts, a public library, rural telephone cooperatives, fiber optic lines, gas and oil lines and the Western Area Power Association."[4]

Had MATL really tried to negotiate, instead of suing the landowner, the whole mess would probably never have happened. But, after losing in court, MATL sought out a solution in the state legislature. They got HB 198 introduced to solve their problem.

With solid and powerful support, House Bill 198 sped through the House of Representatives, achieving final passage in a month by an overwhelming vote of 69-30. By the time the bill reached the Senate, however, the concerns of numerous landowners had reached the Senate Energy and Telecommunications Committee, and the bill languished there, unable to gain a majority, for more than six weeks.

However, those who wanted this bill passed weren't about to let it die. The Democratic Governor wanted it. The Republican legislative leadership wanted it. Eventually, 26 of the 50 senators voted to "blast" the bill out of committee.

People from all over the state contacted senators to urge them not to be stampeded into passing this bill. Some of them had already traveled hundreds of miles to the state capitol to testify against it before the House and Senate committees. Some had called or written their representatives earlier in the session.

They had strong feelings. There are plenty of other landowners who also face the condemnation of their land for projects that do not serve the people of our state or nation, projects that will only line the pockets of private developers. There's yet another power line being developed, and a lot of landowners in its path are very unhappy with how they've been treated. There was the Keystone XL pipeline being advanced in northeast Montana by another Canadian company to carry diluted bitumen from the Canadian tar sands mines all the way to the Texas coast for refining. There's the Tongue River Railroad, which for almost forty years threatened ranchlands in one of Montana's most truly rural and non-industrialized valleys.

To these landowners and many others, House Bill 198 – by handing private developers the power of eminent domain – would prevent real negotiations from ever taking place between developer and landowner because it would take away any semblance of a level playing field. When one party has the power to condemn the other party's land, this is very far from being a "willing seller, willing buyer" transaction. As attorney Hertha Lund, who won the district court case, described it, "This is not negotiation – this is an ultimatum."[5]

The state Senate's debate over HB 198 was long and passionate, and it divided both political parties. On the Republican side, you had those who consistently favored the power of corporate developers over individual citizens, joined by those who favored any kind of energy development and would not tolerate obstructing it, and opposed by fellow Republicans who held deep beliefs in the rights of property owners. Among the Democrats, you had those who sided with the little guy, opposed by those who had been convinced that this power line was vital to creating clean energy jobs (and that this law was necessary to allowing it), and also opposed by legislators who simply didn't want to get crosswise with the Governor.

In the end, the state Senate voted 28-22 to concur with the House and enact HB 198. Landowners in the path of power lines and pipelines and railroads knew that they had been severely wounded. *Kelo* has come to Montana.

Two years later, a bill was introduced to repeal this law. Again, people from both parties intermingled for vastly different reasons to defend the expansion of eminent domain powers and to defeat the repeal bill. The power of private parties to condemn private property for private projects remains the law in Montana.

Want an Industrial Railroad Through Your Place?

This new route will leave the Tongue River valley floor a few miles north of Ashland, Montana, then cut westward past an Amish farm, then take a course that will cut the Rocker 6 in half.

. . . .

Someday, someone will write a history of the Tongue River Railroad. It will stretch from 1977 – or even before that – through 2016. The story will include family ranch operations placed under dire threat for over 30 years, first by a speculator, then by a pair of billionaires, a major railroad company, and one of America's largest coal companies.

It will include the Northern Plains Resource Council, a citizens organization with deep roots in the ranch country of southeast Montana that fought this project from the beginning. The story will tell of changing alliances among conservationists, cattle ranchers, Northern Cheyennes, labor unions of coal miners and railroad workers. It will weave in and out of courtrooms and federal agencies.

It will involve politicians, power plants, and everyday people in Montana, other states like Washington and Minnesota, and China.

Most of all, though, the story of the Tongue River Railroad will run through the lives of several families who live in the Tongue River valley of southeast Montana. These are families who earned a living, raised families, and worked year in and year out to defend their homes from a coal industry project that threatened to cut their places apart.

. . . .

Wally McRae's Rocker 6 Land and Cattle Company sits on an irregularly-shaped piece of land where Rosebud Creek and the Tongue River turn toward each other for a few miles. Between those streams there's good grass, with 16 springs fed by shallow aquifers in coal beds.

Wally grew up a few miles down the road, but has lived along Rosebud Creek all his life (except for college at Montana State and a hitch in the U.S. Navy). He and his son Clint operate the Rocker 6, where they raise Black Angus cattle. Both of them look like archetypal cowboys, rugged figures with thick mustaches.

Ranch history means a lot here, and Wally has long been the unpaid caretaker of the little cemetery that sits on a small rise in the valley. His cowboy poetry is known and admired nationally, and he supports all the cultural and historical activities in his sparsely populated neighborhood.

Clint has a fine eye and hand for painting and for pen-and-ink drawings. He and his youngest daughter Elizabeth have spent many hours on another project, a hot rod '36 Chevy pickup they call the "Cowboy Coupe." (She is now working on a project of her own, a '55 Ford pickup.)

The Rocker 6 lies in coal country, and the specter of seeing his place strip-mined drew Wally to take action back in the early 1970s. Because the ranch lies above coal beds, it will always be threatened. The biggest threat of late has been the Tongue River Railroad, a coal-hauling project that's been on the drawing board since 1977.

Since that time, the Tongue River Railroad was a project looking for a purpose. Originally, it was proposed as an 89-mile spur to service a planned coal mine near Ashland. That project received a permit from the Interstate Commerce Commission (now the Surface Transportation Board) in 1986. But the Northern Plains continued to fight it while members like Wally raised hell about the threat to their land and livelihood. Over time, the economics for the mine didn't pencil out, so it never came to be.

However, the speculator behind the Tongue River Railroad came up with a new incarnation, eventually winning a new permit in 1996. This time, the railroad would extend for 131 miles, connecting up with tracks near Decker, Montana, just north of the Wyoming border. That revised route, first proposed in 1990, was opposed by everyone from the ranchers in the valley, to the railroad workers who would be displaced by the new arrangement of crew stations, to the Montana coal miners who saw the proposal as a way to weaken their advantage in transportation costs over Wyoming coal mines. The proposal languished.

Another route change was approved in 2007. Still, the Tongue River Railroad was never built.

Later, the Tongue River Railroad's reason to exist became another proposed coal mine in the area – the largest new coal mine being planned in the United States at the time. To be located on a tributary of the Tongue River called Otter Creek, this mine – if it were built – would have been just the thing to make the Tongue River Railroad a reality. Much, perhaps all, of the coal from that mine would go to Asia, and the Tongue River Railroad would be the first stage of that long trip.

Its route as originally proposed would have crossed the Rocker 6 for four miles, cutting pastures off from the river, severing parts of the ranch from one another, and isolating some parts of it. Isolation and severance. What it would have meant mean to Wally McRae was a ranch cut to pieces.

But Wally's worries got a whole lot worse on December 17, 2012. That day, the Tongue River Railroad announced yet another route, and it was exactly what Wally had most feared. This new route would leave the Tongue River valley floor a few miles north of Ashland, then cut westward past an Amish farm, then take a course that would cut the Rocker 6 right in half for nine miles. It would condemn Wally and Clint's land, and cut off their winter pastures from summer range. It would run right next to the corrals they use for branding.

After passing the corrals, the coal trains would then climb a divide between the Tongue River and Rosebud Creek, going past a lovely sandstone outcrop where Wally told me he once picked up the best arrowhead he ever found anywhere.

The railroad would condemn Wally and Clint's property using the power of eminent domain, and Wally was told he would have to herd his cattle through culverts to get them to the river. His lifetime of experience has told him that range cattle don't like culverts and won't go into them, and he wanted the rail-road (if it were to be built) to put in bridges instead of culverts. To a cow, he told me, that far side opening of a culvert looks about the size of a dime.

But even if the cattle would go through those long culverts, the fact remains that Wally's day-to-day ranch operations would become more complicated and more costly.

Moving cattle each spring and fall would become a very different process. Today, it's a fairly low-key affair. Cows and calves walk together in a long line, allowing calves to easily stay with their mothers. Once across Greenleaf Creek, they're gathered into corrals where the calves are branded. Then those calves re-join mothers for a summer of grazing.

If this new version of the Tongue River Railroad were to be built, moving cattle would change from a slow and easy process to more of a cattle drive. Wally and Clint would have to hire hands to drive the cattle to big culverts. Then, they'd have to drive range cattle into these culverts. This may not even be possible.

In fifty years on the Rocker 6, Wally and Clint have developed a ranch oper-ation that a family can run efficiently. The Tongue River Railroad would have wrecked that operation.

The railroad, if it were built, would likely start wildfires from train exhaust, brakes, or wheel bearings, or from maintenance work. The Rocker 6 is in dry country – train-sparked fires would spread quickly in dry summer grass and fires may not be spotted until they have grown to dangerous size. This is country that knows the danger of wildfire, and this is a family that knows how a fire can upset an entire operation for years. Roughly 25% of the ranch was burned in the giant Ash Creek fire of 2012.

But train-caused wildfires aren't the only problem. If the Tongue River Rail-road were built across the Rocker 6, it would have blocked the McRaes from getting to fires started by lightning or other causes.

Wally and Clint have listened to politicians for many years affirm their sup-port of private property, yet be perfectly willing to sacrifice good Montana ranch land to the coal industry. Clint says, "What you've got here is a private corporation being granted the power of eminent domain so they can condemn my land in order to ship coal to China. I've got a problem with that."

·· ··· ·· ··· ·· ··· ·· ··· ·· ··· ·· ··· ·· ··· ·· ··· ·· ··· ·· ·· ·

That early-1990s proposal to extend the Tongue River Railroad to Decker, Montana, would have cut the Alderson place in two, going right through the bull pasture. Irv Alderson said, "We will have two pastures, one with water and one without."

The historic Bones Brothers Ranch is thirty-some miles upstream from the Rocker 6, along a small tributary called Hanging Woman Creek. Irv's daughter Jeanie Alderson reflects, "Everything that my family has been, is now, or will be is tied up in this place."

Irv is in his eighties now; Jeanie and her husband Terry Punt have fought as hard as they could to save the Bones Brothers Ranch, working with Northern Plains, with their ranch neighbors, and with their Northern Cheyenne neighbors. They hosted several ranch barbecues over the years to help raise money for the fight and to build solidarity with neighbors in the Tongue River valley.

During this period, speculation on coal bed methane also hung over the ranch. It was Jeanie who discovered that the BLM had – without informing the family – leased minerals underlying three-quarters of their ranch to five different parties speculating, most likely, on coal bed methane. That nightmare could still happen if market conditions in the natural gas industry change from what they are right now.

The family's fight against the Tongue River Railroad went on for a quarter-century. When the railroad was re-proposed as a spur line for the Otter Creek strip mine, the Alderson place was no longer a target for the project. But Jeanie and Terry never stopped fighting on behalf of their neighbors down the valley. Up to the very end in 2016, they remained leaders in the campaign to stop the Tongue River Railroad.

·· ··· ·· ··· ·· ··· ·· ··· ·· ··· ·· ··· ·· ··· ·· ··· ·· ··· ·· ·· ·

In contrast to Wally and Clint McRae, Mark Fix doesn't look much like a stereotypical cowboy. You're more likely to see him in tennis shoes or hiking boots than cowboy boots. He is soft-spoken and has a gentle demeanor. He smiles readily.

I don't know if I'd smile as readily as Mark does if I had to face what he had to face for over 20 years. For that long – from when he bought the ranch until December 17, 2012 – Mark's ranch was right in the path of the Tongue River Railroad. Starting on that day – like Irv Alderson's place – his ranch was no longer on the railroad's preferred route. But he knew that the situation could change just as suddenly again before all was said and done. And he never stopped fighting it.

The Fix Ranch is about 30 miles downstream (as the crow flies) from the Rocker 6, and mostly produces beef cattle. On good years, Mark may also have hay to sell.

I visited Mark's place one day during a year when his pastures and hay meadow had enjoyed the first wet spring in 15 years. The Tongue River, which flows near the house on the Fix ranch, was twice as wide as usual, and the pastures were as green as they could be. He and his son Justin had been out swathing hay.

The place was in full bloom. Alfalfa was flowering, along with the beautiful prickly pear and the yucca, as well as the scarlet globemallow and wild roses. Many of the grasses were blossoming as well.

Mark took me to his side-by-side, a small utility vehicle that can get him almost anywhere on the ranch, and we crossed the wooden bridge over the Tongue River. Nearby, swallows were gracefully swooping after flying insects. Killdeer ran on the ground and flew past us almost everywhere. Lark bunting flitted above the grasses of the open pasture. A mule deer doe and her fawn kept their distance down near the river. Pronghorn and hawk checked us out on one of the low ridges. As for the cattle, they were off in their summer pasture.

He first took me past his calving area, a flat field bounded by cottonwoods on one side and a low ridge on the other. We drove across the hayfield, which was partially mowed, and he showed me a hay yard where his bales had been struck by lightning a few years ago and burned up, every one of them. Just northwest of his hay meadow was his winter pasture, a broad, gently sloping plain divided by another low ridge. South of that ridge is a small stock dam.

All of these places – his calving area, the hayfield, and his winter pasture – had been in the path of the Tongue River Railroad for as long as he's owned the ranch, up until that day in 2012 when the bulls-eye landed on the McRaes. If that railroad had been built along its long-planned route, it would have torn through both of the low ridges and cut his ranch in two. It would have forced him to completely change his day-to-day operations. It would have reduced the value of his ranch. It would have killed cattle from time to time, started wildfires, and spread weeds. Coal trains, empty and full, would have rumbled through his place, day and night, about 16 times each day.

The speculators behind the Tongue River Railroad had the power to do this to Mark or any other landowner in their path because they had the power of eminent domain, the power to condemn property and "buy" it from the owner, whether the owner wants to sell it or not.

Mark Fix didn't want to sell.

Mark grew up on his family's cattle ranch near Ekalaka, Montana. He left Montana for a time, working 13 years as an engineer at Boeing. Eventually, though, he and his wife Debbie headed back to eastern Montana to take up ranch life. They managed to buy a place on the Tongue River about 20 miles upstream of Miles City.

He had never been involved with environmental issues or organizations, but when Mark learned that his new ranch lay in the path of the proposed Tongue River Railroad, he realized it was inevitable that he'd join the Northern Plains Resource Council, because Northern Plains had already been fighting this railroad for years. He figured this was the best prospect to save his ranch.

Quite a few miles upstream – upstream from the Rocker 6 and the Bones Brothers – a billionaire, the late Forrest Mars, had bought himself a large hobby ranch in the early 2000s. Unlike Mark and Wally, Forrest Mars had the good sense to be born into a family of colossal wealth, the Mars family, who sells us Snickers bars, M&Ms, Mars bars, and such. He is estimated to be worth more than $20 billion.

Forrest Mars did not like the fact that his large hobby ranch was vulnerable to the energy industry. When coal bed methane drillers got permits to drill on his land (because he didn't own all the minerals beneath it), he tried and failed to stop them in court. When it became apparent that the Tongue River Railroad would cross seven miles of his ranch, he tried to get the state legislature to change Montana's eminent domain law to give more protection to landowners (like him). That failed, too.

When you can't lick 'em, join 'em.

In 2011, Mars sent a letter to several members of Northern Plains revealing that he had bought a one-third interest in the Tongue River Railroad. He had partnered with Arch Coal, the St. Louis company planning the coal mine at Otter Creek, and with the BNSF Railway, owned by Warren Buffett's Berkshire Hathaway, Inc. Forrest Mars explained in his letter that he used his one-third interest to ensure that the Tongue River Railroad wouldn't connect with the line at Decker, Montana, meaning it wouldn't go through his ranch.

But this partnership ensured that the railroad would run through other people's ranches – Mark's place and Wally's place and other ranches on the lower part of the Tongue River. And as a one-third owner of the railroad, Forrest Mars would make money on cutting these other people's ranches in half.

"It's kind of sad to feel like a neighbor basically sold you down the river," Mark told a reporter.[1]

At the end of 2011, the Ninth Circuit Court of Appeals agreed with Northern Plains and ruled that the railroad would have to re-do its environmental impact statement, because the previous study had sidestepped the law and had relied on data that was decades old.

After submitting a new permit application, after holding a series of ten "scoping" meetings to inform the public of its plans and ask for the public's input (required by law as part of the EIS process), after showing the public maps of what it planned to do, the Tongue River Railroad Company announced more new plans, in the form of a new route.

The public was told about one set of plans, and allowed the chance to comment on those plans. Then – on December 17, 2012 – the railroad simply changed its plans. No new hearings. No new maps made available. No new public comment on the new plans. It was this sudden change that more than doubled the railroad's impact on the Rocker 6 ranch.

In 2015, a draft environmental impact statement was released for the Tongue River Railroad. In its approximately 4,000 pages, some astonishing claims were made. One such claim was that the coal from the proposed Otter Creek strip mine – the railroad's sole customer – would be sold to power plants in the American Midwest. But coal-fired power in the U.S. has been in decline for several years, and many coal plants have closed down.

Nobody who was familiar with coal markets believed this claim for a second.

Even at the height of coal use in the United States, very few (only ten) American power plants within a profitable distance were ever equipped to burn high-sodium coal like that found at Otter Creek.[2] Some of those have closed or have converted to natural gas, and more will no doubt close in coming years. No customers exist for this coal, but the EIS still insisted the coal is not going to Asia, but to the Midwest.[3] This was because Arch Coal knew that exporting coal to Asia is unpopular with many people.

Another eye-popping piece of whimsy in that EIS was that the 1.3 billion tons of coal to be mined from Otter Creek would not add any greenhouse gases to the atmosphere. In fact, the draft EIS claimed that opening the Otter Creek strip mine and burning its 1.3 billion tons of coal would result in a net decrease in greenhouse gas pollution.[4] The firm that prepared the EIS asserted that every ton of Otter Creek coal would displace a ton of coal from someplace else. 1.3 billion tons of coal would be mined, transported by train, and then burned, but all this would somehow reduce greenhouse gas pollution.

Again, nobody believed this. You have to wonder if the people who wrote this claim even believed it themselves.

Still, there remained immense political pressure to go forward with this mine and railroad, and that meant immense political pressure to cut through the Rocker 6 or any other private property that stood in the way. This coal – since it would go to Asia – wouldn't do much (if anything) for America's energy independence, but it would make a lot of money for a St. Louis coal company as well as Chinese industrialists, Warren Buffett, Forrest Mars, and other powerful people.

Late in 2015, the Tongue River Railroad asked the federal Surface Transportation Board to suspend work on the railroad's permit application until the permit for the Otter Creek mine was approved. Northern Plains quickly responded with a formal petition requesting that the Surface Transportation Board put an end to the railroad's permit application, arguing that ranchers on the Tongue River had endured 38 years of speculation over their property, and it was unfair to keep the threat of condemnation hanging over their property any longer for a speculative project.

The Tongue River Railroad Company had insisted to the Surface Transportation Board that the Otter Creek mine remained a viable proposal. What the company didn't reveal was that Arch Coal had already lost half of its coal leases in the Otter Creek valley – the coal owned by Great Northern Properties – because Arch had stopped making lease payments. The remaining coal leased by Arch Coal from the state of Montana would be impossible to mine without the Great Northern lease because the coal is owned in a checkerboard pattern.

The Tongue River Railroad knew of this, and knew of its significance, because Arch Coal is a one-third owner of the railroad. But this critical fact didn't surface for several months. It was Arch Coal's bankruptcy declaration in January 2016 that set the wheels in motion for this information to be revealed. In a bankruptcy proceeding, the court allows certain "interested parties" to see relevant documents, and the fact of this lost coal lease came to light.

In the end, it was Northern Plains that informed the Surface Transportation Board in April 2016 of the lost coal lease at Otter Creek. This meant that Arch Coal no longer had a viable mine project. With no mine, there was no longer a reason for the Tongue River Railroad to exist. Eleven days after Northern Plains notified the STB of this fact, the STB finally denied the Tongue River Railroad's permit application. It was a sudden and relatively quiet end to a 38-year battle.

....

These families have also worked to keep coal bed methane drillers from polluting the Tongue River with salty discharges from their wells, and from ruining aquifers as they dewater them to get at the methane. Many families rely on the Tongue for water that their cattle need. Other people need water from the Tongue River to irrigate crops and hayfields. The last thing any of them need is salty water, especially those who rely on irrigation. People in the valley rely on springs and wells to water livestock, springs and wells that could dry up if methane wells discharge large volumes of water from shallow coal bed aquifers, or if strip mines mine blow giant holes in the aquifers.

Some of Mark's neighbors have been told so many times that environmentalists are enemies of farming and ranching, it's hard for them to get past that notion.

Mark knows that "environmentalist" is a loaded word, but he doesn't particularly mind being known as one. He knows for a fact that Northern Plains has stood up for him and his ranch more than any other group and, to him, it's these actions that tell the truth of the matter.

Wally's sense is that, while most people who ranch near him don't want to join an organization because they don't want to be labeled, "on the balance, most people understand it and appreciate my taking a stand."

He feels that the term "environmentalist" has been widely misused, on purpose, to destroy people's credibility and make it easier to dismiss them.

Though miles apart, these ranches are about family.

Wally and Mark and Jeanie and Terry, different as they are from one another, all know that energy development projects like the Tongue River Railroad, the Otter Creek coal mine, and coal bed methane aren't just threats to the environment; they are threats to their property and to their families' livelihoods. And these aren't the only threats family ranch operations like theirs face.

These families know that ranchers and farmers need to talk to townspeople (their customers), and even to environmentalists. They know that stereotypes of environmentalists – as well as stereotypes of ranchers – are intended to keep people from working together, intended to make sure the coal miners and railroad speculators and gas drillers win out over everyone.

If the Tongue River Railroad had been built, it would have seized property, devalued additional property, and made it harder for family-based ranch operations to survive. The coal it had planned to haul would have gone to China, Korea, Japan, or India, and much of the cost would have been borne by the Rocker 6, the Fix Ranch, the Bones Brothers Ranch, that Amish farm, or other places up and down the river.

If it had been built, it would have served one purpose – to ship coal from the Otter Creek strip mine, coal primarily intended for shipment across the Pacific Ocean to customers in Asia. In order to do that, if it had been built, the Tongue River Railroad would have condemned and ruined good Montana ranch and farm land under a grant of eminent domain from the United States government. People own this land, yet it would have been forcibly "purchased" from them so that a St. Louis coal company, Chinese industrialists, and a railroad owned by Warren Buffett and the late Forrest Mars (and that coal company) could make a tidy profit.

Most of us, given the choice, would steer clear of such powerful adversaries. But what do you do when you're just minding your own business – earning a living and raising a family – and one day they come after you? If you're lucky, you have friends who will fight for you.

CHAPTER TWENTY-THREE

Where Your Home Is

Mining has already taken place under Ellen Pfister's land, and large cracks (big enough to swallow a horse) are appearing on hillsides of her ranch.

· ·

They first came after Boyd Charter's ranch when his son Steve was a teenager. As a boy, Steve just wasn't all that enthusiastic about ranching. During sixth grade, he turned in a class project, an autobiography, in which he wrote, "My father owes his success as a rancher to child labor."[1]

Steve left home as a teenager to attend Shattuck, a military boarding school in Minnesota. Boarding schools were a common path for ranch kids who lived far from the nearest high school, and Steve was ready to get away from the ranch. He became friends with other Montana ranch boys there, and the school suited his overall outlook on the world at the time.

He recalls arguing in favor of the Vietnam War when he was fourteen years old. His father, a World War II veteran, opposed the Vietnam War. Boyd was very conservative politically, and generally suspicious of the government. At the same time, he was very conservation-minded, and protective of the land upon which his ranch operation depended. And he absolutely would not tolerate being pushed around.

Steve wonders today how his life might have been different if the coal companies hadn't come sniffing around the ranch when he was in high school. First, the Northern Pacific came to drill core samples to "inventory" the coal reserves beneath the mountain ranch. Later, Consolidation Coal showed up, announcing its intention to strip-mine the area.

The Charter ranch has two parts. The lower part, near the road between Billings and Roundup, was where they lived most of the year and where the cattle wintered. The mountain ranch is much-beloved, up in the Bull Mountains, with trees and springs and lush grass for summer grazing. This is also where the coal beds are.

The land there is checkerboarded. Bull Mountain Properties, a subsidiary of Signal Peak Mining, owns every other section. This land was originally part of a railroad land grant from the 1800s, and the Charters lease those sections for grazing. The other sections in the checkerboard are owned by the Charters, but the minerals beneath are owned by the federal government.

The summer after high school, Steve and fellow Shattuck classmate Paul Hawks (also from Montana) wrote to everyone they could think of to raise awareness of what was about to happen to the Bull Mountains. Later, when he attended the University of Montana for a time, Steve told professors there about the looming coal development near his home. The threat posed by the coal companies sparked feelings about the ranch that had been buried inside him for much of his life.

Boyd Charter appealed to the Montana Stockgrowers Association for help, but was rebuffed. The Stockgrowers wanted more coal development, even at the expense of some of its own members' ranches. This helped Boyd Charter realize that some whom he had considered friends would not help him save his ranch from the coal companies.

Afterward, Boyd and Anne Charter, along with neighbor Ellen Pfister and several other people, formed the Northern Plains Resource Council. Through Northern Plains, they made a new family of friends with whom they worked shoulder-to-shoulder to help family-owned ranches survive the specter of being strip-mined. Some of these new friends were fellow ranchers, some were just people who cared.

Steve Charter left college and went to work as a volunteer for the newly-formed organization. His work sent him across Montana, doing his best to help landowners understand the implications of a new power line being planned from Colstrip westward. He enjoyed the work; although the power line went through, Steve felt he helped some ranchers to protect themselves a little better with the information he gave them. In public meetings, the 20 year-old Steve Charter often had to face off with an array of Montana Power Company officials. He recalled later seeing a letter that surfaced during a court case in which an MPC attorney was instructed to dig up "dirt" on Steve.

Steve eventually married Jeanne Hjermstad, a young Illinois woman who graduated from Wellesley with a degree in Greek and Latin, and from the University of Michigan with a Master's in Environmental Studies. Jeanne had come west to work for an organization in Helena, Montana, but she later went to work for Northern Plains, where she met Steve. Jeanne took to ranch life quickly.

Steve and Jeanne worked the ranch and raised two children, son Ressa and daughter Annika. When the coal issues subsided for a number of years, Steve and Jeanne became very active in trying to restore competition to the meatpacking industry, a dysfunctional marketplace dominated by just four big companies. The days of large cattle auctions are disappearing as the big packers take more control over the industry and have cooked up a stew of strategies to depress and manipulate prices.

Steve and Jeanne took on great personal costs as they challenged the cozy arrangements that funnel mandatory Beef Checkoff payments to a program run by the National Cattlemen's Beef Association, an industry association that claims to represent cattle producers, but marches in lockstep with the big meatpackers. The Beef Checkoff is a fee that every cattle producer in America is required to pay when they sell an animal. Steve and Jeanne absolutely did not appreciate that they were forced to make these payments, and their own money was used against them to promote the monopolistic practices so pervasive in the industry.

The couple sought to get locally produced beef carried in more grocery stores, but grocers were effectively bullied out of carrying local meat. The Charters were dragged into federal court when the U.S. Department of Agriculture sued them on behalf of the NCBA for not paying the Beef Checkoff.

Steve and Jeanne worked on a wide range of ideas for improving the viability of family-run ranches, such as alternative grazing rotations, producing biodiesel on the ranch (and using the leftover residue for cattle feed). They built a house in 1981 that runs on solar energy and is built into a hillside to protect it from the Montana winds.

For many years, the ranch has managed its grassland with an eye to the long term, keeping those grasses healthy, able to absorb plenty of carbon from the air, and able to build the soil.

Jeanne Charter was named as a "Farmer Hero" by Farm Aid in 2008. She was also a "keystone" member of a Billings-based food-buying club, which put consumers in direct contact with area food producers. That club, and many other projects to help family ranches survive were dealt a hard blow in 2011 when Jeanne was killed in a wreck on the highway near their ranch.

Jeanne's death came less than a year and a half after Steve's mother, Anne, died.

For all the experimentation at the Charter ranch, many of its operations are very traditional. Every summer, they trail their cattle on a two-day trip from the home ranch, across Dunn Mountain, to their mountain ranch. Every fall, they trail the cattle back to the lower ranch. Neighbors help neighbors with this and other necessary work.

Coal mining is back in the Bull Mountains. Several years ago, the state licensed the Signal Peak mine, a longwall operation in which the highly mechanized mining takes place underground, but which creates hard-to-forecast impacts when the land surface collapses over the mined-out areas. Mining has already taken place under Ellen Pfister's land, and large cracks (big enough to swallow a horse) are appearing on hillsides of her ranch.

In 2011, a subsidiary of the Gunvor Group, a large Swiss commodity trading company (owned by a Swede and a Russian-born Finn) bought a one-third interest in the Signal Peak mine, announced plans to increase production nearly threefold over the prior year, and to ship most of that coal to Asian customers.[2]

The coal beneath that Charter ranch is part of that expansion plan, and the U.S. Bureau of Land Management leased thousands of acres of coal, including coal beneath their mountain ranch, in 2012. The lease amount (30¢ a ton) was regarded by many as a bargain-basement price, and the BLM had refused to add stipulations that Steve and his son Ressa had requested to protect the land surface from damage by the mining.

In 2014, Northern Plains sued the BLM for its failure to even study what mining that coal would do to the land surface and to the people who ranch there.

Adding to the pressure on the ranch, Congress passed a defense funding authorization bill at the end of 2014 that included a coal "swap" in the Bull Mountains. The bill authorized trading coal owned by the United States to Great Northern Properties (railroad spinoff corporation, the largest private owner of coal reserves in the U.S.). It could open parts of the Charters' mountain ranch to strip mining, including the springs where he and Jeanne got married, the cabin where they took the kids when the cattle were at the mountain ranch in summer, and the places where his family's ashes are scattered.

It's been a long fight. Steve is in his sixties now.

I asked him about his neighbors and how they felt about his family's longstanding environmental activism. He told me that most of his neighbors didn't think very highly of environmentalists in general, but they always acknowledged his and his family's right to speak up in defense of their ranch. He told me that, "It can be easy to fall into fighting, but we've always tried to treat each other with respect, even if we disagree."

CHAPTER TWENTY-FOUR

Public Lands

These places where all of us are equal are among the few forces left that
bind Americans together, that make us equal to one another.

..…..…..…..…..…..…..…..…..…..…..…..…..…..…..

When I was growing up, Dad and I lived in rented apartments and houses. He was never a property owner. We never had a yard that was ours. Nor a garden. Nor even furniture.

Luckily, when we lived in Sioux Falls, there was an area of undeveloped woods just down the hill from our apartment building. And when we moved to Rapid City – I was 10 at the time – there was an undeveloped hill not far from where our little one-bedroom house shared a lot with two other rentals.

Our occasional excursions into the Black Hills gave me more than Dad realized. They gave me new places where I was allowed to walk around, to climb rocks and wade creeks and look for wild animals. I didn't know about public lands or land management agencies then. But for a kid who had lived in rental units all his life, these open spaces became important to me. They were a place where I had just as much right to go as anybody else. When you grow up living in furnished rentals, that's a strong feeling.

Some people think that those who advocate for the public lands – for national parks, for wilderness, for wild places in general – are elitists. But in my own life, those places were always an outlet for a kid from a below-middle-class household.

I could learn in those places. I could become a stronger person there. I was equal to anybody in those places, and it didn't matter whether I came from a poor household. As I grew, those lands became a great equalizer to me, a place where every American has as much right as anyone else, where we are all equally welcome.

Today, our nation is gradually losing our great Middle Class, and that's a shame. We are becoming more and more divided economically and culturally. And for that reason, I believe these public places, whether national parks, national forests, national grasslands, or the other public domain lands of the West, are more important than ever.

Terry Tempest Williams summed it up pretty well. "Public Lands are our public commons and they belong to everyone."[1]

These places where all of us are equal are among the few forces left that bind Americans together, that make us equal to one another. While the outcomes of today's unregulated marketplace are pulling us apart – by economic class and by culture – the public lands remain in my mind a place where we can share whatever we have left in common.

None of us own these lands, yet all of us own these lands. And all of us are responsible for them.

Twenty-first-century America is full of forces that put some of us above others. Public places, however – they could be the Lincoln Memorial as well as the Canyonlands – are anything but elitist. They are a symbol of Americans' equality to one another, a reminder of something we have in common.

CHAPTER-TWENTY-FIVE

Private Property, Part 2

This water right would be unlike traditional water rights because the water would leave the basin from which it was withdrawn. It would not supply water to crops, nor livestock, nor households; it would be "marketed."

···

Some people want water to become private property. Corporations around the world have moved to acquire ownership of water rights and water delivery systems. In the United States, troubles from years of under-investment by public water systems has caused many cities to turn over water delivery systems to private companies, a transaction that turns citizens into customers, that can prevent citizens from having full access to information about how the water they drink is handled. Water has been termed "blue gold" and the "oil of the 21st century."

A coal bed methane company withdrawing large amounts of ground water from beneath the arid plains of southeast Montana had plans to pump a lot more before the price of natural gas fell sharply starting in 2008. Pumping the water to the surface is what allows the methane to be accessed, but the water is a significant problem to methane drillers. The ground water in the region tends to be salty, so it's not considered viable for irrigation, especially on the clay-rich soils common there. The company applied for a water right to its discharge water. The company even sought the right to pipe that ground water from the near-desert plains of eastern Montana to other states. This water right would be unlike traditional water rights because the water would leave the basin from which it was withdrawn. It would not supply water to crops, nor livestock, nor households; it would be "marketed."

This would amount to privatizing the water, and it would come at a great cost to other water rights holders in the area. Methane drilling, over time, depletes aquifers. That depletion has been modeled by hydrologists and, once depleted by large-scale drilling, the aquifer would take many years – in some areas, lifetimes – to recover. Granting this water right would amount to privatizing a public resource, and would damage the rights of the other water users who depend on that aquifer. It would also change the system of rights and responsibilities that other water rights holders have relied on for more than a century.

Not every piece of nature is appropriate to become a piece of private property. I believe this is true of water, of air, of wild animals.

And, much as I am comfortable with the marketplace and with business, not every human activity is appropriate as a profit-making venture, and not every profit-making venture is free enterprise. Police departments, fire departments, public parks, and public libraries are obvious and immediate examples of enterprises that should not be established simply out of the profit motive. But some people would like to do it that way. Some people would put private corporations in control of our drinking water supply. Some people would put our national parks – the Grand Canyon, the Statue of Liberty, the Lincoln Memorial – into the hands of private corporations.

It's important for Americans to remember that not everything should be bought and sold. We need to remember that, at one time in this country, human beings were private property.

CHAPTER TWENTY-SIX

Another Wacko Environmentalist Song

My country, 'tis of thee,
Sweet land of liberty,
Of thee I sing:
Land where my father's died,
Land of the pilgrim's pride,
From ev'ry mountainside
Let freedom ring!

My native country thee,
Land of the noble free,
Thy name I love:
I love thy rocks and rills,
Thy woods and templed hills;
My heart with rapture thrills
Like that above.

We love thine inland seas,
Thy groves of giant trees,
Thy rolling plains;
Thy rivers' mighty sweep,
Thy mystic canyons deep,
Thy mountains wild and steep,
All thy domains.

Thy silver Eastern strands,
Thy Golden Gate that stands

Wide to the West;
Thy flowery Southland fair,
Thy sweet and crystal air –
O Land beyond compare,
Thee I love best!

(*Gloria: a hymnal for use in Sunday schools, young people's societies, and devotional meetings*, Editor: Benjamin Shepard, A. S. Barnes & Co., New York, 1916, verses *1-2: Samuel Francis Smith; verses 3-4: Henry van Dyke* [http://www.hymnary.org/hymn/G1916/page/240])

CHAPTER TWENTY-SEVEN

Gasoline and Groceries

Refining oil is a dirty business. Bringing food to our table is sometimes a dirty business. But whether we're buying cars, filling up our cars, choosing a store, filling up our shopping cart, or buying a light bulb, we have choices.

....

For decades, American taxpayers have been subsidizing the oil industry. We've subsidized it when the nation prospered, we've subsidized it while Americans struggled. When the economy and the budget deficit got so bad that some politicians talked about privatizing Medicare, the Obama White House proposed reducing some of these subsidies for the oil industry. After all, the President reasoned, this industry was raking in huge profits at a time when most Americans were struggling and millions of Americans were desperate.

Conoco-Phillips, in a press release, called this proposal to reduce oil industry subsidies "un-American."[1]

That's the company from which I routinely buy gasoline. So why would I prefer to do business with a company that is so arrogant, and that has such twisted values? It's all a matter of the choices I have.

There are two oil refineries here in Billings – ExxonMobil and ConocoPhillips (spun off in 2012 to Phillips 66). There's another refinery just up the road in Laurel (Cenex). I almost always buy Conoco.

However you go about it, the oil business is dirty. Getting it out of the ground is dirty. Refining it is dirty. Transporting it is dirty. Most of the end uses (burning it) are dirty. Driving around in my Toyota sedan is one of those dirty uses. Buying groceries that are shipped from all parts of the world is dirty. Bringing my daughter home from college for Christmas – whether by plane or train – was dirty.

But here in Billings, ConocoPhillips has historically run the cleanest of the three refineries. Its output of sulfur dioxide is a fraction of the SO_2 that Exxon's refinery releases into our airshed. And it is more willing to let the public know what's going on with their operation, having established a citizens advisory council years ago.

Is ConocoPhillips a great company? Nope. It's heavily involved in Alberta, extracting the filthy bitumen from tar sands (or "oil sands" as the oil industry wants us to call them), and piping this thick, corrosive goo across American farms and rivers on its way to refineries in Texas. ConocoPhillips is one of the world's biggest oil companies and its refinery spinoff – Phillips 66 – is one of America's biggest air polluters.[2] But I drive a car, and that means I have to buy gasoline from an oil company that pollutes the land, the water, and the air.

Sulfur dioxide is an "indirect" greenhouse gas. It also makes breathing difficult for people like the late Nettie Lees, people who suffer from asthma and other respiratory problems.

Back in the mid-1990s, Exxon was discharging more than six times the sulfur dioxide *per unit of production* that Conoco was putting out from its stacks, and Cenex discharged more than four times Conoco's output.[3] The three companies were all refining sour crude from Alberta, but Exxon was by far the dirtiest.

By the end of 2008, Exxon-Mobil (so named because of a merger) was spewing twenty times as much sulfur dioxide as ConocoPhillips. To be fair, by 2008 Exxon had reduced its SO_2 output considerably, but so had ConocoPhillips. The difference is that Conoco had invested heavily in pollution controls, Exxon had to be forced by federal regulators.[4]

Some people may think of Exxon whenever they think of the Exxon Valdez oil spill off the Alaska coast. Others may know Exxon as the company that has bankrolled so much junk science in an effort to create a phony controversy over climate change, controversy that doesn't really exist in the scientific community. And some people will no doubt think of Exxon when they recall its profiteering when Americans were suffering through record-high gasoline prices. A lot of people around here think of Exxon as the company whose pipeline burst beneath the Yellowstone River in 2011, spewing about 1,500 barrels of oil into one of America's best rivers (and recovering only about 10 barrels).[5]

I think of Exxon as the company that has to be dragged, kicking and screaming, to make any progress on reducing its pollution. I think of Exxon as the company that tries (with considerable success) to buy the goodwill of the community with nickel-and-dime charitable contributions. And, yes, I also think of the Exxon Valdez, the corporate-sponsored junk science, and the profiteering. I don't buy Exxon's gasoline.

The ConocoPhillips / Phillips 66 refinery is still an oil refinery. It still pollutes the air and still contributes to global warming. (So do I when I drive my car and heat my house and cook my food.) From time to time, an operational upset at the ConocoPhillips refinery still stinks up downtown Billings. But I will give them credit for making an effort to operate a less terrible refinery here.

My preference for Conoco gasoline is political. So is my weekly grocery trip.

I'm not as well-informed a shopper as I should be. And I'm sometimes – much too often – less conscientious than I should be.

All things being equal, I'd rather buy from a local business. I want my dollars to help keep jobs in my community, to help keep small businesses alive in my community. Of course, all things aren't always equal, and my support for local business is far from perfect.

I like to buy locally-produced food. That used to be easy enough in Montana, but it isn't any more. Try finding locally raised meat in your supermarket. The handful of big meatpackers have a lot of market power (another market failure) and they sometimes use that power to keep grocery stores from making room in their display cases for local meat.

Sometimes you can find local meat at the grocery store, but it usually costs significantly more. When it's anything more expensive than hamburger, the price difference can really get your attention.

I'm fortunate to know where the vast majority of my meat comes from. There's Steve Charter north of Billings, and there's the B Bar Ranch near Melville, Montana. I know that the cattle grew on grass, and that the meat is processed at a smaller packing plant, the type which used to operate all over the country.

I know that these families don't routinely feed antibiotics to their cattle. We're having enough trouble with antibiotic resistant bacteria – we certainly don't need to breed more such deadly bacteria by feeding animals antibiotics when they aren't sick. That practice translates directly into stronger bacteria that antibiotic drugs can't treat. In a study published in the scientific journal *Clinical Infectious Diseases*, researchers bought beef, chicken, pork, and turkey at grocery stores in different parts of the country and tested them for bacteria. Nearly half the samples contained strains of Staphylococcus bacteria, and more than half of those staph bacteria were resistant to at least three classes of antibiotics.[6]

In the last few decades, the meatpacking industry has become more and more concentrated. "Concentrated" is a polite term for "monopolistic." Monopolies aren't exactly what we learned they are in high school; that is, they don't usually result in reducing the number of players in a given market down to just one. Monopolies usually mature as shared monopolies – in this case, an oligopsony – where a small handful of players effectively run a given marketplace. This is what's happened in meat, poultry, and several other agricultural commodities.

The price for most cattle is no longer established through an open and competitive bidding process at the local livestock auction. It's established by private contracts, with one buyer representing one company in an area. The market power of each big meatpacking company allows it to keep prices that they pay for cattle low. The big packers own substantial numbers of cattle so that, if prices start to climb, they can dump more cattle into the marketplace and drive the prices back down.

And why is this an environmental issue?

Harm to the land. In the end, the proportion of your food dollar that reaches the rancher has shrunk over the years, and the proportion of your dollar going to the big packers has grown. The ranch family, meanwhile, doesn't have as many of those "good years" that help keep dollars in their rural communities. They are under constant pressure to find new ways to survive. Sometimes this means selling off land for subdivision. Sometimes it means allowing their community to be targeted for some really nasty development project. This happens in a community that's desperate for dollars because so many farmers and ranchers have gone out of business, and the ones that survive have fewer and fewer good years. Healthy, economically viable rural communities aren't as vulnerable to this. But monopolization has helped depopulate farm and ranch country and force the people who remain there to open themselves to environmentally damaging developments that they wouldn't have had to consider when agriculture sustained the community.

Public health. As their packing houses become larger, the monopolists realize that they can make more money if they produce more by running the production line faster. This doesn't leave much time for meat inspectors to work, so inspection at these packing plants has been largely reduced to an exercise in paperwork that relies on self-reporting by the operator of the plant. Since 1998, a system of "Hazard Analysis Critical Control Point Plans" at the U.S. Department of Agriculture has led to a meatpacking system in which the big packers largely police themselves and the USDA inspects paperwork more than it inspects meat.

John Munsell used to run a small meat processing plant in Miles City, Montana. Back in 2002, a federal meat inspector notified Munsell that traces of *e. coli* 0157 bacteria had been found in a sample of meat processed at his plant. Munsell informed the inspector that the meat had been originally processed and then sent to him from a large ConAgra packing plant in Greeley, Colorado. However, the USDA didn't trace the meat back to its original processing point. Instead, the USDA focused on ordering Munsell to comply with an onerous new reporting requirement and forcing him to recall several hundred pounds of hamburger. Months later, the USDA did discover *e. coli* 0157 at the ConAgra plant in Greeley, leading to a recall of 19 million pounds.[7]

This new hands-off system was desired by the big packers, and it clearly favors those large corporations over the small because they have a better capacity for completing paperwork. Physical inspection of the meat has become a peripheral concern, and periodic outbreaks of disease originating in packing plants have been the result.

Abuse of power. The big packers got their new "inspection" system because they are huge companies and they have lots of political clout, far more than the small operators.

For years, the big packers have been pushing for a system that they claim will improve food safety. Dubbed "National Animal Identification," it is really just an attempt to shove liability onto ranchers for health problems that originate in over-sized, high-speed packing plants. Another attack on the family rancher by the big packers.

Jobs. And in this age of globalization, jobs in meatpacking plants are no longer the good-paying jobs they used to be. It's just too easy to bring in low-cost labor to work at a fraction of the former wage. And, speaking of jobs, where is the butcher that used to be part of every grocery store? Today's packing plants produce "value-added" products like boxed meat, or meat already packaged with a "brand name" label. There's not as much need for the butcher in your local store.

I want meat that's locally raised and locally processed; I have far more faith in its cleanliness. And I have far more faith that family-scale ranching is better for the environment than corporate farms, animal factories, and economically desperate rural communities.

You might guess that I don't buy ConAgra's products at the grocery store when I can avoid it. Nor Tyson chicken. And I sure as hell don't eat veal because confining a calf like that for its entire lifetime is just plain wrong.

Still, if I walked over and looked in my kitchen cupboard right now, I would find canned soups, boxed cereals, and other products from giant agribusiness corporations. If I were more diligent, I would buy less of those things, and more through the local food co-op. I would be a better gardener. I would spend more time cooking and less money on prepared foods.

Of course, I'm pretty lucky compared to a lot of people. I heard a speech on the radio by LaDonna Redmond, a resident of Chicago. She spoke of how neighborhoods that are predominantly African-American have one-fifth the number of grocery stores, per capita, as the rest of the country. She began noticing inexplicable illness in her own children and realized how difficult it is for people in her neighborhood to have any shopping choices at all. She spoke of how, in her neighborhood, she could buy crack cocaine, she could buy heroin, she could buy a semi-automatic weapon. But, she said, "I cannot purchase an organic tomato."[8]

How we shop affects our lives, our health, our local economy, our environment. Shopping is not trivial. Wendell Berry reminds us in his essay "Conservationist and Agrarian," that...

...mostly urban conservationists, who mostly are ignorant of the economic adversities of, say, family-scale farming or ranching, have paid far too little attention to the connection between their economic life and the despoliation of nature. They have trouble seeing that the bad farming and forestry practices that they oppose as conservationists are done on their behalf, and with their consent implied in the economic proxies they have given as consumers.[9]

I'm not a very good shopper, and I should be a better one. This is no small matter. Pope Benedict XVI said in 2009 that "Purchasing is always a moral – and not simply economic – act."[10]

Refining oil is a dirty business. Bringing food to our table is sometimes a dirty business. But whether we're buying cars, filling up our cars, choosing a store, filling up our shopping cart, or buying a light bulb, we have choices. They are choices we all make.

But I need to reiterate one important point: we will not make the world better by being better shoppers. Our dollars do have some power, but that power is very limited. People who are serious about protecting America's environment know that shopping is not going to get us there.

Filmmaker Annie Leonard said in her film, *The Story of Change*:

If we actually want to change the world, we can't talk only about consumers voting with our dollars... As Gandhi said, "Be the change." Living our values in small ways shows ourselves and others that we care, so it is a great place to start.

But it's a terrible place to stop. After all, would we even know who Gandhi was if he just sewed his own clothes and then sat back waiting for the British to leave India?[11]

CHAPTER TWENTY-EIGHT

Agriculture

For the only sure way to preserve rural land is to have a thriving rural economy on the land. – Wendell Berry

....

Many of the people I contacted while writing this book are farmers and ranchers, and others grew up on farms. In recent years, a perception seems to have become widespread that farmers and ranchers are consistently at odds with environmentalists. Working for an organization that was formed by ranch families, this has not been my experience.

It's true there are some ag groups that maintain persistent anti-environmental postures. Before Northern Plains was founded in 1972, Boyd Charter and other ranchers had gone to another organization for help, an organization where several of them were members – the Montana Stockgrowers Association. Had the Stockgrowers stepped in to help these ranch families protect their property and the natural resources they relied on, Northern Plains might never have become necessary. However, the Stockgrowers would not come to their aid and, to this day, the Montana Stockgrowers Association is just about as reliable an ally as there could be for metal mining, oil and gas drilling, coal mining, and other extractive industries. The Montana Farm Bureau is much the same.

But there are also ag groups that don't have such a knee-jerk reaction against environmentalists.

It's true that some people in rural areas, from the time they're children, hear a lot of venom directed toward environmental organizations. It's true that some ag publications take a solidly anti-environmental position at every opportunity. It's true that some people in farm and ranch country paint environmentalists with a very broad brush – environmentalists are all vegetarians, they want to take away private property, they want to turn farm and ranch country into some kind of back-to-nature preserve where they can smoke their pot and worship their pagan gods.

And it's true that there are environmentalists who conceive of ranchers and farmers as a bunch of agribusiness lackeys who want to kill all wildlife, pollute all the rivers and streams, and sell us food products laced with dangerous chemicals. Stereotyping goes both ways. A couple of environmental groups have expressed reservations about working with Northern Plains because our farm and ranch background makes us just not "green" enough.

So there really is a gulf between *some* ag groups and *some* environmental groups. In my experience, though, the hostility toward agriculture among some environmentalists is not nearly so widespread and institutionalized as is the gospel preached against them in some ag organizations and news outlets.

In their efforts to cultivate allies in farm and ranch country, extractive industries have usually been eager to play on these stereotypes and this hostility. The perception they nurture is that environmentalists are dangerous to farming and ranching, and the farmers and ranchers must stick with their friends in the mining industry and logging industry and the oil and gas industry.

Back in the 1990s, Pegasus Gold ran a cyanide heap leach gold mine in north-central Montana. In the late 90s, Pegasus walked away from the operation, and the state realized too late that the bond Pegasus had posted wouldn't nearly cover the costs of stabilizing the site and treating the tainted water that would perpetually leach out of the rock as the rain and snow came. So every Montana taxpayer is paying for that water treatment, forever.

But when the mine was still operating, Pegasus used to pass out refrigerator magnets that said, "If it can't be grown, it has to be mined." It was an effort to solidify support among ag people, based on supposition that the extraction of minerals was similar to the growing of food and fiber, and that the two industries had better cover one another's back. Their common enemy? Environmentalists, of course.

The hard rock mining industry hammered home its key message to enlist support from ag groups: "You're next."

I don't know how many farmers and ranchers bought into the Pegasus line that they were natural allies. Some did, I'm fairly sure. But agriculture at least carries the possibility of being a sustainable enterprise, one that can continue indefinitely without degrading the natural resource base it depends on. Not all farms and ranches operate sustainably, but most of them have that potential. The extraction of minerals does not.

I want to see a healthy agricultural economy in Montana and the rest of America. Those of us who don't live on farms and ranches benefit in many ways, including the food we buy (especially when it's raised by independent, family-run operations), the wildlife habitat, open space, and other natural resource conservation afforded by the presence of cows rather than condominiums. Stronger rural communities, surrounded by economically healthy farms and ranches, are a positive value for people who care about America's environment.

Unfortunately, we don't often see such communities anymore. Many rural areas of Montana and other states are depopulating. Many rural communities are economically desperate. And monopolistic agribusiness corporations exercise an increasing dominance over the way farming and ranching is done in the United States (and the rest of the world, too). In many regions, the oil and gas industry (as well as the mining industry) makes it harder to operate a farm or ranch.

"By ruin of farmers and rural communities, by erosion, pollution, and various kinds of industrial development," Wendell Berry tells us, "we have ominously degraded and reduced the long-term food-producing capacity of our country."[2]

It's important to remember that not all farming is good farming. Some farmers and ranchers have bought into the corporate ideal of genetic engineering, overuse of antibiotics and poisons, and practicing monoculture. Some support the political agenda of the big meatpackers, as contrary as that is to their own self-interest. And some rural areas are dotted with large feedlots and concentrated animal feeding operations – more appropriately called "animal factories."

These animal factories have no resemblance to a farm or ranch. They confine cattle, hogs, and poultry for feeding before slaughter, sometimes hundreds of thousands of animals in densely crowded conditions – the animals that most of us cook and serve as meat on our dinner tables. The sheer volume of waste generated in these animal factories creates a gigantic pollution problem that affects ground and surface waters, and forces everyone living in the area to breathe a putrid stench every day and every night. The property values of those unfortunate neighbors often wither away in that stench. Large volumes of chemicals, including the non-medical use of antibiotics, add to the pollution threat.

Has the spread of these animal factories helped farmers and ranchers? Hardly. While the corporations running these factories have prospered, there has been no ticket to prosperity for farmers, or for rural communities, or for most employees who work in these factories. Low prices paid to farmers are not reflected by low prices in the grocery store. But the political power wielded by these animal factories and the corporations that run them has bent public policy and regulatory agencies to do their bidding in many places.

Away from these animal factories, there are farmers and ranchers who do their best to make their practices fit with what the land and water and weather bring them. They don't pump their cattle full of antibiotics and they fight for a marketplace that has room for local packing plants. They fight for clean water when methane drilling or coal mining threatens it. As long as they can survive economically, they won't subdivide.

Montana farmer Dena Hoff once told me that "the best fertilizer is the farmer's shadow." It means that the farmer is present, is tending to things, and the farm is better for that attention. We need more farmers like that. And those farmers need more good customers who want locally grown food, organically grown food, food that gives us health and sustenance and that that sustains the land and water we all need.

And just as much, environmentalists and the agricultural community need each other. They are confronted by a corporate economy that measures nothing but dollars, and that places no value on family, on country, on the next generation. These are the corporations that generate record profits at the same time many farmers and ranchers teeter on the brink of bankruptcy. These are the corporations that reduce the world's people, water, beauty, genetic wealth, and everything else they touch to dollars. These corporations don't give a damn about the hungry people of the world. They sure don't give a damn about whether American farmers and ranchers are able to earn a decent living from the land.

Wendell Berry, long a thoughtful commentator on agriculture in America, reminds us:

The great centralized economic entities of our time do not come into rural places in order to improve them by "creating jobs." They come to take as much of value as they can take, as cheaply and as quickly as they can take it.[3]

I want family-scale farming and ranching to survive and thrive again in America. It will be good for our environment and it will make our rural communities healthy again.

CHAPTER TWENTY-NINE

Environmentalists on TV

Another CBS program, "CSI: New York," featured an environmental group that set off a deadly bomb with a solar-powered detonator.

·· ··

I admit it, I watch too much television.

I recall watching an episode of a short-lived CBS drama called "Eleventh Hour" in which the villain was a crazed environmentalist who deliberately poisoned Lake Michigan with mercury to make people more aware of pollution.

Another CBS program, "CSI: New York," featured an environmental group that set off a deadly bomb with a solar-powered detonator. (Yes, I did laugh out loud at that one!)

The crazed, evil environmentalist has become a standard plot device on TV, mostly in cop shows. Sometimes they shoot people, sometimes they blow people up. But they are a convenient class of villain that lazy television writers will no doubt continue to produce indefinitely.

Yet another CBS show, "NCIS," included an episode in which an environmental terrorist attempted to murder the crew of a U.S. Navy submarine.

The investigators in a spinoff show, "NCIS: Los Angeles," went after a screwball environmentalist scientist who wanted to turn loose the smallpox virus onto mankind. "The earth is dying, and we are the disease," said the villain. I can't help but wonder if the writers giggled aloud as they constructed that plot and dialogue.

And still another CBS program, "Blue Bloods," featured a fanatical environmentalist who shot and killed people driving cars that get poor gas mileage.

(OK, OK, I watch too many cop shows.)

If you're as old as I am, you may remember the days of TV westerns in which a fight in a barn ended when someone fell onto the business end of a pitchfork that was left standing, tines-up, in a stack of hay. I've never seen a pitchfork left that way in the real world, but it was a common plot device on TV.

And in the real world, of course, there have been damn few environmentalists who have turned to violence. So how do I feel about seeing so many evil environmentalists on TV?

I suppose I feel the same way deeply religious people must feel when television's most frequent portrayal is of them is the psychotic anti-abortion murderer or the corrupt priest. I try not to take it too seriously. After all, I have my own stereotypes of television writers. And I'm sure my stereotypes are at least as valid.

CHAPTER THIRTY

Mining

When the company declared bankruptcy in 1998, it became apparent that the amount of the bond wouldn't come close to the actual costs of treating the poisoned water that was migrating off the mine site and downstream.

....

Right after high school, I took a summer job as a tour guide at an old gold mine in Keystone, South Dakota, leading walking tours into an unsuccessful early-twentieth-century gold mine. I worked there a couple more summers after that, and enjoyed most of the people I met. I also learned a lot. My boss often took me and the other employees on outings to other old mines in the Keystone area, of which there are many.

We visited the nearby Peerless Mine, the Hugo, the Etta, the Ingersoll, the Dan Patch, and the Holy Terror (named after its original owner's wife), as well as many unnamed tunnels and pits. Keystone is a great place to start a rock collection. While the early miners there sought gold and other precious metals, later mining took a variety of minerals associated with the many pegmatite dikes in the area: ores of metals like tin, tungsten, lithium, and beryllium. A rock collector there can pick up beryl, spodumene, lepidolite, feldspar, mica, tourmaline, and more.

Most of the mining in Keystone had been finished by the time I worked there as a tour guide, and had become more a part of the town's history than its economy. The mountains in that area are full of unreclaimed mines.

Those unreclaimed mines are externalized costs that the mine operators left behind when they closed up. But the pegmatite mines of the Black Hills create nowhere near the problem of many other kinds of mines – coal, uranium, certain metal mines. Some mines will leach toxic chemicals into watersheds for centuries, maybe longer, after the mines have closed down. Preventing that won't happen by itself. Somebody has to take action, and that action has to be enforced by the rule of law.

Many people who don't live near mining activity tend to be blind to its impacts. I have repeatedly heard people refer to "pollution-free" electric cars or even electricity that is "more than 100 percent clean" – if the pipe dream of "clean coal" could somehow be realized.[1] Statements like these are oblivious to the impacts of mining itself.

The mountaintop removal mining that plagues Appalachia is a recent technology that our government has allowed, a technology that leaves behind decapitated mountains, ruined watersheds, and people living with the constant prospect of being flooded by toxic coal wastes.

In the mountains of the West, the advent of cyanide heap leach mining in the 1970s changed the game for gold mining. It became the way most gold is mined, and it vastly amplified the damage that gold mining does to the land and water. It's the reason that I don't wear a wedding band made of gold.

What cyanide leach mining meant to the industry was that you didn't need to have a high-grade ore to make money; all you needed was a big enough body of ore. Cyanide leach mining became widespread at a time when gold prices were high, which pushed the technology into use very quickly.

The idea of such mining is this: if gold prices are high enough, you can turn a profit from very low-grade ores. You can tear apart a mountain that's filled with low-grade ore and still make money because your costs are so low – labor costs and facility costs. You just grind up all that low-grade ore and set it outside in big piles, then percolate a solution of cyanide through the piles. The cyanide captures the gold. At Pegasus Gold's Zortman-Landusky mine in north-central Montana, they were making money even when it took 69 tons of rock to collect one troy ounce of gold – 69 tons for one ounce. The mountain, of course, was never reclaimed.

As you can imagine, this creates another mountain of waste rock. But, while the mine is operating, the great outdoors is being used as the processing facility. The big ore piles, and the cyanide solution percolating through them, are sitting outdoors, in drainages that go somewhere. Technical failures, or even something as simple as a heavy rainstorm, can cause that cyanide, acids, and heavy metals to leave the site and flow downstream.

Pegasus Gold operated Montana's first cyanide heap leach gold mine just outside the Fort Belknap Reservation from 1979 to 1998. They developed the Zortman-Landusky mine (actually two connected mines) on land that the Assiniboine and Gros Ventre tribes were forced to sell to the U.S. government after gold was discovered there in the late 1800s.[2]

During its operations, Pegasus applied for and was granted 11 expansions, the last one nearly tripling the permitted area of operations. The mine repeatedly violated state and federal water laws, some involving large spills of toxic chemicals, and Pegasus was eventually required to develop an improved water treatment plan and post a bond with the state of Montana. When the company declared bankruptcy in 1998, it became apparent that the amount of the bond wouldn't come close to the actual costs of treating the poisoned water that was migrating off the mine site and downstream. As of this writing, about $1.5 million is being spent every year – half of that is tax dollars – to treat water at the site, and additional funds are being spent to improve or repair water treatment on the abandoned mine site.[3]

In a free market, the mining company would never have been allowed to get away with shoving that cost onto the public. Public agencies are notorious for accepting bonds from mining companies that are nowhere near enough to pay the real cost of cleanup. It isn't that unusual for a mining company to walk away from an operation. In many cases, that's what they have the financial incentive to do.

By the way, our nation is filled with abandoned mine sites. U.S. government estimates range from 100,000 to 500,000 abandoned mine sites in the United States.[4]

Financial incentive is what leads many mining companies to fight tooth and nail against laws or standards that would require them to prevent pollution or reclaim the sites of their operations. Preventing pollution creates jobs and reclamation creates jobs. But a job represents an expense, and mines and other pol-luters will avoid creating these particular jobs (expenses) as much as they can and as long as they can.

Some mine sites contain toxic chemicals (e.g., mercury), or even explosives, left behind by the companies that walked away from them. Some sites are leach-ing chemicals into watersheds, chemicals that come from the rock that was ex-posed during mining (e.g., sulfuric acid). These chemicals can kill life in the streams. Or they may simply contaminate that plant or animal life, then concen-trate the poison as it passes up the food chain. Abandoned uranium mines con-tain radioactive materials in their tailings piles. Some abandoned mines and mine infrastructure facilities are so bad that they're designated as Superfund sites, though the federal Superfund has been chronically under-funded for its purpose of cleaning up heavily polluted locations.

Even if nothing toxic is migrating off the site, unreclaimed mine sites can lead to the silting of streams. Dust can blow off the site and some dust, like the dust at Libby, can be dangerous all by itself. When money is spent to clean up these sites, much of it is *your* money.

Dad tried to teach me when I was a boy; if I make a mess, I need to clean up after myself. For a mine, cleanup is (or should be) a cost of doing business.

Instead, we have allowed mining practices – mountaintop removal for coal and cyanide heap leach mining for gold – for which there is no cleaning up, not even the possibility of cleaning up.

Fifty or a hundred years ago, we knew a lot less than we do today about the impacts of mining. We also had less capacity to inflict large-scale ruin upon the land and the water then than we do today. Mountaintop removal mining. Strip mining. Longwall mining. Cyanide heap leach mining for gold is bad enough that the voters of Montana decided in 1998 to outlaw any new cyanide heap leach mines.

Mining is more than just a hole in the ground. It's the largest producer of toxic waste in our nation. It's the energy-intensive process of smelting ore. It's burning the energy minerals, and then disposing of combustion waste that contains heavy metals and other toxins. It's the scarring of the land. It's the depletion of aquifers and the pollution of rivers.

When I got married in 1980, my bride and I exchanged wedding bands made of silver, which is a less rare metal and therefore requires less mining than a comparable amount of gold. A friend of mine who got married in 2006 bought wedding bands of palladium that came from the Stillwater mine in Montana, a responsible operation that has worked hard to prevent pollution. Her rings still required mining, and even responsible mining still creates impacts, but it's a lot less damaging than the typical gold mine. (There was a responsible gold mine that operated near Jardine, Montana, in the 1980s and 90s, responsible in its behavior toward the land and water, and also in its behavior toward the community downstream from its operation.)

Mining enterprises must deal with many variables: geological uncertainty, fluctuating prices for the product, variations in ore quality, recoverability of the mineral reserves, total size of the ore body, labor costs, labor productivity, transportation costs, availability of water, capital costs, presence of conflicting land uses, and so forth. Mining has always been a very volatile industry.

But it's also an industry that, most of the time, wants to have things its way, that lobbies hard against regulation, and that tends to blame every slowdown in production and every increase in prices on environmentalists or on overzealous regulation by government. This is something I hear when an aging oil refinery is shutting down or when a mine approaches the end of its ore body. The true cause could be any combination of variables, but the industry often blames it on those who work to protect the environment.

I saw a newspaper article several years ago about a convention of the Montana Mining Association. The headline read, "Miners told that environmentalism must be destroyed."[4]

As an environmentalist, am I against mining? No, I'm not.

What I'm against is killing people by poisoning them with asbestos fibers that the mining company knew was dangerous and hid from their workers and the public.

What I'm against is mining companies that simply walk away from an operation, leaving taxpayers to clean up the mess.

What I'm against is decapitating mountains and filling in watersheds with coal mine waste.

What I'm against is polluting water and the soil with heavy metals and toxic chemicals.

What I'm against is passing off a boom-and-bust economy as a path to prosperity.

I use mined products every hour of every day. I'm using their products right at this moment. I use their metals, I use their energy, I use their stone and concrete.

Whatever problems mining creates, I am party to them. I must do my part to ensure that those problems are lessened – the pollution, the health problems, the externalizing of mining's costs onto the taxpayer and the general public, the destruction of America's landscape. I must work to ensure that mining companies are held accountable for the impacts of their operations, or to reduce those impacts. I must be willing to pay a little more for the mined products I use in my daily life so that the prices of those products really reflect their true costs. I must recycle metals as much as I can. I must try my best to use energy wisely and efficiently.

CHAPTER THIRTY-ONE

Good Neighbor Agreement

Some people, upon reading about the agreement, got the impression that it was some sort of "love fest" between the mining company and the citizen groups.

....

Is it possible to change the traditionally sour relationship between environmentalists and mining companies?

Montana's Stillwater Valley is a beautiful place, but it's no stranger to mining. Starting in the late 1800s, various metals have been dug and blasted from the rocks of the Beartooth Mountains in the upper reaches of the valley. At first, it was chromium, copper, and nickel. Today, it's metals like platinum and palladium.

The first actual mining for platinum group metals began in 1986 in the upper Stillwater Valley. A few years later, the operators – Chevron and Johns-Manville – divested themselves of this operation, and a new company was incorporated. In the late 1990s, the new company – Stillwater Mining Company – began work on an additional adit (or mine tunnel) from another watershed, the upper reaches of the Boulder Valley.

In each of the two affected watersheds, a group of citizens organized, affiliated themselves with Northern Plains, and did their best to keep their respective communities educated about the likely effects of the mine on the natural and human environment. *High Country News* reported that these groups "studied and commented on five different environmental impact statements, as the mine expanded on private and U.S. Forest Service lands."[1] Northern Plains also took the state of Montana to court in 1993 for issuing the mine a waiver from water-degradation laws, even before the mine had applied for a permit. Northern Plains had filed another lawsuit on a state EIS early in 1999.

There came a time, though, when the price for palladium skyrocketed because of increasing demand for its use in catalytic converters on automobiles. This prompted the Stillwater Mining Company to make plans for accelerating production. However, there were serious obstacles with the company's requests to expand its mine on the Stillwater and discharge wastes into the Boulder (a prime trout fishery). Many local citizens were concerned about a plan by the company to develop "man-camps" rather than establish places for its employees to live in local communities.

In 1999, Northern Plains and the two local affiliate groups made an offer to Stillwater Mining: come and negotiate with us, and we won't fight your permit. They urged the company to become a "good neighbor" by committing itself to preventing pollution and operating as cleanly as possible. Many mining companies would have rejected this offer without a second thought, but Stillwater Mining was at that time led by a CEO whose background was business rather than mining. He recognized the value in negotiating an end to the chronic legal and regulatory battles that plague mining companies *and* environmental groups, and he agreed to negotiate.

The negotiations lasted just over a year. The parties disagreed strongly on numerous points, and they argued – sometimes on their feet – across the table from one another. At one point, the citizen groups walked out of the negotiations. However, this impasse came several months into the talks and, by that time, the participants had developed personal relationships and a level of trust. They were able to resume the negotiations and, in May 2000, the parties signed the "Good Neighbor Agreement."

Some people, upon reading about the agreement, got the impression that it was some sort of "love fest" between the mining company and the citizen groups. The fact is that the negotiations would never have taken place if the citizen groups hadn't had leverage in the form of a potential lawsuit and permit challenge. Trust between environmentalists and mining companies has always been in short supply... the company and the three groups in the negotiations faced skepticism from mining companies and from environmental groups. One environmental activist publicly criticized Northern Plains for even talking to a mining company.

The agreement was much more than a handshake; it was a written, legally binding, 102-page contract. It set up a process to:

- Provide citizen oversight of mining operations – including the right to inspect mine facilities with independent technical consultants – in order to ensure that the area's quality of life and productive agricultural land would be protected;

- establish clear and enforceable water quality standards above and beyond state requirements;

- provide local citizens with access to critical information about mining operations and the opportunity to address potential problems before they occur;

- establish a program of citizen involvement in studies of ground water, the water quality of the rivers, and the biological health of the rivers;

- ensure public safety and security while protecting the interests of miners through traffic plans designed to reduce mining traffic on winding country roads;

- set goals and objectives for developing new technologies to reduce the impacts of mining.

It established a process through which citizens in the local communities would be involved in monitoring the impacts of the mine operations. It set specific goals for completing baseline water studies, established strict water pollution limits for the Stillwater and East Boulder rivers; and provided for independent environmental audits. It created a plan to establish conservation easements that would protect area ranchland that the company had purchased over the years. Over 4,000 acres have been protected using these conservation easements.

Some provisions of the Good Neighbor Agreement were re-negotiated in 2005 and 2008, but the fundamental structure, processes, and purpose of the agreement have continued.

It hasn't been an entirely smooth ride. For one thing, mining is a volatile industry. The company went through a buyout by a Russian mining company. The price of platinum and palladium dropped substantially, as did the value of the company's stock. When the worldwide economic recession hit in 2008, Stillwater Mining lost its biggest customer, General Motors. The company had to lay off hundreds of workers. In 2013, the company went through a hostile takeover by a hedge fund called the Clinton Group. The new management, though, affirmed the value of this agreement to the company's long-term future.

Upholding their obligations under the agreement demands time and hard work from the people on the citizen oversight committees. The obligation continues for the life of the mine operation, which could be another three or four decades. Or more, if new deposits are found in the area. And there's always a possibility that new management at the mine could someday take a belligerent approach to the agreement.

But for more than sixteen years (as I write this), the Good Neighbor Agreement has established that it's possible to run a responsible, profitable mining operation. Mining has impacts, and reducing those impacts does cost money. Still, reducing impacts also reduces other kinds of costs. It reduces the uncertainty of regulatory compliance, it reduces the money spent on attorneys.

Right now, the mining industry isn't exactly rushing to negotiate more agreements like this. Eventually they may discover that avoiding lawsuits and the traditional conflict that accompanies mining development is worth something. They may discover that there is a value to increased certainty. They may discover that it's possible to be a good neighbor and a profitable mining operation at the same time.

CHAPTER THIRTY-TWO

Overzealous Regulation?

The power of corporations over our daily lives, including foreign corporations, was not part of the world in which the Founding Fathers lived.

....

Let's say a mining corporation is polluting a river where you live. How many ways can you think of that would make them stop?

Do you go to the company and reason with them? Do you demand that they negotiate with you? Do you threaten not to buy their product? Do you think any of this will really make a difference?

It's not absolutely impossible to get a company's attention, even to change its behavior. But certain conditions must exist that give you leverage, that make the company feel like it has to talk with you. It can happen, but not often.

On occasion, I've heard a commentator suggest that environmentalists (or maybe some other kind of community activist) should "demand a seat at the table." This is an astoundingly naïve suggestion.

You don't get a seat at the table just by demanding it. You get a seat at the table by possessing leverage. The polluting company has to see some interest in talking to you. Otherwise, it has no reason to do anything but ignore you.

Leverage means that you have the power to substantially affect the polluters' plans or activities. Maybe they need a certain permit and you have a good case to challenge that permit in court. Or maybe they have big plans that you could slow down by pointing out how those plans violate the law. Or maybe you have the power to unleash some really bad publicity about the company.

I remember seeing an episode of a 1970s television show called "Happy Days," in which the "everyman" character Richie asks the "tough guy" character Fonzie to show him how to get a reputation as a tough guy. It doesn't really work out too well for Richie. Finally, Fonzie tells him that, "at some time, you have to have actually hit somebody."

It's a lot like that for citizen groups. If the company or the industry you are challenging doesn't believe you could ever actually "hit" them, they have little reason to talk to you. But if they do have a reason to talk to you, then you have leverage.

Maybe a polluting company would talk to you because their CEO is a nice guy. Don't count on his niceness outweighing the company's focus on the bottom line.

Just getting a corporation to negotiate with your local environmental group is a major accomplishment in itself. For most polluters, let's face it, there just isn't a compelling reason to talk to a environmentalists who are making trouble, and who want you to change your business practices.

So the mining company is dumping poison into the river. And they won't listen to you, won't negotiate with you. What do you do?

One choice you have is to exercise your right as a citizen, petition your government to put a stop to that company's poisoning of the river. There are three branches of government –legislative, executive, judicial. Which one do you choose?

Let's start with the legislature. If the passage of a law will help protect the river from being further poisoned, then maybe this is the option you take.

If you do, the cards are stacked against you. You'll try to find a legislator to sponsor your bill. If you succeed in getting the bill introduced, you'll testify in a committee hearing where you are a stranger and the company's lobbyist may know several members of the committee personally. That lobbyist will talk about all the jobs provided by the company, about all the taxes it pays, and about how all that will be jeopardized if it's prohibited from polluting that river. That lobbyist's testimony will be accepted at face value by many committee members, whether or not he has any real evidence supporting what he says. Your testimony, even if it's supported by scientific evidence, may well be greeted with skepticism or simply disregarded.

But let's say your bill is approved by the committee. Then it's passed by that full house of the legislature. Then it's passed by the committee in the other house of the legislature. Then it's passed by the other full house of the legislature. Then it's signed by the Governor. Let's say all that happens and your bill becomes law.

What will likely occur next is that a regulatory agency will be tasked with writing the provisions of that law into the state legal code. Now it becomes a regulation. This is a very long journey.

Or, instead of going through the legislature, you might try to deal directly with the executive branch. You identify the regulatory agency that deals with the subject at hand: rivers that are being poisoned. If the polluter is doing something illegal, then the point is to get the agency to enforce the law. If there's no rule against what the polluters are doing, then you can begin the long process of petitioning for government rulemaking. Either way, this is a slow, hard process.

And the outcome isn't always productive. Montana rancher Ellen Pfister joined with fellow members of Northern Plains, along with citizens from other coalfield states, working for several years to convince Congress to pass – and the President to sign – a federal strip mine law. A bill was passed multiple times in the 1970s, but Richard Nixon and Gerald Ford each vetoed it. It wasn't until Jimmy Carter was in the White House that the Surface Mining Control and Reclamation Act was signed into law.

It was a good bill, but it didn't accomplish nearly as much as Ellen and other citizens had hoped. "Regulations are what weakened SMCRA," she told me years later.

Rulemaking is probably preceded by a hearing (or multiple hearings). If it becomes apparent that the rules you propose are controversial (which they probably will be), the agency may want to insert a "consensus-building" process before rules are written. The idea here is that they hope your group and the industry you want to regulate can come to a "friendly" agreement about what should be contained in any new regulations. Slim chance.

In my own opinion, such efforts at reaching consensus between directly opposed interests are a cynical effort to delay action and frustrate citizens. Negotiation may be possible, but only if you have real leverage over the polluter. Without it, you will have no serious negotiations.

After you've wasted a few months on seeking an impossible consensus, the agency board may again take up the question you raised in the first place – would the agency write rules to prevent the pollution of the river and ensure that the people who did it are required to clean it up?

So the agency board holds a couple hearings. You have to get your supporters to those hearings, because you know the company you want to regulate will be there. If your state capital is a couple hundred of miles away (or further), and if the hearing is held on a weekday, it may be tough for your members to make the trip. Even if they do, the agency board might re-schedule it at the last minute, or re-arrange their agenda at the last minute, or add some last-minute restrictions to your testimony.

But let's say you hang tough in the hearings and the board decides to adopt some of what you wanted. Then the process is turned over to agency staff to write the rules. That will take still more months.

But when the regulations are finally written, your problem will be solved, right?

It's funny how things get delayed, get "complicated," get watered down. The final regulations may not fully address the problem you were trying to solve.

First, does the agency have the manpower to enforce the new rule, standard, or regulation? Here in Montana, legislators in recent years have used the budget process to weaken the capacity of state agencies to enforce regulations.

They're not alone. Many state legislatures love to weaken regulatory agencies. (We all hate to be regulated, right?) By weakening the capacity of regulatory agencies to protect the environment (or collect taxes, or protect the rights of wage-earners or renters, or oversee lobbying activities), lawmakers are able to say they're "cutting red tape" or "streamlining government."

A lot of people who wish government would stand up for them feel these days that regulatory agencies don't enforce laws so much as they negotiate with polluters.

And then we have to go back to the question of the agency's capacity. Is the agency understaffed, particularly with field inspectors? It could be years before any meaningful enforcement action is taken.

But even if the agency has the capacity to enforce a new regulation, does it have the will? Does its field staff desire to enforce the regulation? Or are the field staff too closely tied to the industries or companies they regulate? Are there political considerations that make it more convenient to overlook enforcement, or to enforce with a very light hand?

And when it does, you may find that, instead of actually enforcing the rules as written, the state negotiates with the polluter about what will be done and what the fine will be (if there is a fine). Often there's no fine at all and, if there is, it may amount to a tiny fraction of the penalty authorized in law.

Even if the agency adopts a rule and effectively enforces it, the state legislature might pass a law later on that undercuts the rule, as the Montana legislature did in 2015 to a rule protecting water quality which citizens had worked hard to get adopted a few years earlier.

....

For all the dislike of regulations and mistrust of agencies that enforce them, some folks have a naïve faith that someone in some level of government is protecting them against hazards in the environment. I first came across this outlook many years ago when I was collecting petition signatures for the Black Hills Energy Coalition in South Dakota. A lot of people assumed rules were in place to protect us against every possible hazard.

Some people still believe that. One example is the safety of our drinking water. William K. Reilly, who led the EPA under President George H. W. Bush, said in 2009, "For years, people said that America has the cleanest drinking water in the world. That was true 20 years ago. But people don't realize how many new chemicals have emerged and how much pollution has occurred. If they did, we would see very different attitudes."[1]

He was referring to the fact that the Safe Drinking Water Act regulates fewer than 100 contaminants in drinking water, fewer than 100 out of the 60,000 chemicals used in the U.S. Some people assume that contaminants in drinking water are regulated, but that's often not the case. Many contaminants that cause cancer and other diseases are simply not regulated. Among contaminants covered in the law, the standards have not kept up with scientific knowledge. The

New York Times reported in 2009 that the standard for arsenic remains at a level where "a community could drink perfectly legal water, and roughly one in every 600 residents would likely develop bladder cancer over their lifetimes."[2]

To make it even more complicated, diseases originating in contaminated drinking water typically take years to become apparent, so it's very hard to make the link between a person's illness and the contaminants that caused it.

Drinking water will typically contain more than one contaminant, but the Safe Drinking Water Act doesn't deal with the kinds of risks presented when multiple chemicals are in the water.

Government scientists who have sought to conduct research on more chemicals have been threatened with dismissal.

....

The "Iron Triangle" is a concept that describes the relationships among legislators, regulators, and the constituency being regulated. It was often used to describe the federal government and its relationship with the defense contracting industry. But the Iron Triangle works just as well in state government. Interests that pollute are often the beneficiaries of the Iron Triangle, frustrating citizens who want their government to help them when their land or water or air is being polluted.

The way it works is pretty simple: legislators want to stay in power, so they want to get re-elected. Regulators want their agencies to keep power, and to sustain or even increase their agency budgets. And the interests being regulated want to do whatever it is they want to do. Most of the time, that means they want to generate as much profit as possible.

Legislators need campaign donations to get re-elected. They know that a substantial part of those donations could come through or from polluting industries that operate in their districts. Therefore, most legislators will not want to turn those industries into political enemies. In fact, they have every incentive to do favors for influential constituents such as polluting industries. Agencies are a convenient way for a legislator to do a favor, they are tools that can "fix" problems.

Regulatory agencies need the support of legislators to maintain their budgets. They know that that they'll face political difficulties with the legislators who control the agencies' budgets if they come down hard on a company or industry that's key to the re-election of one of those legislators. They have political incentive to go easy on polluters that are powerful figures in the state or in a key legislator's district. If the polluter has little political influence, the agency has a greater incentive to enforce regulations strictly.

Those polluting companies or industries don't want to be regulated because they'll make more profit if they're able to externalize some of their costs. They know that they can prevent, weaken, or delay enforcement actions against their pollution if they become active in supporting or opposing certain legislators – the legislators who control the purse strings of the agencies that would regulate the industry. Or it doesn't need to be so direct – the polluter can generate political opposition against a regulatory agency and a smart legislator can see which way the wind is blowing.

But sometimes, the influence of money over government policy is less direct. Sometimes it's a simple as this: people who work for regulatory agencies have regular contact with the people they're regulating. They may even have social contact and may know the people being regulated on a first-name basis. If some citizen environmentalists walk in and want something done about pollution, those citizens are usually strangers. Those citizens aren't the ones who exercise control over the agency's funding.

All this was before the 2010 Supreme Court decision (*Citizens United v. The Federal Election Commission*) that made corporate money (and, to a far lesser degree, labor union money) even a bigger factor in determining who gets elected. And in what laws get passed. And therefore what government regulators are allowed to do.

As you work to end the pollution of your river, you must also consider whether the political appointee who heads the agency is competent to do the job. "Competence" may refer to the simple question of whether the agency chief has the capability of running a regulatory agency. Some do, some don't. Some are politically ambitious, and some will do anything to avoid upsetting powerful interests. Some years ago, the head of Montana's primary environmental law enforcement department officially muzzled his water quality bureau's chief enforcement officer from speaking publicly.[3]

Some regulators are as corrupt as can be. And some regulators were appointed for the specific purpose of not enforcing the law. Or for twisting the law.

Ronald Reagan is beloved by many, but he knew which side of his administration's bread was buttered. He appointed a former timber industry lawyer to head the U.S. Forest Service. He appointed a Director of the U.S. Fish and Wildlife Service who had utterly no experience nor education in the field. He appointed a head of the Environmental Protection Agency who made it her mission to dismantle environmental protections.

And then, of course, there was James Watt, a lawyer for development interests whose hostility toward environmental protection – from wildlife to national parks to national forests – was manifest in almost every action he took as Reagan's Secretary of the Interior. Watt's positions were so far out of the American mainstream that many Republicans began to call for his ouster (which came, eventually, because of his outlandish remarks, not because of his policies). Yet critics were reminded by Reagan's Chief of Staff James Baker III that Watt's actions "represent the President's views" when it comes to the environment.[4] Watt himself saw to it that federal appointive boards were stacked with a preponderance of people from extractive industries.[5]

The George W. Bush administration was full of department and agency heads whose objective was to undermine the protection of America's environment. His first Interior Secretary, Gale Norton, oversaw a pattern of dismantling environmental protection before resigning and going to work for Shell Oil. Her deputy for fish, wildlife, and parks, Julie MacDonald, ensured that several animal species lost needed habitat, discounting scientific findings all along the way.

Another Norton deputy, Sue Ellen Wooldridge, eventually resigned in a scandal that involved her giving ConocoPhillips a break on paying federal fines after she and her boyfriend J. Steven Griles bought a million-dollar beach house in partnership with a ConocoPhillips executive. Griles, like Norton, was a protégé of James Watt. After accepting a high-ranking post with the Department of the Interior, Griles continued to accept compensation from his lobbying firm, and he continued to meet with his past clients. He worked to weaken standards on mountaintop removal mining, tried to weaken clean air standards as they applied to power plants, and later helped grease the wheels for lobbyist Jack Abramoff. Griles eventually resigned in disgrace and later pleaded guilty to obstruction of justice.

Officials with the G.W. Bush Interior Department's Minerals Management Service – which was charged with collecting royalties for oil removed from public land –partied with oil company executives (booze, sex, drugs) while allowing those companies to avoid a billion dollars in royalty payments.

One MMS official, Greg Smith, was revealed to be using drugs and coercing subordinates into having sex with him. In addition, he accepted gifts from oil company executives and, while in service to the U.S. taxpayer, was moonlighting for a company that does business with oil companies, some of the very companies from which he was supposed to be collecting royalties.[6]

This was just the tip of the iceberg for the G.W. Bush administration, where the "revolving door" spun faster and faster between agencies and regulated industries. People came into "public service" from polluting industries they were to regulate, and left "public service" to go to work for those industries. They were involved behind closed doors in preparing important legislation (e.g., the Bush Energy Bill), and they would often seek industry's pre-approval for agency decisions.[7]

The Bush administration's Environmental Protection Agency declared hydraulic fracturing, a process used to increase the amount of natural gas extracted from rock, to be safe, despite the fact that it leaves known carcinogens like benzene underground and in potential contact with ground water. The EPA's declaration of safety was based on the fact that the EPA had refused to even study the health effects of "fracking." Abetting the EPA's head-in-the-sand approach, Congress in 2005 exempted hydraulic fracturing from the Safe Drinking Water Act, thus taking away any legal basis for the EPA to regulate the health effects of these chemicals (the constituents of which are largely kept secret by gas drilling companies).[8]

In the weeks following the great 2010 oil spill from BP's (formerly British Petroleum) Deepwater Horizon drilling rig in the Gulf of Mexico, a conservation group – the Center for Biological Diversity – discovered that the MMS had granted BP a categorical exclusion from the National Environmental Policy Act, waiving a requirement for detailed environmental studies.[9] The MMS did this hundreds of times yearly, just in the Gulf of Mexico, and continued doing it in the weeks after the spill began.[10]

Oh, and in the weeks following the BP oil spill – as people and businesses along the Gulf Coast watched while their livelihoods and homes changed forever – the director of the Minerals Management Service in Alaska served a cake at a staff meeting with the words "Drill, baby, drill" written on it.[11]

The Minerals Management Service continued its friendly relationship with the oil industry for a time. "They went hunting and fishing on the companies' tab," reported the *New York Times*, "accepted company meals, went skeet shooting at the companies' expense, and in one case flew on a private jet to watch Louisiana State University in the Peach Bowl... One inspector negotiated a job with a company while inspecting its platforms."[12] Finally, in 2011, the MMS was reorganized into three divisions to segregate its duties of enforcement, leasing, and revenue collection.

Regulatory failures can happen at the state level, too. For example, Montana's Board of Oil and Gas Conservation is perceived by many citizens here to be less interested in oversight of oil and gas drilling than in promoting oil and gas drilling. A few years ago, the BOGC published a paper on its website that was produced by a methane industry contractor, a paper with few citations and no peer review whatsoever. Eventually, the BOGC was shamed into removing the industry paper, but the incident served as a demonstration of the agency's institutional favoritism toward an industry it was supposed to regulate.

I don't want to give you the impression that every agency administrator is corrupt or incompetent. For example, Dudley Butler was appointed to head the Grain Inspection, Packers and Stockyards Administration in 2009, an agency within the Department of Agriculture that is supposed to ensure agriculture markets are competitive and fair. A Mississippi farmer and attorney, Butler took action at GIPSA to make the marketplace fairer to family-scale farmers and ranchers by slowing down the big meatpackers in their ongoing effort to turn the marketplace in beef into an oligopoly. He proposed rules to restore integrity and competition to the meatpacking industry. He was working for people, because that was his job.

Unfortunately, Butler's efforts were throttled after an intense lobbying campaign by corporate agribusiness. Members of Congress allied with the big packers used their power to undercut Butler's effort to restore competition to the meatpacking industry. Higher-ups in the Department of Agriculture and the Obama administration failed to fully defend Butler's proposal. The rules he sought were dropped in 2011. In 2012, he resigned his position at GIPSA to return to his farm.

．．．．．．．．．．．．．．．．．．．．．．．．．．．．．．．．．

During the Reagan administration, a new approach was taken toward enforcing environmental regulations – voluntary compliance. States have also adopted voluntary compliance and voluntary reporting. Even when reporting is required, it's often merely self-reporting. The incentive to hide violations can be strong.

Of course, agencies that are serious about enforcing the law – say, the Montana Highway Patrol – tend not to rely on lawbreakers to report their crimes.

As you may have surmised, I have a lot of skepticism about using the regulatory process to resolve pollution problems. The process is hard and tedious and frustrating, and the deck is stacked against citizen groups. You may have done all your homework, you may have all the science on your side, your members may be dedicated and committed for the long haul, yet the decision probably rests on factors completely beyond your control.

And yet I do believe that government is *supposed* to work on behalf of the people. I do believe that people have (or should have) the ability to petition their government for a redress of grievances, whether those grievances be political corruption or the pollution of water or air that people depend on. I have so far refused to give up on the regulatory process, even though my experience – and the Iron Triangle – tell me that regulation does not usually work very well for citizens.

At times the facts may be so clear that an agency cannot ignore its duty. It might be that some appointees to an agency board are willing to listen to the concerns of citizens.

I've met some environmentalists and other people who have a lot more faith in the regulatory process than I do. I've met some environmentalists who've developed an amazing level of expertise about the regulatory process, about the science behind issues, about the inner workings of agencies, about the politics behind an agency's behavior. I've met some environmentalists who are dedicated to making agencies really work for the citizens.

It's not just about the environment, of course. It's about fairness to the citizens of our country. It's about insisting that our government work for the people and not just the powerful interests that give big campaign contributions and that leverage political support for politicians.

But will the rules mean anything in the end? Will they be enforced? If your water or air is being poisoned, if the polluter won't stop, and if the politicians won't stand up for you, then regulation is an option. Sometimes it works.

Sometimes it doesn't. Sometimes the regulatory agency fails, or the regulatory approach itself fails. These are complex problems – trying to find the best way to reclaim land and aquifers that have been strip-mined, trying to figure out how to keep an animal species from going extinct, trying to arrive at the best way to clean up a town contaminated with asbestos, trying to predict how polluters will behave when being asked to change their behavior. Sometimes the regulatory approach isn't well designed or implemented. Sometimes other approaches may work better.

After all,

- Environmental regulations can sometimes be expensive to enforce and/or expensive to comply with.
- It's very easy to create loopholes (officially or unofficially).

- Agencies have only a limited capacity to enforce regulations or even inspect what polluters are doing. If an agency falls out of favor with politicians, those politicians – through the budget process – handcuff the agency and make it harder for it to do its job.

- Because of agencies' limited enforcement capacity, regulations will affect different parties unequally.

- Political pressure makes enforcement inconsistent over time, and this inconsistency makes the business climate less stable.

- Regulations are widely seen as an infringement upon liberty.

- Some agency administrators are inept; some are even corrupt.

- Agency staff are sometimes too close to the parties they regulate.

- There are the other problems which commonly afflict agencies, including the Iron Triangle.

What _are_ our choices?

Is doing nothing an option? Do we just let polluters do whatever they want? If a corporation is polluting the river near your home, who is going to make them stop?

Or should we get rid of environmental laws and regulations, then just let people file a lawsuit against the polluter if they feel their health or their property has been damaged? That would mean, of course, that the only people who get any kind of justice are those who can afford to take on a multi-national corporation in a courtroom. And good luck proving your case if your health problems don't develop for twenty years.

Some people advocate for controlling pollution with market-based approaches instead of regulation. Typically, this means using a tax to replace regulations, arguing that this would free up the polluting companies to reduce their pollution in the most efficient way. The tax, in essence, is what structures the market and creates the incentives for polluters to clean up their operations. Some say this would spur innovation and give polluters a continuing incentive to reduce their discharges. Back when Congress was debating "cap and trade" legislation to deal with the mounting levels of carbon dioxide in the atmosphere, many environmentalists (including most of the ones I crossed paths with) opposed it. Many instead favored an approach that would levy a tax on carbon pollution.

A tax is usually less expensive to administer than regulation. And the government can actually raise revenue while improving the quality of our environment.

Much has been said about how market-based approaches can work better than regulation. That's probably true in some cases.

Still, I'm a little uncomfortable with a system that gives someone the legal right to pollute, as long as they pay the tax. This is not a small issue, especially if you live downstream or downwind from where the pollution is discharged. This is not a small issue if your child is breathing polluted air or if the value of your home is being reduced by a polluting facility nearby.

I'm also a little uncomfortable with a system that puts a dollar value on things that have no price, including a human life.

Someone would have to create the "market" that will reduce the pollution. And all this would still be subject to political pressure and would require an agency to enforce the rules of the market. Something as simple as setting the tax (or fee) too low would fail to create the necessary incentive to reduce pollution.

Still, this is something we should probably be willing to think about and talk about.

....

Then there's that larger question – how much influence should the government have over our lives? I don't really know the answer to that question, except I know there isn't one "ideal" solution. In the end, though, we have growing problems in our nation that we can't just ignore.

But we also have to ask ourselves, how much influence should corporations have over our lives? My liberty is more threatened by the power of corporations than by the government. When it comes to government, at least I have the right to vote. At least I have the Constitution to protect me. At least I have the courts (if I can scrape together the money) to protect me.

When it comes down to it, you and I aren't strong enough by ourselves to defend our children from some corporation that pollutes the air they breathe and the water they drink. If not our government, who will stand with us and help us defend our children?

Is the answer for the government to "free us" by getting rid of laws and rules and standards that protect our air and our water? If Congress and the President were to set such a course, it would mean they would have also decided that the right to pollute is more important than protecting the lives and health of Americans.

We have to ask ourselves whether this path would really make us more free. The power of corporations over our daily lives, including foreign corporations, was not part of the world in which the Founding Fathers lived. In their world, corporations were relatively small entities that were chartered for specific and usually temporary purposes.

But in your and my world, these entities – these modern corporations – have an amazing amount of power over us. We don't get to vote on their leadership and we have nothing to say about their policies. In these times, we are in very real danger of allowing the democracy for which our forebears sacrificed and fought and worked to be overwhelmed by this power.

These entities have the capacity and the financial incentive to (for example):

- withhold information about what's in the food we buy,
- lie about how much pollution a car discharges from its tailpipe (like Volkswagen diesels),
- sell us cars that are unsafe,
- industrialize every place they want to (like Wally McRae's ranch),
- send jobs overseas where labor is cheaper,
- jack up the price of medicine for toxoplasmosis from $13.50 per pill to $750.00 for no reason other than to make more money (like Turing Pharmaceuticals did in 2015),
- hide their taxable revenues in offshore bank accounts,
- hide information from their own shareholders,

- destroy the free market by destroying competition,

- institutionalize discrimination against women and any other class of people they want to and, yes,

- dump pollution into the air and water.

What do corporations care about? They care about making money for shareholders (although even that thin slice of concern has often been sidestepped by corporate executives who put their own interests ahead of the interests of their shareholders).

In dealing with America's environment, none of us will get exactly what we want. I guess that has to satisfy us for the time being. It had to satisfy the people who drafted the Constitution and the states that ratified it, because they wanted to move our young nation forward.

I know that there are some people who advocate for a "big brother" sort of government, or a "nanny" state. I'm not one of them, and I don't personally know anyone who is.

But I believe government is a tool that Americans can use to realize many of our values. Profit-making corporations are tools for making money. That's fine, for what it is. But it's not everything, and it's certainly not the end-purpose of America. As a nation, we are about much more than making money.

If someone tries to tell you that making money is the purpose of America, read the Constitution. If someone tries to tell you that America exists so people can get rich, read the Constitution.

I've tried to have faith that my government can behave honorably and that it can act on my behalf as a citizen. But I don't see it happen all that often and, during my adult life, I've generally seen government act mostly on behalf of the politically powerful and the greedy.

Polluters and their political allies complain about overzealous regulation. As you can tell, this hasn't been my experience with agencies that are supposed to safeguard our land, water, air, and wildlife. I've heard the cries by some to get rid of the U.S. Environmental Protection Agency because they believe EPA is over-zealous in enforcing environmental regulations. Here are three problems I have with that argument:

1. It isn't true. It's not even close to true. In 2012, the Associated Press published the results of a study of EPA enforcement that extended back for a decade. The study found that the EPA's enforcement actions fell from 224 actions in 2002 to 87 actions in 2011.[13] Instead of overzealous enforcement, environmentalists should be raising hell about lax enforcement at the EPA.

2. Even if the claims of overzealous EPA enforcement were true, would that be a legitimate reason to dismantle the primary agency that enforces pollution laws in this country?

3. This argument isn't applied to other law-enforcement agencies.

I've seen and read about cases where the U.S. Department of Justice was overzealous in law enforcement, where a U.S. Attorney or FBI official over-reached in order to make a name for himself by unjustifiably prosecuting and bullying someone.

Still, I've never heard anybody call for dissolving the Justice Department. Such radical "solutions" seem to be reserved for the agencies that enforce environmental laws. On the whole, under-enforcement is a more widespread and more persistent problem than overzealous enforcement when it comes to environmental laws.

The Iron Triangle ensures that regulatory agencies are not "the answer." Still, there are professionals out there in the agencies, and we need them, even if we were to adopt a taxation approach to some environmental issues. We need science so that our decisions are based on something besides who is the most powerful or who has the most money. We need a body of law that's based on legitimate and consistent processes. Most of all, we need a fair referee.

Yet we hear a continuous drumbeat from politicians to get rid of regulations and to weaken the agencies that enforce them.

What if baseball were played without rules and without umpires? If there are no rules and no umpires (or police, courts, regulatory agencies), then the game will eventually begin to fall apart. One team might decide to put twelve players onto the field instead of nine. They might insist on no walks for the other team. They might insist that every close play goes in their favor, and they might even use open intimidation to get their way. They might not do any of these things, but what if they do? Who stands up for the real game of baseball if there are no rules and no umpires?

In my experience with organizations, I've seen a few small groups try to adopt a model that operates without rules, that reaches consensus rather than taking votes, that eschews having leaders with defined roles. Here's why such groups don't usually work: sooner or later, they end up being dominated by bullies. Rules (e.g., bylaws) and the enforcement of those rules are what keep that from happening. If you don't have rules, you don't have democracy. If we didn't have our Constitution to start us off, democracy wouldn't have had a chance.

So, if your water is being polluted, where can you turn?

Of course, regulation doesn't apply just to protecting America's land and water. It applies to:

- Whether we keep markets from being swamped with monopolies;
- Whether we protect the integrity of financial markets instead of allowing the financial system to be overrun by duplicitous practices that amount to gambling with other people's money;
- Whether we inspect sanitation practices in restaurants;
- Whether we get truthful labels on the food we buy; and
- Whether we require people who practice medicine on your child to have completed medical school.

I don't want people dumping toxic chemicals in my water. If it happens, where do I go?

Can I convince the polluter to stop? If not, then what? If the legislature doesn't help, and if the agencies don't help, then the courts are what I have left.

CHAPTER THIRTY-THREE

Sue the Bastards

In granting the water right, the state had ruled that ground water discharged by a methane company isn't really ground water, but that the water instead originated in the company's pipes.

....

If I have a pollution problem to resolve, I surely wouldn't want to go to court. I know that it would cost much more than I think it would, and take far, far longer than seems possible. I've seen organizations resort to court action a few times when laws were being broken and nobody was enforcing them. Every time, it's been a slow and expensive process, with outcomes almost always falling short of their hopes. But there were times when court action was a necessity.

For example, the Montana Board of Oil and Gas Conservation began issuing permits to drill for coal bed methane without requiring any kind of environmental study. It took a lawsuit by Northern Plains to make sure that environmental impact studies were conducted, and it took additional court actions to ensure that the resulting EIS actually met the requirements of the law.

It took a lawsuit to establish that the salty water being discharged by methane wells is a pollutant that can be regulated by the federal Clean Water Act.

It took a lawsuit to require a methane company to remove several impoundments it had illegally constructed across stream drainages without a permit (the same permit that any landowner would be required to obtain when building an impoundment in a drainage).

In the West, water rights are a big deal, because access to water will make or break an agricultural operation. When you have a water right, you don't own the water, but you have established a legal right to use a certain amount of it for a certain beneficial purpose. If you have a legal right to use the water you take from a stream or a well, then you have the right to defend yourself when someone else comes along and tries to take that water.

If you have a right to use ground water in an area that's being drilled for methane, there's a good chance your water well might eventually go dry if the industry pumped out the massive volume of water it was originally projected to do. (The massive gas deposits of the Marcellus Shale drove down the price of natural gas and slowed methane development in other areas – at least for a time.)

The water that's discharged by methane drilling, at least in Montana's portion of the Powder River Basin, tends to be quite salty. Not as salty as ocean water, and not salty enough to harm you. You can drink it and livestock can drink it but, over time, it could ruin your soil. If you're using the water to irrigate a crop, you could eventually ruin the soil that your livelihood depends on. Still, many ranch families don't irrigate. They use the discharged water for domestic purposes and for watering their livestock. To such families, this water is precious.

One methane company operating in Montana decided on a new strategy to fend off any lawsuits by landowners who want to protect their water rights. If the methane company could obtain a state-recognized water right to the water it pumps out of the ground, then nobody would be able to sue them over a dried-up well. The company applied for and, with limited restrictions, was granted a water right by the Montana Department of Natural Resources and Conservation.

Ranchers in Northern Plains recognized the threat this would pose for people who depend on well water. In granting the water right, the state had ruled that ground water discharged by a methane company isn't really ground water, but that the water instead *originated in the company's pipes*. One Northern Plains member observed that this is like saying milk originates in a carton or a jug, and not in a cow.

Northern Plains sued the state of Montana over this water right, and the judge agreed that water which comes out of the ground is ground water. People shouldn't have to go to court to establish a principle that's so clear and simple. But the state's failure to protect water rights meant that someone else had to do it in a courtroom.

In the end, it's important to remember that court cases don't exist in a vacuum. Courts and judges may not be as susceptible to political winds as are legislators, but they aren't completely insulated from them, either. On top of that, any citizen organization going to court – over an environmental issue or something else – may well find itself outgunned by expensive corporate lawyers who may even belong to the same country club as the judge. If you live in a small community, you may find that every attorney in town has already been doing legal work for the industry that's creating the problems you need to deal with.

Montana rancher Carol Nash was concerned about possible damage that could be done near her home by an oil company that was exploring in the area. She said,

> When we were talking to the county commissioners about this, they said, "Oh, well, you can always sue them." And I thought, "you're kidding, right?" I said, "first of all, who's got money to sue an oil company?" and secondly, I've heard of people suing who die before the suit is ever settled! And meanwhile, they're living with all this, the damage is done, and then they die. So the oil company wins. So, no, suing an oil company is not a viable option.[1]

Some polluting companies prefer to take their chances in court for these very reasons. They know they have an edge, and the court case may cost a lot less than it would to simply follow the law and prevent the pollution in the first place. From where I stand, a negotiated agreement, when it's possible, would make a lot more sense. But that will never happen if you don't have the leverage you need in order to have "a seat at the table."

The courts exist as a last resort for citizens when the other branches of government are too corrupt or too ineffective to deal with issues constructively or to enforce the laws that are already on the books.

We've all heard the descriptions of "lawsuit-happy" environmental groups. I know there are some environmentalists who are quicker to think of courtroom solutions instead of other strategies. It may be that they are lawyers in their professional lives, so they naturally think that way. It may be that they have heard of other successful environmental court cases, so they think this is a good approach.

And there are some environmental organizations that specialize in legal strategies, sometimes offering services to citizen groups in need of legal services for a specific matter.

Northern Plains has been criticized in recent years for filing several lawsuits. However, each one was undertaken because laws were being broken or ignored, and the courtroom remained the only option for citizens to redress a grievance.

It costs too much, and it takes too long, and the outcomes are almost never clear-cut enough. But sometimes you have to do it.

CHAPTER THIRTY-FOUR

Environmentalist as Obstructionist

It's absolutely necessary in our free country that we have people who stand up against things that are wrong. Where would America be without these people?

....

People who work to protect the environment are often called "obstructionists" who are "against everything."

I've never met such people, but it's possible some are like that. However, you're likely to hear the "obstructionist" label applied to anyone who dares to criticize someone else's plan to make money by plundering natural resources.

Montana writer Todd Wilkinson said that, "it's inconvenient to be vigilant, it takes courage to act on personal convictions, and it makes other people angry."[1]

The late Ed Swartz, a cattle rancher in northeast Wyoming, had his share of problems with the energy industry, some of it having to do with salt-laden discharge waters from coal bed methane wells ruining his alfalfa meadows. And for speaking up about it, he made enemies and was called an obstructionist. He once warned citizens who speak out against the energy industry: "They will lie, they will cheat, they will try to discredit you."[2]

"Corporations," he said, "have more ability to be heard than you will ever have."

He could also have warned citizen activists that they may threaten you. Or they might bankroll an "Astroturf" (imitation grassroots) organization to say terrible things about you, things the company or industry doesn't want to be accountable for having said. They might try to intimidate you. They might try to divide your members. They may even try to infiltrate your organization or take over your public events.

And it doesn't matter how right or how reasonable you are.

At Northern Plains some years ago, a task force of members drafted a position on coal bed methane development when that industry was just getting started in Montana. Fundamentally, the task force's position was that coal bed methane would be drilled in Montana, but that it needed to have parameters so that this short-term industry wouldn't inflict long-term damage on the natural resources that people need to survive for the long haul. Here's what Northern Plains said responsible coal bed methane development would look like:

1. Effective monitoring of coal bed methane development and active enforcement of existing laws to protect private property rights, Montana citizens, and Montana's natural resources.

2. Surface owner consent, surface use agreements, and reimbursement of attorney fees to help landowners better protect their property rights.

3. Use of aquifer recharge, clustered development, mufflers for compressor stations, and other low-impact, best available technologies to minimize impacts on underground water reserves, rivers and streams, and surface resources.

4. Collection of thorough fish, wildlife, and plant inventories before development proceeds to protect habitat, followed by phased-in development to diffuse impacts over time.

5. Meaningful public involvement in the decision-making process.

6. Complete reclamation of all disturbed areas and bonding that protects Montana taxpayers from all cleanup liability costs.

But many people refused to see these principles as reasonable. Northern Plains was repeatedly referred to as an "opponent" of coal bed methane (including by news reporters).

Look again at some of the language in this set of principles:

- "protect private property rights;"

- "minimize impacts;"

- "fish, wildlife, and plant inventories before development proceeds;"

- "meaningful public involvement;"

- "complete reclamation;"
- "bonding that protects Montana taxpayers."

To those who wanted methane drilling at any cost, the people who advocated these principles were "obstructionists." And, yes, the methane industry bank-rolled an Astroturf group specifically to attack Northern Plains.

Northern Plains' principles on coal bed methane didn't oppose methane de-velopment. Through the organization's history, its members have dealt with plenty of issues where the goal was to prevent the impacts of <u>irresponsible</u> de-velopment, not to simply oppose development.

But there are times when it does come down to outright opposition. At the beginning of the 1990s, Northern Plains and many other groups voiced opposi-tion to a gold mine that was proposed at high elevation in Montana's Beartooth Mountains, in the headwaters of three watersheds, two of which drain into Yel-lowstone National Park. A mine in that location was a bad idea. Reclamation at that elevation would have been impossible. The ore body was full of sulfur-filled pyrite, and an impoundment would have to be maintained permanently to pre-vent the mine wastes from acidifying the three streams draining from the site.

Eventually that mine was stopped. And it should have been. Bad ideas can sometimes be fixed up, but some will always be just plain bad.

There's nothing inherently wrong with being against something. It's abso-lutely necessary in our free country that we have people who stand up against things that are wrong. Where would America be without these people?

Where would we be without the people who fought for generations against slavery? Where would we be without the generations of Americans who fought for the right to vote for women?

Where would we be without people like Lois Gibbs at Love Canal, New York, people who stand up against a wrong that is being done, people who state clearly, and with moral authority, that it must end?

Call them obstructionists if you want. Whether the problem is slavery or the poisoning of someone's water supply, standing up against something that's wrong amounts to standing up <u>for</u> what is right.

CHAPTER THIRTY-FIVE

False Choices

Where is all the prosperity that was supposed to come from weakened environmental laws and from allowing more pollution?

··

The labeling of Northern Plains' position on coal bed methane as "opposition" reminds me that we are often presented with false choices and are then asked to decide on one or the other. Someone will lay out an "either-or" decision, and tell us we have to choose either one or the other.

Is coal bed methane a choice between unfettered drilling and nothing? Of course not.

My wife, Candace Forrette, is an artist. When she was in art school, professors would tell her that she had to make a choice between being a good artist and having children. You can't be a mother, they told her, and a good artist at the same time.

They were wrong, of course. They had presented her with a false choice. In fact, she became a very talented artist, and her work is thoughtful, compassionate, ethical. Did all this add up to financial success? No, it didn't. Does being thoughtful, compassionate, and ethical bring you financial success in most of life's endeavors?

But, the thing is, would eschewing motherhood have made her more talented or insightful, more able to reflect upon life? That's highly doubtful. The professors who presented her with this false choice were either making it up or passing along some tale they had been told.

The biggest and most consistent false choice when it comes to the environment is the choice between having a clean environment and having a robust economy. We are told we can't have both. Even some environmentalists buy into this false choice. News reporters buy into it all the time.

To hear some PR men in the mining industry talk, you'd think that the choice is whether to allow mining companies to do whatever they want – resulting in prosperity – or regulating them and obstructing prosperity.

But when you pass through mining towns – especially older ones that developed before environmental laws existed – you can see with your own eyes that an awful lot of those towns are anything but prosperous, places where the real money has been shipped out of the community. And many of them are stuck with environmental and public health problems left behind years after mining shut down.

Here in Montana, back in 1971, our state legislature enacted the Montana Environmental Policy Act, a look-before-you-leap approach to handling developments that could have a substantial effect on the state's natural resources and human environment.

The state legislator who introduced MEPA was the late Rep. George Darrow, a Republican and a petroleum engineer. He believed that an ounce of prevention is worth a pound of cure.

He understood that actions which affect the environment – stream channels and river valleys reshaped for a railroad, good topsoil lost to a shopping center, minerals depleted and never again available for use in the future, wildlife and fish habitat eliminated for other uses – are, in his own words, "a special class of human activities" because they are "essentially irreversible." Darrow wanted the state of Montana to look before it leaped into such projects.

Forty years later, Darrow described it this way, "MEPA is a program for keeping the harvesting or the mining reasonable and paying heed to what is left for Montanans to use down the road. It's the difference between a forest on the mountainside and a mountainside that's stripped, eroding and clear cut."[1]

The new law declared a state policy "to foster and promote the general welfare, to create and maintain conditions under which humans and nature can co-exist in productive harmony, to recognize the right to use and enjoy private property free of undue government regulation, and to fulfill the social, economic, and other requirements of present and future generations of Montanans."[2]

Much of MEPA's language is reflected in the Montana Constitution:

- That Montanans have the right to a clean and healthful environment (Article II, Sec. 3);

- That Montanans have the right to participate in the operation of state agencies before final decisions are made (Article II, Sec. 8);

- That Montanans have the right to know and observe the actions of their state government (Article II, Sec. 9);

- That the state and each person has the responsibility to maintain and improve a clean and healthful environment in Montana for present and future generations (Article IX, Sec. 1).

In order to achieve the law's goals, Rep. Darrow wrote MEPA to help state agencies make better decisions – decisions that are balanced, decisions that are accountable, and decisions that are arrived at with meaningful public participation. The point was not to dictate any particular outcomes – the point was to identify the environmental impacts of state decisions <u>before</u> the decisions are made.

Nobody testified against the bill, and many organizations testified for it. It was passed 99-0 by a Republican-majority House of Representatives and 51-1 by a Democrat-majority Senate.

From MEPA's enactment in 1971 through July 9, 2013, Montana state agencies undertook more than 58,000 MEPA actions (environmental assessments and environmental impact statements, as well as categorical exclusions for activities determined not to cause significant impacts to the human environment). Of those 58,000 actions, 64 court cases were initiated against the state, 20 of which were eventually dropped or settled out of court.[3]

Barely one action in 1,000 has been challenged in court.

Still, MEPA is often characterized as a tool that allows environmentalists to obstruct projects through litigation. Some politicians say the law is an obstacle to economic prosperity in Montana. MEPA has come under increasing legislative attack, especially since 2001, with bills to create exemptions to the law, restrict the right of citizens to go to court, create strict time limits for environmental reviews to be completed, and further restrict the law's scope. Other laws have been targeted as well, such as the Major Facility Siting Act (MFSA), a law designed to balance varied concerns – community impacts, environmental impacts, public need (that is, whether there is an actual need for the electricity to be generated by a project) – when a major electrical project is proposed in a community. And there's the Montana Water Quality Act.

For 20 years, starting in the 1970s, Montana had maintained a policy of not allowing the state's remaining pristine waters to be polluted (whatever pristine streams remained after more than 100 years of intensive mining activity). In 1993, the Montana legislature repealed that policy. This allowed mining companies to avoid being required to treat the pollution they discharge into clear mountain streams.

In 1995 (the Montana legislature meets in odd-numbered years), the Water Quality Act was again weakened when the legislature re-defined "high quality waters" to exclude some surface waters and most ground water, allowing those waters to be dirtied to the lowest possible standard. That legislature also allowed mining companies that dewater aquifers and to dump that ground water – even if it contains high levels of arsenic or other naturally occurring pollutants – into high quality streams without having to obtain a permit to do so. That legislature also weakened water pollution standards, allowing more nitrates in ground water.

The 1995 legislature was very busy. It also expanded the number of state agencies that would be allowed to grant permit exemptions to polluters, increasing the cases in which ground water could be polluted by mines, oil and gas exploration, landfills, and refineries without even having to acquire a permit to do so. It also weakened the Major Facility Siting Act by tripling the threshold size for projects it applies to. Originally, all projects generating less than 50 megawatts were exempted; the '95 legislature tripled that threshold, exempting all projects of less than 150 megawatts.

But all this would show that Montana is "open for business."

In 1997, the legislature went one better on the Major Facility Siting Act, this time quintupling the threshold from its original level of 50 megawatts, increasing the exemption to the law to 250 megawatts, which is a pretty good-sized power plant.

The attack on the Major Facility Siting Act continued in 2001, as the legislature exempted from MFSA jurisdiction the very kinds of development – electrical generation projects – that the law was primarily enacted to address.

But that year, the Montana Environmental Policy Act became the legislature's primary target – all in the name of jump-starting Montana's economy. The previous (1999) legislature had directed the Environmental Quality Council to study MEPA, and the EQC study reported to the legislature in 2001 that MEPA helps state agencies make better and more legally defensible decisions.

However, the attacks on MEPA were not about to end, despite the results of the legislature's study. The 2001 legislature passed laws to prevent state agencies from putting stipulations onto permits aimed at reducing the impacts of pollution. It put restrictions on the nature of alternatives that could be analyzed under the MEPA process. It also put restrictions on what can be considered in an analysis. All those bills also limited the rights of citizens to appeal agency decisions while allowing the industry creating the impact to appeal at any point of the process.

The 2005 legislature made it optional for hard rock mines to backfill open pit mines. They weakened reclamation requirements for coal mines, and allowed companies to determine when reclamation is "complete."

In 2009, the legislature enacted a proposal for coal reclamation bonds to be released before reclamation is even complete.

In 2011, reflecting great confidence in state agencies to issue permits to developers, the legislature affirmed that those permits, even if they fall short of legal requirements, cannot be stopped or even modified by a state court. The Legislature declared that information on environmental impacts which is gathered in MEPA-required studies of projects that are planned by some party other than the state cannot be used in making regulatory decisions about such projects. Coal mining giant Arch Coal got the legislature to add a provision that declared its proposed coal mine on Otter Creek (where roughly half the coal is state-owned) to be such a non-state project, ensuring that none of the information found in environmental studies can be used in state permit decisions. Another change: environmental impacts are to be considered only within Montana – contributions to regional, national, or global environmental problems are no longer to be considered.

In this long process of taking bites out of Montana's environmental laws, the legislature also erected obstacles to citizen involvement. Legislators established a "pay to play" system in which citizens would have to post bonds when challenging a state-issued permit. They established stiff fees if citizens challenging a permit don't prevail. They required large fees when citizens seek a hearing before the Board of Environmental Review. They limited the admissibility of new evidence at a permit hearing.

Over the years, these lawmakers have repeatedly offered us a false choice – protect the environment and allow the public to participate in decision-making, or weaken these rights and achieve economic prosperity. Looking at the years of legislative attacks on MEPA since 1993, and increasingly since 2001, environmental protection in Montana has been degraded significantly. And it isn't just MEPA; other laws pertaining to Montana's environment have also come under a withering attack by every recent legislature.

And it leads me to ask: where is all the prosperity that was supposed to come from weakened environmental laws and from allowing more pollution? Montanans have struggled and struggled to earn a living in recent years, even before the 2008 recession began to tighten its grip. Montanans are among the nation's leaders in having to work at multiple jobs just to get by. Our private sector wages are persistently among the nation's lowest. Our suicide rate is among the nation's highest. Our farm and ranch families are beset with monopolization and other corporate strategies that make it extremely difficult for family-sized operations to survive. The Montana legislature, year after year, gives us a false choice, backed by false promises.

Where is the prosperity? You could look at other states and see the same thing – the states with solid long-term prosperity are not generally the ones with the weakest environmental protections. Weakening protections for our children and the world they live in has not brought us the prosperity the politicians promised.

All through the long, rough wake of 2008's Great Recession, some politicians and lobbying groups offered up a steady cadence of proposals to fix the economy by dismantling protections for the water our children drink, the air our children breathe, and the land where our children's food is grown.

It's just another false choice. The recession wasn't caused by environmental protection, and it wouldn't have been reversed by undoing environmental protection.

While there are plenty of either/or choices in life, there aren't nearly as many as we're told.

In the years to come, we Americans will need to sharpen our decision-making skills. Like it or not, we need to find new energy solutions in the years ahead, and it won't be easy. False choices will not help us. If someone offers you an either/or choice, think about it first. Chances are good that it isn't quite so simple.

Frequently Asked Questions

Are environmentalists against technology?

> *It is obvious that the gain in material power affords opportunity for social betterment. If mankind can rise to the occasion, there lies in front a golden age of beneficent creativeness. But material power in itself is ethically neutral. It can work equally well in the wrong direction.*
>
> Alfred North Whitehead
> *Science and the Modern World,* 1925

I don't know any environmentalists who are against technology. However, I know plenty of people who think technology is often used for ill-conceived purposes. Like factory farms, like whaling factory ships, like coal-fired power plants. But those same people will likely be in favor of other technology, like solar collectors, composting toilets, recycling plastic, and pollution-eating bacteria.

We should probably do a better job of asking ourselves what the purpose of a certain technology is. Does it make the world better? Or does it serve no other purpose than to make someone a buck?

The technology behind solar and wind energy will make our nation more independent, it will make our air and water more healthy, it will create huge numbers of jobs in communities across our nation.

....

Where do environmental organizations get their money?

From different places. Some organizations rely completely on dues or donations from their members and supporters. Some organizations rely heavily on grants from private foundations, churches, or – in a few cases – government grants for specifically designed projects. Funding varies from one organization to another.

Some groups are tax-exempt, which means that you can take a tax deduction if you make a donation to them. Being tax-exempt restricts the activities in which an organization can engage; for example, a tax-exempt organization can lobby for legislation only within certain limits prescribed by the Internal Revenue Service, and it cannot support or oppose a candidate for public office.

When I was in the Black Hills Group of the Sierra Club long ago, our funding reflected the fact that the group was part of a national organization. As a member, I mailed my dues to the national office, and a portion of my dues was returned to my local group. A local group could also receive funds in an annual allocation from the national group, based – if I correctly recall – on the size of the group.

I don't know how the Sierra Club operates nowadays, but I know that the main organization is not tax-exempt. It has a couple of special projects that are tax-exempt, but the main organization isn't. This limits its income, because large donors can't get a tax deduction when they make a contribution, but it also frees the organization to work more in politics.

When I was involved in the Black Hills Energy Coalition, it operated entirely on money raised through dues, donations, and occasional fundraising events, like running a food booth at a neighborhood fair, or serving as a parking lot crew for a bluegrass music festival. The group was not tax-exempt, so nobody got a tax deduction when they made a donation.

To hear some people talk, you'd think environmental organizations were swimming in foundation money. Not true.

At the Northern Plains Resource Council, our funding comes from different sources. Northern Plains is tax-exempt, so donors can take a tax deduction when they make a gift. Membership dues are the basic source of our income. We also ask members for special contributions that go toward specific projects or issues. We hold fundraising events like the auction at our annual meeting, a barbecue in the Tongue River valley for several years, or occasional other events such as concerts or cowboy poetry. We also apply for grants from private foundations and some church funding programs. Raising money is the main part of my job there.

Only a comparatively small number of private foundations support environmental groups that organize people on a local level. Some foundations simply don't deal with small or local groups because they'd rather not handle so many requests for funding. And some foundations focus on nationwide or even international environmental issues. For this reason, they do not fund local or state groups.

Some foundations simply won't fund activism because they don't want to do anything controversial. If an environmental group challenges a powerful economic interest or a government agency, some foundations simply don't want to have any part of it. It's safer to give money to a zoo or a university research project.

Some foundations have geographical restrictions, meaning they will only fund organizations in a certain area. When your group is far away from population centers – say, Montana or South Dakota or other states in the Great Plains – there aren't all that many foundations that will even accept a proposal.

And then there are foundations that don't accept funding requests at all, but instead select the organizations they will support based on their own prior knowledge. If such a foundation isn't already familiar with your group (and it probably won't be if your group is in South Dakota or Montana), then you have no way to introduce your organization to them.

Some people wonder, when an environmental organization accepts grants, does that mean the organization is controlled by the foundations that award the grants?

Not in my experience. Every foundation has its own programs and guidelines and restrictions. If an organization is doing work that fits within a foundation's programs and other restrictions, then the organization can apply for a grant. If the organization is awarded a grant, it's required to spend the money in a manner consistent with the work described in its proposal. And the organization is generally required to submit a report later.

However, no foundation I've ever encountered has asked for control over the organization. If they did, it would be impossible anyway, because the organization where I work has a set of bylaws that describe how the organization is governed. Northern Plains has a board of directors whose members are elected, either at-large or by their local Northern Plains affiliate group. There's no way a foundation could gain a seat on our board or in any other way take part in the governance of the organization.

This is an important fact to remember, because you'll often hear the charge made that, if an organization accepts a foundation grant, it surrenders control of the organization to the foundation which made the grant. In reality, the actual responsibility of the group receiving the grant is to spend the money like it said it would. In accepting a grant, it has not surrendered control of its organization. I have often heard this accusation made, but I've never seen a case where it's true.

As an aside, I've seen some organizations – hospitals, museums, churches, whatever – which routinely invite someone to serve on the governing body because that person is a major donor. This is a separate issue from foundations, but it's worth mentioning. The idea, as I understand it, is that the charitable organization wants to have the major donor on its board because it hopes to connect with other philanthropists that the donor may know personally.

Not all nonprofits elect their board members like Northern Plains does. In the world of charitable organizations, there are many philosophies about governance and whether, or how, governance connects to fundraising. This is a big discussion – way bigger than I could cover in this book – and I suspect there is no single right answer at the end of it.

But when we discuss grant income to environmental groups, all of us need to avoid applying double standards. If it's wrong for an environmental group in our community to accept a grant from a foundation headquartered somewhere else, then it's just as wrong for other organizations to do it. It's wrong for a church, it's wrong for a hospital, it's wrong for a zoo, it's wrong for an organization that helps the poor, it's wrong for a historical society. If we're going to accuse an environmental organization of surrendering its governance to an outside foundation when it accepts a grant, then we must make that same accusation against every other organization that accepts a grant.

Have you ever heard that that accusation made against a local museum or hospital? I haven't. In fact, local organizations that bring foundation grant funds into a community are often congratulated for aiding the community's economy. But I rarely hear this praise extended to an environmental group. To me, that's a double standard.

And if it's wrong for a Montana environmental group to accept a grant from a foundation in, say, Seattle, then why is it OK for a coal company headquartered in St. Louis to operate in Montana with financial support from all over the globe?

In recent years, much criticism has been directed at certain foundations that support environmental work because of their tendency to focus narrowly on supporting specific issue work – usually by larger organizations – and to neglect support of smaller, grassroots organizations. It's those grassroots organizations that must face off with the polluters – which are often major international corporations – and with those who support the polluters politically. But it's those very organizations that seem to have the toughest time attracting funding from foundations.

Some foundations have adopted business-oriented reporting requirements that focus on measurable outcomes, with statistical data to support them. Such requirements, of course, measure almost nothing about the kind of progress that must be achieved against large polluters that enjoy comfortable support among politicians of both parties. They measure nothing of what has enabled movements for social change in America to succeed.

Such reporting requirements would have stymied the Civil Rights movement. The Women's Suffrage movement – dragging on for a lifetime – would have been able to report little measurable progress for most of its existence.

Most grassroots organizations therefore do their best to avoid becoming too dependent upon foundation funds. That's why they charge membership dues, and send out fundraising letters, and hold fundraising events.

But you know what really matters about fundraising? What really matters is when a member from Fishtail, Montana, enclosed a hand-written note with her $30 donation, a note that says, "The amount I send is necessarily small, but the hope is large."

....

Are environmentalists all Democrats?

No, but if I had to guess, I'd think that the majority of them probably vote Democratic these days. At the same time, many of them are also very frustrated with the Democratic Party because of what they see as a lack of understanding and commitment by the Democrats when it comes to protecting America's public health and the environment.

The late Ed Swartz was a Republican, as are many other environmentalists I have known. But if you care about the environment today, the modern Republican Party probably doesn't give you very many candidates to vote for. There was a time, in Montana and nationally, when at least some Republicans showed leadership in environmental protection. I think of the late George Darrow here in Montana. But since the beginning of the Reagan era, the Republican mainstream has veered sharply toward protecting the interests of corporations – Wall Street, Big Oil, and so on – and it's become routine to hear Republican leaders and candidates attack environmental laws and standards. If elected, they often try to weaken or dismantle environmental protections, or to make it impossible to enforce those standards. And, as I've already said, it's not just about allowing more pollution of water, land, air, and destruction of the American land – it's also about attacking the rights of citizens to participate in governmental decision making.

In a time when many Democratic politicians don't care all that much, and most Republicans are openly hostile, who does an environmentalist vote for?

Some get involved with third-party candidates. Personally, this has never been an attractive option. Few third-party candidates are ever elected to office.

That doesn't mean there's no place for third-party candidates in American politics. But I'm not one who places much faith in them.

If most people who care about the environment vote for Democrats, I suppose it's because they feel they've been forced to. Those moderate Republicans whose natural tendencies were pro-business but who also saw a responsibility to exercise good stewardship of our land and water and air – those Republicans are harder and harder to find.

....

Are environmentalists all liberals?

Somewhere along the way, a lot of people – including quite a few environmentalists – have gotten the idea that protecting the environment is an issue of the left. But in my job, I regularly cross paths with people who have very different reasons for becoming involved with environmental issues.

For example, some ranch families, conservative by nature and by upbringing, got involved when their property (or their water, or their ability to earn a living) was threatened by some kind of mining or drilling activity. Even if they held a certain suspicion of environmentalists, they often came to realize that being conservative and protecting natural resources fit perfectly well together, that being conservative and protecting property rights are perfectly consistent.

At Northern Plains, I work with some very liberal and some very conservative folks. Many of them have come to find that they have important things in common. They may come from different backgrounds and have different political predispositions, but they often come to see that clean water isn't a liberal cause. Shutting citizens out of the decision-making process isn't a conservative cause.

The most conservative politicians take steps to centralize government, strip power from states, and advocate spying on American citizens. Liberal politicians have done many of those same things. And all of them have kowtowed to corporate polluters to get re-elected. When it comes to the environment, "liberal" and "conservative" labels just don't mean very much.

Retired Rear Admiral David Titley observed that "Conservative people want to conserve things. Preserving the climate should be high on that list."[1]

....

Are environmentalists all annoying and self-righteous?

Of course not. But, yes, some of us are. There are some environmentalists who annoy the heck out of other environmentalists with self-righteous attitudes and talk. Sanctimonious preaching, some would say.

In 2011, the U.S. Postal Service issued a series of "Go Green" stamps that I personally found preachy. Each of the 20 stamps admonished us to do something: fix water leaks, recycle more, ride a bike, insulate the home, use public transportation, maintain tire pressure, share rides. You get the picture. Even though I see value in every one of those admonitions, I get tired of being preached at. So do most people. And some environmentalists need to understand this better.

Anybody, environmentalist or otherwise, who talks as if they know more than anybody else is annoying. Anybody, environmentalist or otherwise, who talks as if they are morally superior to everybody else is annoying.

Environmental writer David Roberts asked readers for advice, comments, and suggestions when he was shopping for a new car for him and his wife, their two sons, and their large dog. He was looking for something smaller and more efficient than the minivan they had been driving. In addition to plenty of honestly useful tips, he received a few suggestions that:

I should get rid of my dog, or leave the dog at home, that I should stop being a cosseted hypocrite and start getting my kids to school and doing my errands by bus or bike, and that above all, I should never, ever say anything nice about cars generally or any car specifically and that by doing so I have disgraced myself, disgraced Grist *(the online* magazine for which he wrote), *and most likely disgraced the baby Jesus.*

Roberts continued:

The dolorous monks among the commenters reflect, I fear, what the great mass of non-environmentalists expect from environmentalists: scorn, condescension, and above all, judgment. When I tell civilians that I write for an "environmental website," they immediately take on a guilty mien and start shifting from foot to foot, stammering about how they try to recycle, as though they're trying to apologize for or justify their daily habits. They expect me, as an environmentalist, to be a kind of monk, full of virtue and contemptuous of their lack.

It is not a role I want any part of. And it is not to environmentalism's benefit that people think of it that way, as a kind of ascetic order standing outside U.S. consumer culture, condemning those within as weak and fallen.[2]

There's no denying that some environmentalists act as if they know better or are more moral than other people. Those individuals have failed to understand these simple truths of human living: *none of us have perfect information, none of us are right all the time, and pretty much all of us have to make compromises in life.*

There are a few environmentalists who have their own "litmus test" for whether they think a person or an organization is smart enough or moral enough. Maybe they believe you can't be a real environmentalist if you eat meat or drive a car. Maybe they have an in-your-face style and degrade anybody who disagrees with them.

Fortunately, I don't cross paths with these people very often. I honestly don't think are very many of them. But they're out there. They seem to have the ability to get noticed. And they can be annoying.

I was reading a piece in an online magazine, an angry essay in which the author wrote about "why poor Americans often f…ing hate eco do-gooders…"[3]

"They're smug as shit," the author wrote. She described having written an earlier article about the struggle of feeding a family of five on little money, and then receiving a comment from a reader who chastised her for having three children. She describes writing about the anguish of her mini-van being stolen, and then receiving a comment from a reader advising her to buy a cargo bike (a very expensive bicycle, which she could not have afforded even if it were a viable solution, which it wasn't).

Indeed, these were thoughtless, even heartless, responses. But the author made the mistake of attributing those responses to environmentalists in general. She failed to understand that these were the responses of jerks, not environmentalists. She assumed these responses represented "the environmental movement." She was stereotyping. She was reciting pieces of "The Narrative" about environmentalists.

At Northern Plains, when we interview people who apply to work as field organizers, we try to talk about this unusual and demanding job to give them an idea of what's involved in working with diverse people from diverse backgrounds. For example, in the course of an interview, we let job applicants know that they may be an overnight guest in the home of a member who raises cattle for a living, and may be served an evening meal that includes a big slice of roast beef. How will the person respond to that situation? We've had a few staffers who are vegetarians but who also believe in courtesy and deference to their hosts and eat what their hosts have prepared for them. And we've had some job applicants who exhibited a self-righteousness that told us they would not work out in this very people-oriented job.

It gets back to the main point I'm trying to make on these pages – environmentalists are just like other people and, yes, some of them can be annoying and self-righteous.

There's a guy who has spent part of almost every Saturday for several years at a busy intersection on the west side of Billings – now, he's annoying. He stands on a stepladder with a portable loudspeaker and microphone, yelling at all the cars with his message about accepting Christ. He's loud and abrasive and hard to understand, and I can't believe he's persuaded anyone to convert to Christianity.

Does he represent Christians in general? Of course not.

And if you run into a guy who's annoying, or self-righteous, and who claims to be an environmentalist, just remember – that guy's a jerk. Like it or not, there are a lot of jerks out there. Some of them are Christians, some of them are environmentalists, some of them are car mechanics. But not all car mechanics are jerks, are they?

I believe a number of environmentalists are angry, and angry people aren't usually too much fun to be around. I can get pretty angry myself sometimes about things I see happening, and I can understand why others feel that way as well.

I think some environmentalists probably have developed sort of a siege mentality. After all, when they look around, it's easy to get the feeling that powerful forces are actively hostile – not only to environmentalists, but even to the environment itself. It appears that some people – including political and cultural leaders – really do want to destroy wild nature and wild animals. It appears that some people actively oppose developing energy sources, like the sun and wind, which would help America become more energy-independent. Look at what some of the people early in this book say about environmentalists – "nature Fascists," "fanatics," "a spreading cancer" – and it's not that hard to understand why some environmentalists might be angry or defensive.

Since protecting the environment requires democratic processes and the access of citizens to the decision-making process, some environmentalists are angry that these democratic processes seem to be under attack in recent years. National and state lawmakers seem to be looking for ways to shut out the voices of citizens, to deny them legal redress, and to give polluters more ways to control the outcomes in public agencies that are supposed to be working on behalf of the people.

When government functions on behalf of corporations instead of citizens, it should make any American angry. It's a dead-end path, and that end is a place that means ruination for our water and land, for our public health, and for our freedoms. Oh, it means swollen corporate profits, too. But you and I both know that corporate profits are not what America is about.

However, if you say so, somebody will certainly think you're annoying and self-righteous. Sometimes all it takes for someone to find you annoying is to say something that somebody else doesn't want to hear.

....

How common are eco-terrorists?

While definitions of "terrorism" vary, the common thread among those definitions is the use of violence to achieve political ends. Whatever an "eco-terrorist" would be, it implies that the person uses violence to achieve his or her ends.

I've heard the term "eco-terrorist" thrown around quite a lot. Let me tell you how it was used against Wade Sikorski, a soft-spoken Montana wheat farmer.

Like many farmers, Sikorski is also a philosopher. But unlike many farmers, he has a Ph.D. after his name. A graduate of Montana State University who went on to earn a doctorate in Political Theory from the University of Massachusetts, Sikorski reads and writes serious stuff, tackling contemporary issues, and exploring them from different scholarly angles. His scholarly pursuits, however, helped make him a target on the World Wide Web.

Sikorski wrote an article titled "On Mad Bombers," which was a critique of the manifesto written by "Unabomber" Ted Kaczynski. *Theory and Event*, an online journal produced by Johns Hopkins University, carried Sikorski's article in 1997.[4]

At the time, there was much debate over Kaczynski's sanity, for he was adamant about not using an insanity defense in his trial. He insisted that he was behaving rationally, and that idea is what Sikorski explored in his article.

Wade concluded that there was certain logic to the Unabomber's thinking, for Kaczynski was concerned about real issues, and had devised a response to them that, in his own thinking, made some kind of sense. Wade wrote: "The Unabomber has done nothing, absolutely nothing, that does not find, at some point, justification within our civilization." After all, Wade recounted, we based our national military strategy on the theory of Mutually Assured Destruction for many years. As a society, we have been comfortable with violence on a large scale for quite a while.

Wade also pointed out that, while Kaczynski's fairly random killings put him in jail for the rest of his life, we as a society don't hold everybody to the same standard. Wade's article recalled that the 1995 Montana legislature raised the legal level of arsenic pollution so that, instead of one cancer death in a million being the acceptable threshold, the State of Montana would be OK with arsenic pollution if it causes one cancer death per thousand exposed people. That's a thousand-fold increase.

Wade's article imagined how society would respond to a random killer who fired a gun into a convention hall packed with a thousand people and killed one of them. This one-death-in-a-thousand is fundamentally the policy that the 1995 legislature adopted when it decided that one cancer death per thousand people was acceptable if a mining company was administering the arsenic.

Subsequently, multiple websites used Wade's description in order to make it appear as if he was defending the Unabomber. One such site, based in Wyoming and sponsored by an organization called the "Wyoming CBM [coal bed methane] Group" placed Wade's name and an out-of-context quote at the head of a section about "eco-terrorism."

So why did Wade's relatively obscure article in an academic journal make him a target on the World Wide Web? Why did a website sponsored by the Wyoming coal bed methane industry want to label him an "eco-terrorist" just for writing about a controversial subject in an academic article?

Actually, I don't believe Wade was the real target at all. His involvement in the coal bed methane issue was no different from hundreds of other people who testified about their concerns for water quality and aquifers.

However, earlier in the 1990s, he did represent his local affiliate group on the board of the Northern Plains Resource Council. And Northern Plains had definitely gotten the attention of the coal bed methane industry. If the methane industry could paint Sikorski as a supporter of terrorism, maybe they could succeed at making Northern Plains look like a supporter of terrorism.

If you actually read Sikorski's article (you can obtain a copy online or through your local library), you'll see for yourself how preposterous it really is to claim that he's defending the Unabomber.

But there's something worse than the out-and-out dishonesty of this claim. It's the public, worldwide targeting of a private citizen as an "eco-terrorist," simply for writing an academic article about a controversial subject.

It's the deliberate attempt to ruin a man's reputation as part of a cynical strategy to discredit a citizen organization, simply because that organization dared to demand water treatment, aquifer recharge, and reasonable protection for natural resources.

Remember the definition of "terrorism." Accusing Wade of "eco-terrorism" means they accused him of threatening or using violence. What kind of people think it's OK to lie like that about a man?

The Canadian corporation TransCanada wanted to build more pipelines through the United States, the biggest being the Keystone XL pipeline, to carry diluted bitumen from the horrific tar sands mines of Alberta to refineries and ports in Texas, where it could be refined and – depending on what the market was doing at the time – exported to overseas customers.

The Keystone XL project brought out many thousands of protesters for many reasons. TransCanada would sure have liked to take those protesters out of the game, and one of their strategies was to paint these American citizens as potential terrorists.

In 2013, TransCanada approached the Nebraska State Patrol to suggest that the state police consider Keystone XL opponents as potential terrorists. The company didn't stop with Nebraska authorities. *Bloomberg Business* later reported that, "Time and again, in private e-mails and closed-door meetings with federal, state and local law enforcement, the Canadian company characterized peaceful opponents engaged in constitutionally protected protest as dangerous radicals or worse."[5]

In 2011, a representative of Anadarko Petroleum told oil and gas companies that they faced nothing less than an insurgency, according to a recording. He urged audience members to download the U.S. Army/Marine Corps Counter-Insurgency Field Manual, the military's guidebook to the age of international terrorism.[6]

I've read about certain acts – violent acts that destroy property – that I would call "eco-terrorism." They're always a big deal in the news precisely because they are very rare (despite their common use as a plot device on TV cop shows and despite the efforts of energy companies to paint their opponents as potential terrorists).

And yet I hear that word "eco-terrorist" thrown around very casually – or very deliberately – in some circles. When anyone uses it, they are accusing a person of being a violent criminal. If I ever hear someone use it, I challenge that person to be very clear about what he or she is saying. I hope you will also raise a challenge when you hear someone use that word.

And if you ever know of an actual eco-terrorist, I hope you call the police. I also hope you call the police if you see someone gun down a wild bear just for fun, or poison an eagle just to sell the feathers.

....

Are environmentalists all just a bunch of NIMBYs?

You know what NIMBYs are. NIMBY stands for "not in my back yard," and these are widely described as people whose concern about an issue is simply a desire to keep an undesirable project away from themselves. Some polluting companies have put considerable effort into portraying people who object to their plans as NIMBYs – selfish, irresponsible, elitist. After all, our civilization creates waste and pollution, and it has to go <u>somewhere</u>. Citizens who stand up to defend their communities and their families from a pollution-filled project are therefore portrayed as NIMBYs, and are said to simply be wishing that project onto someone else's community.

So there we have it, a corporation wants to come in to a community and build a dirty, polluting project that externalizes costs onto the general public, and anyone in that community who objects to it is portrayed as selfish. I'm sorry, but I believe people have the right to speak up for their homes and families without being berated and called names.

On a broader scale, externalizing pollution costs onto the general public is wrong. It's wrong in my town and in yours.

There are some actual NIMBYs out there, but I've never really regarded them as environmentalists. Most of the people I've met who have stood in opposition to polluting projects are *not* selfish, and are *not* simply wishing that such projects would go to someone else's town. They want a real solution that means reducing our pollution and waste. They know it's not right to be polluting anyone's water and air, nor contaminating anyone's soil. They know that the real question is not which town gets stuck with the polluting project, but why we aren't dealing with our pollution more responsibly in the first place.

CHAPTER THIRTY-SEVEN

Are Environmentalists <u>for</u> Anything?

Not this, but that.

………··…··…··…··…··…··…··…··…··…··…··…··…··…··

S ince environmentalists aren't all the same, I can't tell you with any certainty what they are for as a group. They have different positions from one another on all kinds of things. Remember the argument about eating meat?

When it comes to climate change, there are serious disagreements among people who want to protect the environment. Take nuclear power… some environmentalists today feel that more nuclear power will help protect our atmosphere from the effect of greenhouse gases. Myself, I'm still pretty skeptical about that. What I have seen of nuclear power in my lifetime tells me it represents the kind of over-centralized, over-technological, risk-externalizing energy source that has created many of our problems. I worry about security issues, about waste storage, and about the pat answers we keep getting about what the technology can do, when the real-world implementation of nuclear technology has never lived up to promises.

But I could be wrong.

Still, I often hear this accusation that environmentalists are against everything, so I got in touch with a few dozen environmentalists and asked them… "What are you for?"

Most of these people live here in Montana. Some of them work for organizations, most don't. Some live in town, others on farms or ranches. Some of them gave me long lists, some just offered a few ideas that came to mind quickly.

Some of them emphasized preservation of natural landscapes. Others stressed the way we govern ourselves as a nation. Still others reflected on the way we produce food or use energy. And some lists call for us to think differently than we do now.

How many of these things are *you* for?

- **Clean air and clean water.**

Almost everybody mentioned these fundamental needs of life, reflecting deep concerns over pollution and scarcity.

- **Preserving American land.**

Some of these environmentalists talked about protecting wild places where Americans can feel the sense of freedom and responsibility that built this country. Some of them spoke of hunting and fishing, and of open space around our communities. Some of them talked about keeping our soil healthy, some about looking after the places wildlife need in order to live. Some talked about preserving our cultural and archaeological history, while others emphasized safeguarding America's natural beauty.

- **Restoring America's land.**

These environmentalists are for building topsoil rather than destroying it, building a ranching economy on grasslands that should not be converted to croplands, and providing skilled jobs in the woods (restoring streams and habitat, etc.). One person mentioned restoring wild bison herds on public lands.

- **Governing our nation for the good of the people.**

These environmentalists expressed concerns for maintaining honesty, fairness, and transparency in government, and for keeping government decision-making processes open to citizens (this was a big concern). Most want to protect the rights of citizens by reducing the power of corporations over how we live and how we are governed. Some spoke of making sure that environmental costs are paid by those who create them. Others expressed concerns about protecting the integrity of our free elections.

- **Energy to power America.**

These people want America to be energy independent. They are for using energy efficiently, and using renewable energy (e.g., solar, wind, small hydropower, geothermal, tides) as much as possible, especially at the local level.

Some said they want to use energy in a way that doesn't "screw up the planet" and – when we extract fossil fuels – to protect the land and water and the rights and health of people. Some added that they are for protecting the right of landowners to refuse access of power lines, pipelines, and mining projects to their property.

- **How we feed ourselves.**

Many of these environmentalists told me they are for access to safe, healthy food for everyone, as well as access to locally produced food. They're for the economic survival of family-scale farming and ranching. This means they're for national policies that encourage small-scale, sustainable farming rather than corporate agriculture. Some mentioned reducing our use of chemicals in raising grains, fruits and vegetables, and livestock, as well as reducing the use of antibiotics as a feed supplement for healthy animals.

- **Living good lives.**

The environmentalists I contacted offered me a wide range of thoughts about the way we live – good stewardship, respecting God's creation, living with a sense of place. They also talked about minimizing the damage we do to the land and water and air in the way we live. They expressed concerns for ensuring safe and healthy lives for children. Some said they want self-reliant local communities, where people can shop at locally owned businesses. Some talked about treating other people respectfully. One person even mentioned giving ourselves challenges that are hard and uncomfortable, that teach us what we're made of.

- **Thinking differently.**

Finally, some of these environmentalists spoke of their desire for an end to the mythology of "conquering nature" and, instead, seeing ourselves as stewards of the American land. Some other points that they are for: people wanting less instead of always wanting more, being good neighbors, pursuing peace in the world, and understanding that real people and real families are more important to our nation than corporations.

One of these environmentalists told me, "There is so much to be <u>for</u> that it is hard to know where to start."

Another one reminded me that, while environmentalists often say "no," the full message is actually "not this, but that." Not a negative but, instead, an affirmation of something positive. For example, he said:

Not coal and nuclear, but solar and wind.

Not industrial agriculture, but local organic permaculture.

Not conspicuous consumption and planned obsolescence, but well-crafted, durable products that our great-grandchildren will cherish.

Wilderness

Man always kills the things he loves, and so we the pioneers have killed our wilderness. Some say we had to. Be that as it may, I am glad I shall never be young without wild country to be young in. Of what avail are forty freedoms without a blank spot on the map?

– Aldo Leopold

Wilderness made me a better American.

One day, I sat on top of Hay Butte in the South Dakota Badlands and looked out over Tyree Basin to the west. In the distance, I saw a small herd of bison. In the far distance, buttes and grasslands swept off toward the Black Hills.

And I thought to myself how lucky I am to live in this big, beautiful country. I thought of how this land helped to shape us as a people – the great eastern forests, the fertile prairies, the Great Plains, the mountains that form the spine of this content, the deserts, and our thousands of miles of coastlines. I reflected that I owe this great country my best efforts to protect these places – places that are important to us as a nation and to our character, even if we can't all go there.

But some people seem to hate the very idea of wild places. Why?

Is it that these lands could be put to more profitable use and are being wasted? Is it that these lands represent something scary, like dense forests and wild animals? Is it that we can't drive our cars into these lands? Is it that these lands are defended by people we just don't like?

Protecting America's wild places used to have broader support a few decades ago. I came across a full-page ad in the April 1966 issue of *National Geographic* titled, "How to keep a forest from becoming a neon jungle." The text of the ad began:

America's wild and beautiful lands are going fast. Each newly born baby has one-quarter acre less of such land to enjoy than the baby born a moment before.

What environmental organization placed this full-page ad? It was the Sinclair Oil Corporation.

Some people complain that we should put our public lands to multiple uses, not "lock it up" as wilderness. The thing is, we already do apply the multiple-use concept to most public lands and, in law, wilderness is one of those uses. The Multiple-Use and Sustained-Yield Act of 1960 prescribed managing national forests for different values and purposes. It specifically listed outdoor recreation, range, timber, watershed, wildlife and fish. The law includes a passage specific to wilderness:

The establishment and maintenance of areas of wilderness are consistent with the purposes and provisions of this Act.[1]

In the years before the Multiple-Use and Sustained-Yield Act was passed, America's national forests were under heavy pressure from timber cutting, and the law was a tool to ensure that our national forests wouldn't simply become cut-and-run tree farms for the logging industry.

From his farm in Wisconsin, retired biologist Aldo Leopold wrote of big ideas and little details of the life and land around him. One chapter of his book *A Sand County Almanac* is an important essay on wilderness. Another chapter is entirely about one chickadee that lived in the woods on his farm.

Yet another chapter tells of two young men he encountered canoeing on the Flambeau River. The young men had enlisted in the Army and this trip on the Flambeau was a last "taste of freedom" for them before basic training.

It was freedom along with the responsibility that inevitably accompanies it. Leopold writes:

No servant brought meals: they got their meat out of the river, or went without. No traffic cop whistled them off the hidden rock in the next rapids. No friendly roof kept them dry when they misguessed whether or not to pitch the tent. No guide showed them which camping spots offered a nightlong breeze, and which a nightlong misery of mosquitoes; which firewood made clean coals and which only smoke... The wilderness gave them their first taste of those rewards and penalties for wise and foolish acts which every woodsman faces daily, but against which civilization has built a thousand buffers.[2]

The Flambeau is not an officially designated wilderness area. In fact, Leopold described his first trip on the Flambeau as a trip through a wilderness "on its last legs." The wild stretches of the river had been chopped up by cottages and fake "log" cabins, by resorts, and highway bridges. It had been logged over, first for its pines and later for its hardwoods. The flow of the Flambeau's forks was interrupted by a number of dams and, in Leopold's time, a new mile-wide hydroelectric dam was on the drawing board right in the middle of a prime stretch of the river. He never contemplated the open pit copper, gold, and silver mine that would operate later on the upper reaches of the watershed.

Still, decades of restoration efforts led by the State of Wisconsin, dating back to the 1940s, have helped restore some parts of the river.

Author Wallace Stegner recalled a night on the prairie when he was still a young boy in 1915.

Then in the night I awoke, not knowing where I was. Strangeness flowed around me; there was a current of cool air, a whispering, a loom of darkness overhead. In panic I reared up on my elbow and found that I was sleeping beside my brother under the wagon, and that a night wind was breathing across me through the spokes of the wheel. It came from unimaginably far places across a vast emptiness, below millions of polished stars. And yet its touch was soft, intimate, and reassuring, and my panic went away at once. That wind knew me. I knew it. Every once in a while, sixty-six years after that baptism in space and night and silence, wind across grassland can smell like that to me, as secret, perfumed, and soft, and tell me who I am.

It is an opportunity I wish every American could have.[3]

The official designation of "wilderness area" is only for places that meet the standards expressed in the Wilderness Act of 1964, and those standards are impossible for some public lands to meet. The federal lands from which wilderness areas may be designated include those managed by the Department of Agriculture (national forests and grasslands) and the Department of the Interior (national parks, national monuments, Bureau of Land Management lands, etc.). It takes an act of Congress to set aside a piece of land as a wilderness area.

There are lands that simply can't get congressional approval, even if they are still worthy American places. There are plenty of places in our country that need saving, plenty of wild places that will help our fellow Americans understand this nation of ours.

Wallace Stegner in 1982 lamented about those who are "bent upon undoing all the environmental legislation of the past seventy-five years and turning us back to the damn-the-consequences practices that have left us, in all the ways of true civilization, poorer than people so naturally blessed have any right to be."[4]

Some people resist protecting wilderness, saying, "How much wilderness is enough?" Author Edward Abbey replied with these questions: "How many cities are enough? How large a population do we really need? How much industrial development must we have to be content?"

It's a false choice, really. Wilderness isn't the enemy of civilization. In fact, as Abbey reminds us, "Wilderness complements and completes civilization."[5]

Wilderness doesn't just complement civilization… it is part of our heritage of personal liberty as Americans. Edward Abbey continues:

At least in America, one relic of our ancient and rightful liberty has survived. And that is – a walk into the Big Woods; a journey on foot into the uninhabited interior; a voyage down the river of no return. Hunters, fishermen, hikers, climbers, white-water boatmen, red-rock explorers know what I mean. In America, at least this kind of experience remains open and available to all, democratic. Little or no training is required, very little special equipment, no certification of privilege. All that is needed is normal health, the will to do it, and a modicum of courage.

It is my fear that if we allow the freedom of the hills and the last of the wilderness to be taken from us, then the very idea of freedom may die with it.[6]

Wild American places are among the important values all of us today owe the next generation of Americans. We owe them the Constitution and a nation that follows it. We owe them a love of liberty and the right to make a difference in their nation. We owe them the capacity to see what needs to be fixed in our country – as our predecessors did when they ended slavery and stopped denying women the right to vote – and we owe them the moral and political will to fix the problems they face. We owe the next generation a viable middle class and fair chance to improve their lives. We owe them a country where the lives of people are not measured in dollars.

And, among all these and many more things, we owe the next generation the chance to experience the grandeur of our nation, the kind of grandeur that our ancestors walked through in their lives. We owe them a few places where the great American continent is left intact, where there is quiet, where we can drink from streams, where we can challenge ourselves, and space where we can – as the first real American poet Walt Whitman said – "stretch around on the wonderful beauty."

We owe them this.

One Montana Coal Mine

The committee chairman "noted approvingly" that the presidents of Montana's two public universities and others present at a hearing were wearing coal industry lapel pins.

....

Speculation for a massive strip mine in southeast Montana's Otter Creek valley began high in the mountains above Yellowstone National Park. Like many speculative undertakings, it involved a lot of promises and a lot of politicians. And like many speculative undertakings, it fell apart.

But it was an ambitious plan! If it was developed, it would be the largest strip mine ever in Montana.

Cooke City is a tiny little town at the northeast corner of Yellowstone. High in the mountains above Cooke City, Crown Butte Mines wanted to open a precious metals mine (focusing on gold) on a property consisting of privately owned mineral claims and U.S. Forest Service land. The land had been scarred from earlier mining, and had never been reclaimed.

In fact, reclamation would have been a doubtful enterprise here, because of its high elevation – near timberline – where growing seasons are extremely short. The ore body itself contained large amounts of iron pyrite, which would mean perpetual weathering of iron and sulfur from the exposed rock. The site drains into three mountain watersheds, one flowing into Yellowstone's Soda Butte Creek, one into the headwaters of the Stillwater River, and one into the Clark's Fork of the Yellowstone. The company proposed to prevent acid runoff into these watersheds by building a 77-acre impoundment dam. Impoundments, however, have a chronic problem of failing, sometimes dramatically and sometimes little by little.

In all, it was a bad site for a large mine, and the Clinton White House became convinced of that in the mid-1990s. The Administration brokered a buyout of the mine in the interests of protecting Yellowstone National Park and other precious natural resources in the Beartooth Mountains. In that buyout, the company received money, the owners of the private mineral claims received money, and a fund was created to begin reclaiming the site from the damage caused by prior mining. However, important Montana politicians – the Governor, a Congressman, and a U.S. Senator – insisted on a payment to the state to replace the potential value of this mining development that had never actually existed. Of course, none of those politicians gave a damn about the Otter Creek valley, nor the people who live there.

That federal payment to the state would have been $10 million in cash, but the Montana politicians, lobbied by coal speculators, turned it down and instead wanted ownership of certain federal mineral resources within the state. They could have gotten federal coal reserves in areas within existing coal mine plans, but they turned that down, too. They insisted on coal beneath Otter Creek, a little ranching valley about 200 straight-line miles east of Yellowstone. Eager to wrap up the deal, the Clinton White House went along with it.

Several ranchers from southeast Montana, as part of a discussion within the Northern Plains Resource Council, talked it out and eventually decided not to fight the buyout, even though they knew it was likely to create massive headaches for them in the years ahead. They viewed it as a matter of solidarity, and they didn't want to save themselves by shoving the destructive gold mine project onto the residents of Cooke City.

So the New World Mine buyout went ahead, culminating in the final piece of property acquisition in 2010. The state of Montana received ownership of approximately 572 million tons of sub-bituminous coal in the Otter Creek valley, coal that could be consolidated with 730 million tons of coal already owned by Great Northern Properties, a carryover from the federal land grant to the railroad in the 1800s. GNP is the largest private owner of coal in the U.S.[1]

Altogether, that makes approximately 1.3 billion tons of coal. (Around 1.5 billion tons of coal were mined in all of Montana from 1889 to 2010.[2])

The land above the Otter Creek coal covers 18,220 acres (about 28.5 square miles), in three "mineable" tracts.[3]

....

Let me tell you a little bit about Otter Creek. The valley runs roughly parallel to the Tongue River, just to the east on the other side of a small ridge. As it nears the town of Ashland, Otter Creek turns northwest and flows toward the Tongue to become one of its small tributaries. Most of the ranch houses are strung along the valley floor.

Otter Creek is a long way from almost everywhere.

By about 1500, the Crow tribe had moved into southeast Montana from the woods of the Great Lakes region. Allied with the Kiowas, the Crow dominated the region, acquiring horses around 1700, which led to a major change in their lives and economy.

However, Cheyenne and Lakota were also moving westward from the Great Lakes region, and acquired horses a few decades after the Crow. The Crow were pressured by these tribes and pushed out of some areas. Eventually, the Crow allied themselves with the U.S. Army against these other tribes. As reservations were established, the Northern Cheyenne Reservation occupied land along the banks of the Tongue River where Otter Creek empties into it.[4]

After white settlers moved into the area in the 1870s, horses remained important. Transplanted Englishman Lord Sidney Padgett raised race horses, army horses, and even polo ponies (for other English transplants who, for many years, held regular polo matches in the region). Oliver Henry Wallop (son of the Earl of Portsmouth) came to America after graduating from Oxford, spent some time in Miles City, then started a ranch on Otter Creek. He raised horses there until the early 1890s, when he moved on to Story, Wyoming.

Horses were a mainstay in the valley until the Army largely stopped using them after World War II. Since then, cattle ranching has been the backbone of the valley's life, though I've been told there's a horse racing oval still visible in a hay meadow on the valley floor.

Near the lower end of the Otter Creek valley is a little cemetery called "Willow Crossing." Some of the gravestones there are blank. Some tell of long marriages and long lives. Some tell of infants who spent hardly any time at all in our world. Some tell of local families that were joined together in marriage.

The valley rises to hills and sandstone bluffs, with plenty of areas on those hills wooded with ponderosa pines and some junipers. There are a few narrow strings of cottonwoods in the creek bottoms. Sagebrush and other shrubs join blue grama and other grasses to provide plenty of plant diversity is this semi-arid part of Montana.

The open grasslands, shrubs, and pines, the bottomland and rocky slopes, all make the valley home to a healthy range of mammals, birds, and even reptiles and amphibians. Mule deer, elk, white-tails, and pronghorns live here, as do coyotes, raccoons, red foxes, and skunks. Many kinds of birds earn a living here, too – chickadees and magpies, turkeys and wading birds, owls and woodpeckers, golden eagles and turkey vultures. Otter Creek is a little stream but, besides the cattle and people and hayfields, it sustains frogs, salamanders, toads, and painted turtles. Blue racers and prairie rattlesnakes make the valley their home; so do walleyes and white crappies, badgers and jackrabbits, western meadowlarks and burrowing owls. Among the birds, 150-250 species may spend at least part of the year around Otter Creek, and 60-90 species may nest here.[5]

Much of the land in the upper end of the valley and the ridges alongside it are part of the Custer National Forest. Some ranches lease grazing rights on the national forest. There are natural springs in the hills, and the Forest Service has installed a few small reservoirs and pipes to help make water more accessible to cattle grazing there.

On the valley floor, Otter Creek is small, not big enough to use for regular irrigation, though it's sometimes possible to flood-irrigate a hayfield. Just a few days a year of that can make all the difference to a hay meadow in this country. Wells draw water from the aquifer that lies within the coalfield, water that's fine for cattle to drink, but too salty to use for irrigation.

Some Otter Creek ranchers graze their cattle in the hills during the summer and trail the cattle back to the valley for winter. Neighbors help one another with big jobs like trailing cattle, branding, and haying. The closest hospital is in Sheridan, Wyoming. Long school bus rides are a way of life for the kids.

Locals don't much like to talk politics, nor to call attention to themselves by going public on an issue, nor to criticize someone else. They know that they don't see everything the same way – from politics to ranch management – but they depend on each other, and they try to cut each other some slack.

People have known for a long time that there's coal beneath this little valley and the pine-covered hills along its sides.

Coal companies began slowly buying out ranches in the valley, starting in the 1970s, but it still didn't mean a lot to most people. Mining speculation falls through as often as not, and many farms and ranches have dealt with leasehounds who come and go.

For a long time, coal mining seemed like a vague possibility on Otter Creek, something that would never actually happen.

But some ranches sold out over the years. Why?

It could have been that the family was financially strapped and saw no choice but to sell out. Several sustained years of low cattle prices, like the late 1990s for example, can turn a viable ranch operation into one loaded with debt. There was a family that went through a severe health crisis, and selling out was the only way to pay the bills.

Some of these families have stayed on, renting land they used to own.

If a ranch passes from parents to multiple children, selling out may be the only way to resolve the issue of split ownership.

More recently, as the threat of strip mining began to seem more real, it could have been that a family became discouraged about the threat of a giant mine destroying the valley, and sold out because they felt they had no choice.

Whatever the seller's reason, coal speculators have gnawed at the Otter Creek valley for years.

If the specter of a strip mine ruining the valley seemed like a vague possibility years ago, it became much more real when the New World Mine buyout hit the headlines in the 1990s. What made it an imminent threat, though, was the day in 2010 when the checkerboarded ownership of the coal beneath the valley was consolidated.

....

Late in 2009, Great Northern Properties struck a deal, leasing the right to mine its coal in the valley – those 730 million tons – to St. Louis-based Arch Coal. They sold it knowing that the checkerboard pattern of their ownership would not make mining feasible unless the rest of the checkerboard – the state's 572 million tons – was also made available to the project. They were sitting on a lot of coal in that valley, at a time when coal use was beginning to decline in the U.S. The time had come to make sure they got their money out of this asset, before the opportunity passed them by.

Arch Coal and Great Northern Properties had to know that locking in GNP's coal for this project would have the effect of stampeding state officials into making this coal mine a reality. After all, the recession had its grip on Montana as well as the rest of the nation. This one coal lease would bring millions of dollars to the state (and, of course, the politicians promised it would go toward improving our schools). In March, 2010, the Montana Land Board – composed of the five statewide officeholders – voted 4-1 to lease the state's coal tracts in Otter Creek for 15¢ a ton. It would mean almost $86 million right away, with promises of billions more for the state treasury in the years to come. Promises from the coal company. Promises from the politicians.

The destruction of fine ranch country wasn't factored into this bargain. Neither was the destruction of people's property, nor the value of people's property, nor of the irrigation water that many of them rely on. Neither was the destruction of an aquifer nor of hills and wildlife. Neither were the costs to the towns along the route to West Coast ports that would be cut in two by an enormous increase in coal train traffic, nor the cost of new overpasses, nor the costs of repeated traffic jams backed up at railroad crossings every single day for years and years to come. There was no air pollution factored into the bargain, not from the fine particulates that impair the work of the lungs nor from the heavy metals that poison whoever inhales them. And, of course, the bargain utterly ignored the long-term impact to the climate from burning all that coal.

For the sake of our state treasury, the politicians pretended none of this would happen.

Montana politicians – Gov. Brian Schweitzer in particular – pitched the Otter Creek mine, more than anything, as a boon to the public schools in the state. In reality, the mine's tax revenues would have flowed to the state's general fund, and state legislators would have decided how to spend it. This is important because, over the years, supporters of public education in Montana have had to go to court repeatedly to force the legislature to meet its constitutional obligations to adequately fund education.[6]

Depending on where you live, you may remember similar debates some years ago over state lotteries and other forms of gambling. Lotteries were widely promoted as a means to improve funding for public schools. In the end, however, did it really help the schools? "Creative budgeting" allowed funds to be diverted elsewhere, and little, if any, funding windfall, or even funding stability, came to public schools after states legalized lotteries and other gambling. Here in Montana, a state lottery was overwhelmingly enacted by voters in 1986, with the purpose of funding the teachers' retirement system and reducing, or holding the line, on property taxes. Five years later, though, the legislature diverted lottery proceeds to the general fund.[7]

Coal promoters and their political allies have played the same games here in Montana, making promises about school funding that they have many, many ways of breaking. All to convince people that it's OK to destroy Otter Creek.

Of course, these promises of funding put the state's educational officials in the position of literally being forced to advocate for the destruction of Otter Creek valley. In 2013, the chairman of the Montana legislature's Joint Appropriations Subcommittee on Education told university officials that they must lead the fight for natural resource – that is, fossil fuel – development. He "noted approvingly" that the presidents of Montana's two public universities and others present at a hearing were wearing coal industry lapel pins.[8]

Spending that anticipated money, if it ever became real, would be in the legislature's hands. They might allocate it to education after all. It could happen. But when it comes to funding education, Montana's legislature has a history that we probably can't afford to ignore. The money that Arch Coal paid the state for the state for its right to lease coal never went to the schools. We always say we don't believe politicians' promises... we should probably exercise a healthy skepticism for their promises that new coal mining will advance public education.

....

And what of the Otter Creek valley? What would have happened if that strip mine were developed?

The short answer is that this pretty place would have been torn open and industrialized.

Explosions and dust and infrastructure would send the mine's effects far beyond its walls. The groundwater would be screwed up in yet-unknown ways. A railroad would haul the coal down Otter Creek, then down the Tongue River Valley, condemning and cutting through more ranch country on its way to the main railroad line.

This massive strip mine – the largest ever built in Montana – would tear the heart out of the Otter Creek valley. To get at the Knobloch coal formation, the major coal seam in the area and the only one that can be strip-mined, Arch Coal would have to remove the overburden – up to 250 feet of it in some places. By "overburden," I mean pastures and springs, bird nests and cottonwoods, chorus frogs and sagebrush voles and fox dens.

A coal company man told state legislators (verbally) that it wouldn't mine the valley floor. Whether or not that turned out to be true, it almost didn't matter. The mine would tear apart the aquifer. It would rip away the topsoil and rock until it reached that coal. In a little valley like this, ranching can't survive side-by-side with the dust and explosions and constant industrial noise. The Willow Crossing cemetery would witness the end of this little valley's ranch community.

The mine plan for Otter Creek called for tearing up the valley in a series of long strips over a period of 55 years. In addition to the land being mined, there would be a big oval railroad track for loading the coal trains, along with all the equipment used for loading. There would be long conveyor belts to carry the coal from the mined area to the trains, there would be a truck dump, and an office, and a shop, and ramps, and equipment areas, and disposal areas, and storage for explosives.

Just the noise of this mine would have completely changed the character of the valley for 55 years. It would include drilling, explosions, operation of the dragline, trucks, conveyor belts, four diesel locomotives and the cars on each train, as they moved into the mine loadout area (that oval loop of tracks, about two-thirds of a mile long by one-third of a mile wide), and the dumping of approximately 120 tons of coal into each of the 115 to 150 cars on each train.

Once loaded into the train, the coal would have been sent on a journey down the Tongue River Valley, maybe cutting the Fix ranch and neighboring places in half, maybe cutting the McRae ranch and neighboring ranches in half. Long before the Otter Creek mine became a serious proposal, this railroad project had been a snarl of changing proposals that people in the region had to live with every day.

Whatever the route, the coal trains would have spewed diesel fumes – chemicals and particulate matter – for more than a thousand miles, spreading fine coal dust along the way, creating traffic jams, and reducing property values. The region's rail system can only carry so much traffic, so the coal trains would compete with trains carrying Montana wheat to markets, just as oil trains do.

When the trains reached the West Coast, they would have pulled into newly built seaports, excavated and constructed specifically for this purpose – dumping the coal there to be loaded into oceangoing freighters for transport to Korea or India or, mostly, China. All the way, those ships would have discharged more diesel fumes into the atmosphere. Upon arrival in Asia, the coal would have been loaded onto other trains for transport to the places where it would be burned.

After the mine eventually closed, the little valley of Otter Creek would never have looked the same. Coal companies talk about "reclamation," and a lot of people think that means they're restoring the land. But after they blow up hundreds of feet of "overburden" to get to the coal, and after they ship 1.3 billion tons of coal across the Pacific Ocean, there's no possibility that the valley would have resembled anything like what it was before.

Arch Coal's mine application contained maps of pre-mine and post-mine topography. Holding them side-by-side offered a clearer understanding of what would be have been left afterward. The hills and bluffs and slender creek drainages would have been replaced by mounds of rubble. The summer pastures would be gone. The aquifer, of course, would have been ruined. That's if everything went according to plan.

The highest mounds of rubble were to be built nearest the road that runs through the valley. Placing the highest mounds near the road would serve to obscure sight of what the valley would really look like then. I don't know what kinds of plants or animals would eventually have found a home on the rubble mounds. But all that would only have been the first step of what this mine would have done. It doesn't include what the coal smoke would do to the lungs of the people who breathe it (your and my children and grandchildren). And it doesn't include what that coal smoke would do to the climate wherever you (and your children and grandchildren) call home.

But if we (or the Chinese or Koreans or whoever) were to burn the coal from that mine at Otter Creek, its carbon atoms would have combined with oxygen atoms to make carbon dioxide. That heated carbon dioxide, along with nitrous oxide, sulfur dioxide, mercury and other dangerous pollutants in the coal, would float into the atmosphere and begin the first of many, many trips around the world. Your children and grandchildren would breathe in that pollution, whether they live in Billings or Boston or Biloxi. They would also breathe in the mercury and other heavy metals that will go up those smokestacks. And whatever the carbon dioxide would have done to our weather, our children and grandchildren would have to live with it and deal with its effects for many, many years to come.

Most of us, myself included, have trouble thinking of these gases as having weight. If they were compressed into bricks, we could better understand the reality of a ton of carbon dioxide. Or a million tons. Or even a billion tons.

Carbon atoms have weight, and oxygen atoms have weight. If that 1.3 billion tons of coal at Otter Creek were burned (combined with the oxygen), it would have added up to nearly 2.5 *billion* tons of carbon dioxide. (How many bricks is that?) It comes out to more than 700 pounds for every one of us who lives on planet Earth. Of course, those of us in the Northern Hemisphere are the ones who'll be breathing in most of it.[9]

That's just the coal from one mine in southeast Montana.

This little valley came into play because of a never-to-be-developed gold mine that a Canadian company had wanted to build just outside Yellowstone National Park. The plan would have made the Otter Creek valley a sacrifice zone for the Far East. If that were to happen – and it could still happen – it would effectively destroy the valley as American ranch country. Industries would burn the coal in China, and the mining profits would go to Arch Coal's corporate headquarters in St. Louis, or some other corporation's headquarters somewhere else.

Wrecking the Otter Creek valley would do nothing for America's energy situation.

...·...·..·..·...·..·...·..·..·...·..·...·...·..·...·..·..

Montana politicians had been trying for decades to sell coal to customers in Asia. After the turn of the 21st century, the rapidly growing industrial economies of China and India became very important to the coal industry because coal demand had begun to decline in the United States around that time. If the coal industry could reel in these and other Asian nations as customers, it could lock in more coal mining for many years to come, whether or not coal burning continues in the U.S. The American tobacco industry pursued this same strategy beginning in the 1990s.

But exporting this coal to Asia – if the plan worked out – would mean more than just additional strip mines in the West. There's the drastic increase in coal train traffic through communities all the way to the West Coast, the huge new coal ports on Puget Sound and the Columbia River, the coal dust spreading along the route, and diesel fumes and lengthy traffic delays for over a thousand miles. Diesel-powered ships would haul the coal to China or Korea or India, where it would be burned.

If the coal export plan worked out, the particulates, heavy metals, and greenhouse gases would begin circling the globe once the coal was burned. They would float across the Pacific on the same winds that carried Japanese balloon bombs to

Montana during World War II, only they'd stay in the air longer, and accumulate in the atmosphere. Our children and grandchildren would breathe them. The greenhouse gases would alter the weather that our farms and ranches and wildlife and our natural landscapes depend on. All of this was part of the plan.

But, starting in 2012, coal demand began to slow worldwide, especially in China. By late 2015, global coal demand was actually decreasing.[10] A complication for Otter Creek coal was that there was never a market for it. The coal is deeper and harder to mine than coal at many other locations, and the coal in that part of the Powder River Basin is high in sodium. Few American power plants are equipped to burn it.

The coal export scheme that targeted the Otter Creek valley began to look like it might never pencil out. In fact, the project had already begun to fall apart by the end of 2015.

Building a project like this requires a state permit. Arch Coal's 2012 permit application had failed in many respects to meet the standards required of such a project, particularly with respect to its damage to the valley's water resources. When state regulators sent the application back to get their questions answered, Arch failed to respond. Months and months passed. Arch stopped paying the bills for the state's permit-related expenses.

Early in 2016, Arch Coal declared Chapter 11 bankruptcy, hoping to restructure the massive debt load it had accumulated by several years' worth of bad management decisions. The natural gas industry had cut deeply into coal's market share, Asian coal demand was dropping off, and the Obama Administration finally began to insist that America take steps to reduce the damage being done to the climate.

Within weeks of its bankruptcy, Arch Coal made another announcement: that it was suspending its effort to obtain a permit for the Otter Creek strip mine. The company cited "capital constraints, near-term weakness in coal markets and an extended and uncertain permitting outlook." Of course, the "extended permitting outlook" was Arch Coal's own fault, for it had failed to submit a complete application in the first place, then it had failed to respond to the state's questions.

Is the Otter Creek mine dead? Some people think so, but there's much that could yet happen. For one thing, Arch Coal didn't drop its permit application in 2016, the company only asked the state to suspend work on it – they asked for an indefinite "time out." In fact, the state is continuing work on at least one key aspect of the permit application because "there may be a future need for that information" and because of concerns that agency staff could lose familiarity with the project if that work were delayed too long.

Arch Coal kept making payments for its state coal leases even after its bankruptcy. However, Northern Plains discovered that the company had stopped making payments on its coal lease from Great Northern Properties several weeks before declaring bankruptcy. This is over half the coal in the Otter Creek tracts, but it's even more important than that. Since the coal ownership is checkerboarded, a mine is not viable without both the state coal and the Great Northern Properties coal. And Arch cannot sell a lease it no longer possesses. For now, at least, the strip mine on Otter Creek is defunct.

This is a big win – not just for the Otter Creek area, but also for the big picture of America's future energy position. And then there's the worldwide effort to slow down the damage being done to our climate.

Still, market conditions for the coal industry could change. Natural gas prices could increase significantly. Demand for coal could increase in Asia. A future president could undo the efforts to protect our climate from further carbon pollution.

In the meantime, many Montana politicians have positioned themselves in Arch Coal's corner. To date, they have been willing to ignore the damage of carbon pollution to the earth's climate, the ruin of private property and good ranch land, and the fact that coal is a declining industry. Those are long-term problems, and few politicians bother themselves with the long view of things. Failing to take the long view is never good for places like the Otter Creek valley.

CHAPTER FORTY

Why I Don't Believe in Climate Change

We could see for ourselves the prolonged droughts. We knew only too well about the increased frequency and intensity of wildfires. We had been seeing almost every year the early and rapid melting of mountain snowpacks.

....

I'm old enough to remember when some scientists warned that worldwide air pollution could cool the earth, could lead us into another ice age. And, today, scientists are telling us that air pollution will warm the earth.

How can we believe arguments that change so much?

Well, that's what science does. It follows the available evidence. It observes. It gathers facts. It compares new evidence to existing knowledge. Sometimes that existing knowledge has to be corrected. That's one thing that makes science different from religious faith. Science is based on evidence, and evidence accumulates over time. In the world of science, evidence matters, and new evidence can displace old evidence (and old ideas).

Those who inform us of new evidence are not always very popular. Oh, we like the people who bring us new inventions and conveniences. We like scientists who create cell phones and heart defibrillators and high-tech weapons. But we don't seem to care much for scientists who tell us things we may not want to hear.

The U.S. Surgeon General warned us about smoking in the 1960s. A lot of people – not to mention tobacco companies – didn't like hearing that. A lot of people (and tobacco companies) *really* didn't like hearing that secondhand smoke was a substantial health problem to non-smokers who inhaled other people's cigarette smoke. For years, the lack of scientific certainty kept cigarettes (and the companies that make them) from bearing any accountability for the impacts they created in the lives of millions of American families.

My dad smoked two packs of cigarettes daily. Cigarettes killed him and millions of other Americans before there was ever enough scientific certainty to satisfy the skeptics.

Galileo displeased a lot of very powerful people when his observations with the newly-invented telescope verified the theories of Copernicus that earth was not stationary in space, and that the sun and stars did not revolve around us.

The science of biology, unlike physics, is very difficult to replicate with mathematics and this means it's very difficult to achieve the level of scientific certainty that people want. Biologists work with evidence, but it's evidence that is accompanied by many variables. Combine that fact with the difficulty of representing it mathematically, and you can see that it's much harder for biology to predict with certainty than it is for sciences like physics or chemistry.

So, instead of predicting, climate scientists make projections using computer models packed with observations from scientists around the world. Real-world facts are what go into these projections. Still, it's important to remember that those many variables in global climate make every projection ultimately uncertain. Ocean currents change, for example, and we don't know how often or in what ways; this one variable would have a huge effect on what happens to the climate.

Then there are what they call "positive feedback loops," processes that, once begun, accelerate other processes. (Negative feedback loops, on the other hand, tend to keep things as they are.) Scientists are concerned that we're creating new positive feedback loops that will upset the climate's balance to which we – and all the plants and animals that share the earth with us – have become adapted over the eons.

In the Arctic, sea ice (along with the snow that covers it) serves to maintain itself and the kind of weather that local wildlife know how to deal with. But when that sea ice breaks up and recedes due to warmer temperatures, the absence of the ice will lead to even warmer temperatures because open water absorbs and retains the heat from the sun. The more ice that melts, the faster the rest of the ice melts.

This process is already under way, according to a study published in 2014 that found the area covered by arctic sea ice has shrunk by tens of thousands of square miles since 1979.[1]

There are numerous positive feedback loops on our planet, and we don't know how they'll all behave, or at what points we will step over their thresholds for irreversible change. There is a lot of carbon dioxide sequestered in the Arctic permafrost. If the Arctic warms up too much – and we don't yet know how much is too much – that carbon dioxide will be released into the atmosphere, accelerating the warming that's already going on.

Sometimes I've heard people say, "Well, climate change is just a theory," as if to imply that it's not based on anything real, and that it's just a notion someone came up with.

But a scientific theory is based on real-world observations – <u>lots</u> of real-world observations.

A scientific theory has also been subjected to peer-review – that is, it has been published or presented to other scientists for out-in-the-open criticism. Also, a theory is something that could be disproved if enough evidence is found that contradicts it. What a scientific theory does is seek to explain phenomena that have been observed.

Does this mean I believe in climate change? No, it doesn't.

I believe in God. I believe in love. I believe in justice. All these beliefs require faith on my part, and do not rely on evidence alone. Would anything convince me to drop my belief in these things? Probably not.

When it comes to climate change, it's not that I "believe in it," it's that I accept the science behind it. The evidence I've seen convinces me that the science concerning climate change is valid, based on what we know about the world today. That science, like other science about other subjects, may be imperfect and incomplete, and it will surely change. I also accept that enough contradictory evidence could persuade me otherwise. But here's why I think it's valid.

First, there's a fundamental sense to it. We know air pollution can kill people – look at the Great London Smog. Look at the simple risk of sitting in a closed garage with your car engine running… many people who want to kill themselves know that this is one way to do it.

We've dumped a smorgasbord of fossil fuel exhausts into the air – and we've accelerated our dumping of these exhausts since World War II. Can I reasonably believe that it's possible to dump this much fossil fuel exhaust into the air without it having an effect?

The medical journal *The Lancet* published a study in 2015, reporting that climate change threatens to undermine the hard-won gains of the past half-century in development and global health. The study cited direct effects like increased heat stress, floods, drought, and intense storms, along with indirect effects such as increased air pollution, spread of disease, food shortages, and displacement of people.[2]

Second, a lot of evidence has accumulated, evidence that points to the fact that the world is changing, and that the changes correlate with the big increase in our discharging of certain gases into the atmosphere. Is it all just a big coincidence that these changes correlate with the increased burning of fossil fuels? Maybe, but that's just too big a coincidence for me to accept on faith, especially when so much evidence has been brought to bear.

A few years ago, Northern Plains hosted a speaker at its annual meeting who has been deeply involved in studying climate change. Dr. Steven Running is a professor at the University of Montana, but he has also worked with thousands of other scientists around the world as part of the Intergovernmental Panel on Climate Change. At the time Running gave his talk to our members, the IPCC had just received the Nobel Peace Prize for its years of worldwide research on what is going on with the world's climate.

His presentation was geared to a general audience, but it was packed with evidence from all over the world. His many charts and graphs outlined changes to the world's weather, and all of it correlated with the increase in greenhouse gases in the atmosphere.

Some of the evidence he presented was very clear to those of us in Montana. We know that the glaciers are retreating; we can see this happening right now in Glacier National Park. We could see for ourselves the prolonged droughts. We knew only too well about the increased frequency and intensity of wildfires. We had been seeing almost every year the early and rapid melting of mountain snowpacks.

But we could only see so much in our local area. The report Dr. Running had worked on described a wide variety of evidence from all over the world, all illustrating that changes are afoot in the climate:

- the concentration of warm weather worldwide in recent years, continuing a trend that began in the 1950s;

- the concentration of those warmer temperatures in the Northern Hemisphere, where most of the greenhouse gas pollution takes place;

- the increasing areas of the world affected by drought;

- increasing global ocean temperatures (the oceans have taken in far more heat than the atmosphere);

- increasing temperatures at different levels of the atmosphere;

- decreasing glaciers, polar ice caps, and Arctic sea ice and corresponding increase in the number of glacial lakes;

- decreasing areas of seasonally frozen ground, and the instability of permafrost areas;

- decreasing frequency of cold days and cold nights, and increasing frequency of hot days and warm nights;

- increasing intensity of storms;

- increasing flooding;

- earlier spring runoff;

- earlier timing of other events that happen in spring (e.g., bird migrations and nesting, fish migrations, the opening of leaves);

- changes in the ranges of land animals and plants, moving toward higher elevations or toward the poles;

- changes in the range of freshwater algae, plankton, and fish;

- warming of lakes and rivers;

- warming of soils;

- rising sea level;

- increased acidity in the ocean;

- the strong likelihood that the last half of the 20th century was the warmest 50-year period in at least 500 years and likely the warmest in at least 1,300 years.

The IPCC's 2007 report included 29,000 series of observational data, and 89% of that data was consistent with an expected response to warming.[3] The next report in 2014 included more observations and more data, collected from onsite reporting stations, ships, satellites, and remote sensors in soils and floating on the oceans.[4]

Is climate change a scientific certainty? Of course not. The IPCC report addresses the question of uncertainty, and acknowledges that some of their report's evidence was more certain than other evidence, and the report uses terms to clarify the level of certainty or uncertainty on various evidence.

You and I deal with uncertainty every day. We especially deal with it when we're raising kids. "What are the odds my little girl will be kidnapped?" I would ask myself when my daughter was young. I knew from real-world statistics that the odds were extraordinarily slim. But did that stop me from exercising caution every single day? Did that stop me from teaching her to stay away from strangers?

How many threats to our children are out there? If you are a parent, your world is full of threats that are unlikely, but nevertheless worth responding to. You know how much is at stake and, no matter how unlikely the threat is, you take precautions to make sure your kids are safe. You take action even though the threat is uncertain or even remote. We all do it every day. We don't ignore the real-world facts, but we use a reasonable amount of care to avoid an outcome that could be disastrous.

We make sure our children buckle their seat belts.

Wheat farmer Wade Sikorski compares the warming climate to walking on an ice-covered lake in the early spring. There's already an area where the water is open, but changes in the thickness of the ice are gradual. Still, the ice is getting thinner as you approach the open water. "Even though chances are your next step won't be the one where the ice fails, at some point, you are going to take a step that does it."[5]

The American Association for the Advancement of Science (AAAS) employed another analogy to illustrate why it's so hard to state with absolute certainty whether any particular weather event was caused by climate change. During the steroid era in Major League Baseball, home runs were more frequent and were longer. The effect of steroids on hitting couldn't be denied, but it would have been impossible to point to any single home run and state that it was the result of steroids.

"Greenhouse gases have supercharged the climate just as steroids supercharged hitting in Major League Baseball."[6]

We're all well aware that a furious campaign has been going on for several years to discredit the science behind the IPCC's reports, as well as similar reports by other scientists and scientific organizations. Much of that campaign has been underwritten by the oil, gas, and coal industries, and includes a whole lot of junk science. Those guys have a lot to lose if America makes a serious transition away from fossil fuels.

Exxon is best known for underwriting much of this campaign. It's ironic because it was Exxon that, more than any other oil company, arrived at an early understanding of climate change. Back in 1977, a senior Exxon scientist told the company's Management Committee that "there is a general scientific agreement that the most likely manner in which mankind is influencing the global climate is through carbon dioxide release from the burning of fossil fuels." The company funded climate research for several years after that, but refrained from sharing that research with stockholders. By the late 1980s, Exxon had shifted from funding climate research to funding organizations and lobbying aimed at sowing doubt about the science that its own researchers had documented.[7]

And then there are those who denounce the science behind climate change because they just don't like environmentalists, and they see climate change science as supporting what a lot of environmentalists have been saying for many years.

But the evidence continues to pile up. NASA and the National Oceanic and Atmospheric Administration released a joint report that 2010 tied with 2005 as the hottest year on record (since record-keeping began in 1880). It was also the wettest year on record, which climate science also predicts, since the warmer atmosphere can hold more water vapor. We have all heard more news reports about more intense storms in recent years. Heavy rainfall events of more than six inches have increased 27% since 1970.[8] 16 of the 18 warmest years on record have taken place since 1998. As I write this in 2016, the warmest year ever recorded was 2015, according to the National Oceanic and Atmospheric Administration.[9]

Okay, it's getting warmer, some people say, but humans didn't cause it. Therefore, there's nothing we can do about it.

A lot of people want to believe that, but scientific evidence keeps mounting.

In 2010, the National Academy of Sciences announced a new series of reports by the National Research Council. The NAS press release said, "multiple lines of evidence support scientific understanding of climate change. The core phenomenon, scientific questions, and hypotheses have been examined thoroughly and have stood firm in the face of serious debate and careful examination of alternative explanations." Quoting directly from the report, the release said,

Climate change is occurring, is caused largely by human activities, and poses significant risks for – and in many cases is already affecting – a broad range of human and natural systems.[10]

From the American Meteorological Society:

...there is adequate evidence from observations and interpretations of climate simulations to conclude that the atmosphere, ocean, and land surface are warming; that humans have significantly contributed to this change; and that further climate change will continue to have important impacts on human societies, on economies, on ecosystems, and on wildlife through the 21st century and beyond.[11]

From the National Geographic Society:

Scientists have spent decades figuring out what is causing global warming. They've looked at the natural cycles and events that are known to influence climate. But the amount and pattern of warming that's been measured can't be explained by these factors alone. The only way to explain the pattern is to include the effect of greenhouse gases (GHGs) emitted by humans.[12]

From NASA:

...human-caused warming is resulting in a broad range of impacts across the globe.[13]

From the American Geophysical Union:

The Earth's climate is now clearly out of balance and is warming. Many components of the climate system—including the temperatures of the atmosphere, land and ocean, the extent of sea ice and mountain glaciers, the sea level, the distribution of precipitation, and the length of seasons—are now changing at rates and in patterns that are not natural and are best explained by the increased atmospheric abundances of greenhouse gases and aerosols generated by human activity during the 20th century.[14]

From the American Association for the Advancement of Science:

Based on well-established evidence, about 97% of climate scientists have concluded that human-caused climate change is happening. This agreement is documented not just by a single study, but by a converging stream of evidence over the past two decades from surveys of scientists, content analyses of peer-reviewed studies, and public statements issued by virtually every membership organization of experts in this field.[15]

So we have a lot of evidence, but we still have some uncertainty. How much certainty do we need to have before we act? If we wait until we have absolute certainty, will we have waited too long?

Yes.

General Gordon R. Sullivan, former Chief of Staff of the U.S. Army, said "We never have 100% certainty. If you wait until you have 100% certainty, something bad is going to happen on the battlefield. That's something we know."[16]

We also need to remember that carbon dioxide stays in the atmosphere for a long time once we put it there. All the CO_2 we've already put into the atmosphere will be affecting the weather and the world our children and grandchildren live with. The more we add to what we've already done, the greater the effects will be. Those effects could make the world a much more difficult and dangerous place for the Americans who come after us.

Even when we decide to move forward, there are plenty of things we just can't know at this time. How much will new energy technologies cost? How will those costs change as the technologies become more widely used? Can the United States exercise leadership in new energy technologies? Or will we leave it to the Chinese? Will Americans change their personal ways of using energy? If we burn less fossil fuel, what will be the financial benefits of reducing what we have to spend on health care for ailments related to air pollution?

Some say we can't afford to transition away from fossil fuels. But can we afford not to? It's important to remember that there is a cost to inaction, a substantial cost.

We have long bought much of our oil from foreign governments and, as the late energy expert Randy Udall used to say, some of those governments "aren't exactly Denver Broncos fans." The oil boom in North Dakota (and somewhat in Montana) changed that for now. But, as a nation, we burn through eighteen to twenty million barrels every day. Eighteen to twenty million barrels today. Eighteen to twenty million barrels tomorrow. Eighteen to twenty million barrels next Sunday. Do we really think we will never run out?

Energy is going to cost more in the years to come, whether or not we begin the transition to renewables. As oil and other fossil fuels become scarcer in the world, they'll become more expensive. By building vehicles that get better fuel economy, we postponed real shortages in oil, and bought ourselves a hedge against dramatic increases that might have otherwise happened by now. Over the long term, though, extracting oil and other fossil fuels will become harder, using more extreme methods, that are not only more expensive, but also more damaging to our land and water and air.

And all that coal we have in this country? It's the dirtiest fuel we use. Mining it devastates our land, pollutes our water, and damages our aquifers. Burning it taxes our lungs, especially among people who already suffer from diseases like asthma. The ash left over from burning coal is full of toxic heavy metals, and some of that toxic ash gets into the air we breathe and the water we drink.

We pay a high price for the fossil fuels we burn, but much of that price is hidden and externalized. Still, we pay that price, whether it shows up on our electricity bills, or our medical bills, or the taxes we pay so our government can clean up the messes left behind by coal mining. In the future, we may pay that price through increased human misery in the world – more famines, floods, disease – or in sending our sons and daughters to fight in new wars.

So how do we start dealing with a serious threat to our way of life and that of our children, even if the worst effects of that threat won't come around for decades? Thomas Friedman at the *New York Times* said, "I buy insurance. That is what taking climate change seriously is all about."[17]

Friedman recounted former Vice President Dick Cheney's response to concerns that a scientist from Pakistan was offering nuclear weapons technology to Al Qaeda. Cheney said, "If there's a 1% chance that Pakistani scientists are helping Al Qaeda build or develop a nuclear weapon, we have to treat it as a certainty in terms of our response."

Climate change is a "high-impact event." There is scientific uncertainty about the nature of its impacts, and the severity, and the timing. But the effect will be a lot more than just slightly warmer weather. It will affect whether we have enough water, whether we can grow enough food, whether our grandchildren live in a world full of desperate people.

For Friedman, "buying insurance" means preventing the worst impacts of climate change by making the transition to an economy that runs on clean energy. He speculated on what would be the result of taking solid action <u>even if</u> climate change forecasts turn out to be wrong, and he listed these five results:

1. During the transition, energy prices would be higher.

2. We would become less dependent on foreign oil dictators.

3. Our trade deficit would improve.

4. The dollar would strengthen.

5. The air we breathe would be cleaner.

"In short," said Friedman, "as a country, we would be stronger, more innovative and more energy independent."

But we probably shouldn't wait too long to act.

The carbon we put into the atmosphere during the Eisenhower administration is still there. We have been loading more and more carbon into the atmosphere, year after year, and it is still accumulating. Even if we reduce our carbon pollution dramatically – tomorrow – the pollution we generate will be added to what's already up there. Things will get worse before they get better. (When I say "worse," I mean impairing our ability to grow food, increased damage from extreme weather events, water shortages, insect outbreaks, dangerous political instability, and much more.)

The 2014 AAAS report underscored "two inescapable facts: first, the effects of _any_ additional CO_2 emissions will last for centuries; second, there is a risk of abrupt, unpredictable and potentially irreversible changes in the earth's climate system with massively disruptive impacts."[18]

But we probably aren't going to reduce our carbon pollution tomorrow. We have yet to really make a serious start. What are we Americans afraid of? Is it really that intimidating for us to step forward into forms of energy that don't foul our air and water, and that won't run out?

Some people and some organized campaigns against renewable energy claim renewables are too expensive. It's a newer technology and doesn't externalize so many of its costs as fossil fuels do. But if the coal industry had to account fully for its damage to people's health, and its damage to land and water and the air, the entire industry would probably have been abandoned years ago. It keeps its price low by making people sick, tearing up aquifers, polluting rivers and our atmosphere, and taking good agricultural land out of production.

That's not to mention the damage to earth's climate.

The AAAS reminds us that "the longer we wait to respond, the more the risks of climate change will increase. Conversely, the sooner we take action, the more options we will have to reduce risk and limit the human and economic cost of climate change."[19]

Meanwhile, some people still say that climate change is a hoax. Is it? Well, a hoax is something intended to defraud or deceive someone else. Is the world's scientific community intentionally trying to deceive everyone on the planet? If so, why? What would the world's scientists gain from such a deception? Some people say that scientists get more research grants when they produce evidence of climate change. If so, why would governments and scientific institutions want to produce a false scenario of what is happening to our planet? Maybe I'm just not very bright, but I don't see a hoax here. I don't even see a reason to have a hoax.

OK, but perhaps all these scientists are simply wrong. That's what MIT professor Kerry Emanuel thought in the late 1980s. Professor Emanuel teaches atmospheric sciences and was long skeptical about claims that the earth's climate is changing. But as the evidence accumulated, including evidence from his own research, he saw a link between our emissions of greenhouse gases and the change in the earth's climate. "Scientists are being asked to prove beyond any reasonable doubt that there is an imminent danger before we as a society do anything," Emanuel said. "The parallel to that is saying 'You won't buy property insurance unless I can prove to you that your house will catch on fire right now.'"[20]

Another skeptic of climate change, Richard Muller of the University of California at Berkeley, spent two years studying data on the earth's temperatures. He had questioned whether the earth was really warming, but his study published in 2011debunked two key criticisms that climate skeptics had espoused – that data from some weather stations is unreliable and that "heat islands" around cities had skewed the overall results of climate studies. His study came to the same conclusions as previous studies by NASA and the National Oceanic and Atmospheric Administration, and he said, "we have confidence that the temperature rise that had previously been reported had been done without bias."[21]

Nearly all of the world's scientists in the field think climate change is real and the link to mankind's carbon emissions is real. But even if I thought it was a mistake, I know that the consequences of climate change – if it really affects what happens to our long-term weather – could be disastrous. I'd weigh the costs and the benefits of doing something versus doing nothing.

I would ask myself, is America, which used to be known for innovation and ingenuity, so unable to adapt that our economy can't make the transition? I don't think so. I have faith in our capacity to make the most of renewable sources of energy, to use energy more efficiently, and to ensure that our children and their children have a fair chance in this world.

But it won't happen by itself.

CHAPTER FORTY-ONE

It's Not Just an Environmental Problem

The National Intelligence Council... concluded back in 2008 that climate change would contribute to worldwide problems including poverty, environmental degradation, and the weakening of national governments.

....

Environmental journalist David Roberts observed that climate change is not an environmental challenge... it's much bigger than that.[1] It's far more complex than typical environmental issues, and the stakes are far higher. Responding to it will require changes in our culture and in the way we do things. It's about living lives that are free and prosperous, which will mean freeing ourselves of the increasing load of carbon in our atmosphere and the increasing tendency of politicians to go along with whoever makes the biggest campaign contributions.

The National Intelligence Council, which does intelligence analysis for the U.S. government, concluded back in 2008 that climate change would contribute to worldwide problems including poverty, environmental degradation, and the weakening of national governments. Other reports, such as the Quadrennial Defense Review reach similar conclusions.[2]

In 2014, the Department of Defense issued a Climate Change Adaptation Roadmap which identified four types of challenges that climate changes poses for the U.S. military:

- Planning for land, air, and sea operations and instability in other nations
- Training and testing (including fires and climate impacts to training sites)
- The built and natural infrastructure (energy, drinking water, flooding, diseases, etc.)
- Difficulties in acquiring, delivering, and stockpiling needed supplies and materials.[3]

The military has substantial concerns over the impacts of climate change to our national security, and has initiated on-the-ground measures – from green buildings to backpack solar cells – to reduce our soldiers' burden of dependence on fossil fuels. General Gordon R. Sullivan's remark about the cost of waiting until you have 100% certainty is important to keep in mind.

Here are some conclusions of the study coordinated by Gen. Sullivan and other high-ranking military leaders.[4] They found that:

- Projected climate change poses a serious threat to America's national security;

- Climate change acts as a threat multiplier for instability in some of the most volatile regions of the world;

- Projected climate change will add to tensions even in stable regions of the world;

- Climate change, national security, and energy dependence are a related set of global challenges.

Retired Navy Rear Admiral David Titley added that, "Climate change isn't just an environmental issue; it's a technology, water, food, energy, population issue. None of this happens in a vacuum."[5]

Retired Vice Admiral Dennis McGinn said that "Economic prosperity, our environment and national security are inextricably linked and require comprehensive solutions. Building a clean energy economy addresses three major challenges at once."[6]

Clean Coal

They fought against the requirements for reclamation. They fought against having to replace water resources they destroy. They fought against rights for landowners. They even fought against decent working conditions for their own employees.

. . . .

M ost of the time these past several years, whenever I hear a politician from either major political party refer to coal, he or she always says "clean coal." To a politician in a coal state, coal means tax money and high-paying jobs. To get that money into state coffers, to protect those high-paying jobs, he will convince himself that coal mining and coal burning are benign to the land and air and water and people... he will convince himself that coal is "clean."

As a resident of a coal state, I know that more coal mines will be started up, more aquifers damaged and more land ruined in the years to come. I know that more farms and ranches will be cut apart by coal infrastructure projects. And I know that most of it won't contribute even a little bit to America's energy independence because most of that new coal being mined will be shipped to Asia and burned there. That's the hope of the declining coal industry, anyway, to save itself by exporting American coal to Asia. If it succeeds, this plan will dedicate even more rail capacity to coal, aggravating the yearly difficulties American farmers face in getting their harvests to market by rail.[1]

I know that state and national politicians (at least the ones we have these days) will accommodate that industry whenever they can – by finding ways to subsidize the industry, by relaxing standards for how land and water and air can be treated, by keeping citizens the hell out of the process.

Here's just one example of subsidizing the coal industry – the 2015 Wyoming legislature enacted a billion-dollar bonding authority to help fund coal projects outside the state. (That's a billion dollars in a state with fewer than 600,000 residents.) This billion-dollar subsidy was aimed in particular at helping to build a new coal export terminal on the West Coast, which would drive speculative new coal mining to feed speculative markets in Asia.

I know that every dollar we invest in coal development is a dollar that will never be invested in developing the sun and wind and other renewable energy that our nation's long-term future depends on.

(Do you think the Wyoming legislature would ever consider a billion-dollar subsidy to the solar industry?)

Southeast Montana, along with northeast Wyoming, sits atop the Powder River Basin, a large formation of sub-bituminous coal that's comparatively low in sulfur and comparatively close to the surface. The Montana coal in the northern Powder River Basin tends to be higher in sodium; it has to be treated differently when it's burned in power plants because sodium can cause a buildup of melted ash deposits on the inside of the boiler, making it run less efficiently.

Montana has numerous other coal formations, some of which have been mined, and some just speculated upon.

Coal had been mined in southeast Montana for many years, but industrial-scale strip mining – the opening of wide gashes in the earth to fuel coal-fired power plants – came to the Powder River Basin in the 1970s. High oil prices pushed this and other Western coal development, along with a desire to find coal that spewed less sulfur into the air. A 1971 publication called the *North Central Power Study* – a collaboration between the U.S. Bureau of Reclamation and 35 utility companies – called for development of coal strip mines at 42 sites in five states, each site with a coal-fired power plant, most of them massive. Twenty-one of those strip mines and accompanying mine-mouth power plants would be in Montana.

A later study estimated that, by 1980, the need for cooling water for all these plants would amount to 855,000 acre-feet annually. Additional facilities projected to manufacture chemicals and synthetic gas would increase the water consumption to 2.6 million acre-feet per year. Most of that water would come from the Yellowstone River – the longest free-flowing river in our nation. In dry years, the flow of the Yellowstone would be nearly dried up.

Coal development, of course, means infrastructure – roads, reservoirs, railroads, and power lines would spread the impact of coal facilities to people and lands far away. Add in power plants and you have smoke, a lot of smoke. If it's a newer plant which has to "scrub" the smoke to clean out some of the worst pollutants, then you have thousands of tons of ash to deal with. That ash that contains toxic materials which were in the coal and therefore in the smoke.

Thousands of people would move into the sparsely populated region where cattle ranching is the foundation of local economies. Cow towns would have to learn to deal with the high crime, social upset, and high infrastructure costs of a boom-bust economy.

The study forecast tens of thousands of square miles of mined land. Hundreds of thousands of tons of air pollution – particulates, sulfur dioxide, heavy metals – would be spewed into the air every year, air breathed by area residents, their livestock, and all other living things.[2]

Colstrip rancher Wally McRae said simply, "Mining and cows don't mix."[3]

Wyoming rancher L.J. Turner was coming to speak at a Northern Plains annual meeting, and I asked him for a brief biography. This is part of what he told me:

I was raised on the family ranch, married the neighborhood school teacher who taught in a one-room school, raised four wonderful children and have about given up on saving the world, but would like Peabody Coal to leave us the hell alone so that we can save a small part of Wyoming for our family.[4]

The late Anne Charter quoted in her book what her husband Boyd told her about a conversation with a coal executive who wanted to mine their ranch in the 1970s:

They came to buy my ranch. But I told them, you'll always be four dollars and sixty cents short of being able to buy me out. This Del Adams (coal company executive) *walked out that door, he got ahold of the doorknob and he said, "You get as hard-boiled as you want to, but in the long run, we're going to get you. We are bigger than you and we can last longer." Those were his very words: "We're going to get you."*[5]

Many factors – physical, political, economic – intervened and coal was never developed on the scale that had been anticipated. Still, large coal mines and power plants were opened in the region. While driving on Interstate 94 across eastern Montana one day, in the clear sky I could see a ribbon of black smoke coming from the south – from the Colstrip area – crossing high above the highway, and then bending slightly to the northeast. Most days, the visible smoke disperses more readily. But all the particulates and other pollutants are still in the air, even if we can't easily see them.

When you live above coal or other minerals, and someone else owns the minerals beneath your land, there's usually nothing you can do to prevent your land from being turned into a strip mine. The one exception to that is found in the Surface Mining Control and Reclamation Act, the 1977 federal law that governs strip mining. Northern Plains and many other citizen groups worked together to pass a strip mine law in the 1970s, and they fought for a provision that would give surface landowners the right to say "no" to strip mining on their land. Most rural landowners tend to be fairly accommodating to mines and other projects, or they are desperate enough financially that their cooperation can be purchased, so it isn't often that a landowner says "no." Still, they should have that right.

In eastern Montana, well over half the coal is owned by the federal government. Additional coal is owned by railroads or their subsidiaries, dating back to when the Northern Pacific Railway Company received 50 square miles of land from the federal government for every mile of track they constructed across the Northwest (about 40 million acres of land). Still other coal is owned by the state, Indian tribes, and private parties. On any piece of land in eastern Montana, the odds are poor that the landowner owns the minerals beneath his property.

Steve Charter learned in 2011 that a portion of his ranch would likely be leased to a coal company. The word "lease" describes the right to mine. In this case, the mining would use the "longwall" process, a kind of underground mining in which machines bore through the coal seam, leaving behind an empty space that eventually collapses beneath the weight of the earth above. On the land surface, this means deep fissures appear after coal is removed hundreds of feet underground, and some of them may never heal. This is already happening on Ellen Pfister's place a few miles away from the Charter ranch. The elevation of Dunn Mountain, the highest point in the area, was found to be seven feet shorter in 2012 than it was in 2011. How all this subsidence will affect the area's hydrology, and the precious springs that ranchers and wildlife depend on, is still unknown.

Like Ellen before him, Steve is powerless to prevent the coal beneath his land from being leased to the coal company. He and his neighbors asked the Bureau of Land Management to add stipulations to the lease that might minimize the damage. But the federal coal leasing program is not designed to protect a landowner's rights; it's designed to lease a coal company the right to mine coal.

You have probably read or heard about mountaintop removal mining in Appalachia, and I won't write about it here, except for this – like other kinds of coal mining, it demonstrates the fact that coal mining in all its forms depends on creating costs that other people pay. There are the people whose land is mined; the people whose water or perhaps whose entire watershed is ruined; the people whose family cemeteries are desecrated; the people whose property is condemned to make room for mining and infrastructure projects. Oh, and we can't forget the people whose very act of breathing is threatened by the smoke that comes out of the power plant smokestacks – a lot of those people die young because of that smoke. And there are the people whose wells are contaminated or property damaged by gradual or sudden leaks of coal ash.

Water and air and land aren't the only things polluted by coal mining. The political process itself becomes polluted when citizens are shut out of the public decision-making process and when government agencies and politicians maneuver to accommodate the desires of coal companies rather than protect the interests of the public.

Kentucky's Wendell Berry reminds us – even though the politicians forget it most of the time – that "the most vicious fantasy of all is the endlessly publicized notion that the net profit of the coal companies somehow represents the net profit of the whole society."[6]

Janet Keating of the Ohio Valley Environmental Coalition in West Virginia simply observes, "If coal mining has been so good for Appalachia, then why are we so poor?"[7]

You and I don't share their profits. But you and I pay the hidden costs.

"Coal is cheap!" you and I are told repeatedly by politicians and by people and companies whose finances are entangled with coal. And, of course, by the coal companies themselves.

But I doubt if they tell that to the families of the thousands of Americans who die prematurely due to the pollution from coal-burning. The National Academy of Sciences estimated that 20,000 Americans die young because of burning fossil fuels.[8] The NAS studied only premature deaths, and did not look at other costs of coal. Some studies have arrived at higher fatality estimates, some lower.

A study conducted for the air quality organization, Clean Air Task Force, came up with a somewhat lower figure, but observed that, in six years, the figure had been cut substantially as federal clean air regulations forced a reduction in power plant pollution. Those clean air regulations are saving lives, but they are fought at every turn by coal companies, power plant operators, and the many politicians who see their job as making life easier for coal development, no matter what the cost may be in human lives and damage to our natural resources.

For example, Abt Associates' estimate of 13,200 deaths from fine particle pollution in 2010 compares to an estimate of nearly 24,000 deaths per year from existing plants in the 2004 study. Similar public health gains are evident in the estimated incidence of other adverse impacts including hospital admissions (9,700 in 2010 compared to 21,850 in 2004) and heart attacks (20,400 in 2010 compared to 38,200 in 2004).[9]

A study by the Harvard Medical School's Center for Health and the Global Environment took a broader look at the costs of coal, and came up with a range of estimates that would add considerably to your electricity bill (if they were actually accounted for, like they would be in a real free-market economy).[10]

That Harvard study looked at the dollar costs of such factors as coal's impacts on public health in mining regions, air pollution, costs associated with changes to the climate, and pollution by heavy metals and carcinogens (effects on <u>people only, not plants and animals</u>).

What does coal do to people's health? The effects include:

- low birth weight (which can lead to more ailments in adulthood);
- stunted lung development;
- developmental delays in infants (which can lead to a lifelong loss of intelligence);
- kidney disease;
- cardiovascular disease;
- stroke;
- heart disease;
- lung cancer;
- bronchitis;
- chronic obstructive pulmonary disease (COPD);
- asthma (developing asthma, making asthma worse).[11]

Consider the economic costs of these health impacts to families. Consider the costs to families that can never be measured in dollars.

"Simply tallying public health impacts," reported the *New York Times*, "the study found that coal costs the United States economy $140 billion to $242 billion a year."[12]

After adding in other financial impacts from coal, the costs of coal identified in the study came in at a range of $175 billion to $523 billion per year. This is real money. If accounted for on your electric bill, it would increase the rate you pay anywhere from 75% to more than 220%. But these costs are not on your electric bill; you and I and every other American pay them in other ways. These costs are externalized – or socialized – onto everyone, whether or not they buy electricity from a coal-fired power plant. These costs are externalized, most of all, on the 13,000-20,000 Americans per year who die prematurely.

Coal is not clean; nor is it cheap.

And even this Harvard Medical School study came with a long list of costs it did not attempt to quantify:

- impacts of toxic chemicals and heavy metals on plants and animals and the environments where they live;
- certain "ill-health endpoints (morbidity)" aside from deaths related to burning coal;
- direct hazards posed by sludge, slurry, and coal ash impoundments;
- damage to fresh and coastal sea water;
- acid rain and acid mine drainage;
- many long-term impacts on the physical and mental health of those living in coal-field regions and nearby mountaintop removal mining sites;
- health impacts and climate change due to increased tropospheric ozone formation; and
- full assessment of impacts due to an increasingly unstable climate.[13]

Because the ash created from burning coal contains heavy metals, we try to keep it out of the air we breathe and the water we drink. The coal ash (or "fly ash") ponds at Colstrip, Montana, have been leaking since the 1970s, and have ruined several dozen domestic wells that we know of.

Coal ash isn't just dirt. It contains toxic chemicals and heavy metals that are known to cause cancer, birth defects, reproductive disorders, kidney disease, neurological damage, and other effects on people's health.

In December 2008, the wall of a sludge pond failed at a Tennessee Valley Authority power plant near Harriman, Tennessee. The spill released 5.4 million cubic yards of coal ash (525 million gallons) into a drainage where it destroyed several homes and damaged dozens more on its way to the Emory River. The sludge buried approximately 300 acres, six feet deep in some places, covering a road and railroad tracks. It deposited arsenic, lead, chromium, manganese, thallium, and barium onto land and into water.[14]

Coal produces pollution that's way out of proportion to the energy it produces (about half-again as much as conventional oil and twice that of natural gas).

While producing 50% of U.S. electricity (in 2005), coal burning produced over 80% of the carbon dioxide. And that doesn't include the CO_2 produced by methane that escapes from coal mines, nor does it include the CO_2 produced by transporting the coal. It doesn't include all the other chemicals that coal mining, processing, transporting, and burning puts into the air we breathe – mercury (about 67 tons in the U.S. in 2009)[15], along with lead, arsenic, chromium, beryllium, sulfur dioxide, and other toxins and carcinogens.

Older coal-fired plants are the worst. A study published by the Harvard School of Public Health in 2000 found that pollution from two older power plants in the Northeast were linked *annually* to approximately 70 deaths, tens of thousands of asthma attacks, and hundreds of thousands of upper respiratory illnesses.[16]

Without environmental laws and standards, all the coal-fired power plants in the U.S. would be just as dirty as those two.

All these hidden costs of coal – the coal ash, the air pollution that kills thousands of people, the heavy metal pollution, the acid rain, the changes to our climate – none of these costs reflect what would happen to Steve Charter's ranch, Ellen Pfister's ranch, Wally McRae's ranch, Mark Fix's ranch, and multitudes of other people's property that has been (or could be) ruined or devalued by coal mining activity.

And we should remember the costs to American taxpayers in billions of dollars annually through various public subsidies to the coal industry. These include special tax deductions, access to taxpayer-subsidized financing, access to publicly owned coal at bargain-basement lease prices, and other forms of subsidies provided by our tax dollars. More subsidies are cranked out by the legislatures of individual states.

The coal industry and its political allies have made sure these costs are not accounted for in the price of this product. Real people pay these costs – whether a rancher in Montana or a child with asthma in Ohio. But the coal companies still keep telling us how cheap it is to stay dependent on this 19th century fuel.

Today, a coal company operating in Montana might proudly point out the land they've reclaimed. And, yes, it's better than it would have been 40 years ago.

But they didn't start reclaiming mined land just because they're good guys. They started reclaiming mined land only because they were forced to by the enactment of laws like the Surface Mining Control and Reclamation Act. And we need to remember that coal companies fought tooth and nail against the passage of that law. They fought against the requirements for reclamation. They fought against having to replace water resources they destroy. They fought against rights for landowners. They even fought against decent working conditions for their own employees.

And coal companies in Appalachia – some of the same companies operating in the Powder River Basin – have managed to evade responsibility for poisoning watersheds, for permanently burying watersheds, for cutting the tops off mountains – all with no possibility and no intention of reclaiming anything. Some, like Massey Energy, are outright criminals by even the most lenient standard – faking safety reports and keeping employees in constant danger by shortcutting safety rules. This criminal behavior killed 29 employees in 2010, and Massey attempted to sidetrack the investigation. [17]

Even in the West, coal mine reclamation is more of a myth than most people realize. While soil is backfilled, graded, and seeded, full reclamation is out of reach at most Montana mines because of the damage to ground water. A re-seeded field may look pretty good, but restoring damaged water resources underground is not an easy fix. In Montana, less than one percent of the coal mined land has been fully reclaimed.[18]

As rancher Wally McRae reminded me, "you can't see the hydrology." That's why the strip mines have been able to operate for decades without reclaiming the hydrologic balance as the Montana law requires. Their choice has been to forego payment of their bond rather than repair their damage.

The U.S. Office of Surface Mining, Reclamation and Enforcement likes to report that reclamation at Western coal mines looks good because this makes the agency look good. OSMRE likes to emphasize how many acres have been graded and seeded. But when it comes to the hydrology that the land's productivity depends on, reclamation largely isn't happening. OSMRE isn't making it happen, and it's not going to happen by itself.

I attended a public meeting a few years ago that was also attended by several dozen workers from our local (and very dirty) coal-fired power plant. The most outspoken of them maintained that, since coal jobs paid well (he was pulling down more than $100,000 a year), we should do everything we can to encourage more coal mining, not less. What it all amounted to was this: we should damage more land and water because he gets paid more than $100,000 a year. We should keep killing 20,000 Americans a year because he gets paid more than $100,000 a year. We should stay away from renewable energy – after all, it would result in less coal mining – because he gets paid more than $100,000 a year.

Industries change. Whole sectors of our economy change.

When people like the $100,000-a-year man say, "We shouldn't change anything, our industry should just stay like it is now," they're asking for something that has never been part of American life. They're speaking in the tradition of the whaling industry and of Southern plantation owners before the Civil War.

They are saying, "We don't want energy-efficient buildings because that would mean less coal mining. We don't want energy-efficient lighting because that would mean less coal mining."

It's a certainty that coal will be mined in the United States for the rest of my lifetime. The industry has immense economic power and political clout, and continues to supply almost 40% of our nation's electricity. Coal companies will continue to destroy surface and ground waters, continue to decimate and poison landscapes, and continue to kill Americans.

Much as they portray themselves as good citizens and good neighbors, coal companies, at their very best, do only what they are forced to do. They shove as many costs as they can onto the rest of us. Coal is not "clean," and it is not cheap. Using coal costs Americans more than we can imagine. It is not good for our country. And the longer we use it, the longer we delay true energy independence for our nation.

CHAPTER FORTY-THREE

It Didn't Happen by Itself

We Americans are capable of being a practical people. We know, or should know, that preventing a problem is better (and usually cheaper) than trying to recover from a problem. And we know that most problems don't solve themselves.

....

The Dust Bowl of the 1930s displaced millions of Americans and was an environmental disaster. After a drought hit the Great Plains, topsoil was blown away, and farming became impossible. The Great Plains states recovered after the federal government implemented many strategies – soil conservation, tree planting, and education in adapting farming practices to the region. Additional government programs helped the human population make it through the crisis and helped that region stabilize economically. Recovering from the Dust Bowl didn't happen by itself. We Americans took action.

Commercial hunting drove North America's largest land animal – the American Bison – to the very edge of extinction. Our nation may well have lost this magnificent animal if not for a handful of ranchers who stepped in and took action – people like Scotty Philip and Fred Dupree in South Dakota, Charles Allard and Michel Pablo in Montana, and Molly and Charles Goodnight in Texas. The recovery of the American Bison – finally recognized by Congress in 2016 as an important symbol of our nation – didn't happen by itself. Americans – just a few of them in this case – took action to save this splendid and rugged beast.

People who lived in the Love Canal neighborhood of Niagara Falls, New York, suffered miscarriages, birth defects, and other assaults on their health because of a leaking chemical dump buried in their neighborhood. Determined residents and a persistent local reporter discovered the truth. Those residents found remedy because Congress took action to help them relocate and to establish the polluter's financial responsibility. Lives were saved and people were helped. It didn't happen by itself, though.

A pollution "smog" in Donora, Pennsylvania, killed 20 people (plus nearly 800 animals) and sickened thousands more residents in October 1948. The fact that we don't see that kind of event anymore in this country is not mere coincidence, and it didn't happen by itself. Laws were passed – starting with the Air Pollution Control Act in 1955 (America's first clean air law) and the first Clean Air Act in 1963 – to protect air quality (and therefore protect public health).

The Cuyahoga River in Cleveland doesn't catch fire anymore, nor do other American rivers. The Cuyahoga still faces plenty of threats to its health, but 1969 was the last time it ever caught fire. That improvement didn't happen by itself. American cities and states passed laws to clean up rivers, the Clean Water Act was passed, the EPA was organized.

I picked up a copy of the *Statistical Abstract of the United States* (2010 edition) at the public library a while back. Table 362 (Selected Air Pollutant Emissions: 1970 to 2007) showed that certain kinds of air pollution are reduced today from their levels in 1970. Table 362 listed carbon monoxide, nitrogen oxide, sulfur dioxide, volatile organic compounds, and certain classes of particulate matter. Discharges of those pollutants in the United States are all reduced from 1970 levels (or 1990 in the case of some particulates). In many respects (though not all), our kids are breathing better air now than then. This did not happen by itself.

Burning coal kills thousands of people every year in America. As I mentioned earlier, the Clean Air Task Force study estimates that 13,000 Americans are killed annually by fine particulate pollution from coal-fired power plants in our country. This is a substantial improvement from the 20,000 annual deaths their study estimated just a few years earlier. But this improvement didn't happen by itself. It happened because we adopted regulations requiring scrubbers to be installed on smokestacks at power plants.[1]

To the extent that certain pollution problems – toxic neighborhoods, burning rivers, and people dying from breathing the air – don't occur as often as they used to… this didn't happen by itself. Neither did saving the bald eagle by getting rid of DDT, or saving people's lives by getting rid of lead in gasoline.

That's because we Americans have collectively taken action to identify the problems, get an idea of how bad those problems are, establish who is responsible, clean up the pollution, and set a course to prevent the problems from recurring.

But we have a knack for coming up with new problems to solve – new chemicals, new technologies, new kinds of waste, new demands on our land and water.

We Americans are capable of being a practical people. We know, or should know, that preventing a problem is better (and usually cheaper) than trying to recover from a problem. And we know that most problems don't solve themselves.

Yet I've heard some people, even some candidates for the White House, call for getting rid of the very laws that have kept these disasters from revisiting our nation. These are people who believe that problems will solve themselves, that we can deal with our problems by doing nothing.

That's not how America became a great nation.

CHAPTER FORTY-FOUR

Taking Precaution

To this day, you still can't look at one person's health problems and state with certainty that they were caused by cigarette smoke, even if the person was a two-pack-a-day smoker like my dad.

....

We teach our children to take reasonable precautions in life. We were taught as children – as our parents and their parents were taught – that you should "look before you leap," and that "an ounce of prevention is worth a pound of cure."

We teach our children, "better safe than sorry." We teach them this about a wide variety of subjects, from driving a car, to sex, to financial transactions.

A version of that life lesson is found in the "Precautionary Principle."

I've come across various iterations of the Precautionary Principle, but its three components fit neatly into one sentence:

When we have (1) a reasonable suspicion that harm will befall someone, (2) we have a duty to take action to prevent harm, (3) even if the science about cause and effect is not yet certain.

When we find ourselves in such a situation, we should:

1. Consider all reasonable alternatives;

2. Place the burden of assuring safety onto the party whose activities raised the suspicion of harm in the first place;

3. Fully involve the people who will be affected in any decisions that are made.

It only makes sense. How many decades ago did we first start hearing official warnings about the dangers of cigarette smoke? And when did the science of its effects become certain?

Many would say those effects have never been established with scientific certainty. But in the meantime, would we deny that cigarette smoking has killed many Americans? Were we wrong to take action to warn people about the dangers of smoking?

When I was a boy, my dad smoked two packs of Chesterfield regulars each day. I was so accustomed to it that I never really smelled the smoke that must have permeated my clothes and our apartment. But one day – I was around 14 – Dad told me to clean the inside of our car windows. That was when I discovered how sticky that smoke residue was on our car windshield, how hard it was to scrub away. It was then that I began to understand what those scientists were talking about.

To this day, you still can't look at one person's health problems and state with certainty that they were caused by cigarette smoke, even if the person was a two-pack-a-day smoker like my dad. But we know a lot more about what cigarette smoke does and, thank goodness, we took action to convince people not to smoke. And we saved a lot of lives.

Most of the synthetic chemicals in the products we and our children use every day have never been tested to find out whether they are safe or toxic. There are some 85,000 industrial chemicals available for use today. As the *New York Times* reported in 2013, "the overwhelming majority of chemicals in use today have never been independently tested for safety."[1]

Should the burden of proof lie with you to prove those chemicals are unsafe? (Do you even have the financial wherewithal to do this?) Or should the burden of proof lie with the companies that manufacture those chemicals and that put them into the products you and your children use? Should those manufacturers have to prove that the chemicals are indeed safe?

The Precautionary Principle can give us guidance. Better safe than sorry. Look before you leap. An ounce of prevention is worth a pound of cure.

CHAPTER FORTY-FIVE

Building Energy Independence

Home on the Range was using only 21% of the energy that would be used by a new, comparably sized office building constructed to modern building codes. And we had done it for less money than that traditional building would have cost.

....

S ome years ago, Northern Plains had outgrown its rented office space. We had cardboard boxes stacked along the hallway, and the conference room could no longer accommodate the entire staff.

Our board of directors decided we needed to explore a long-term solution to our need for more office space. A committee of members checked out locations around Billings and eventually decided that – after more than 30 years working as an organization – maybe it was time to think about owning our own office instead of renting space.

Our search took us all over town. Eventually, my boss Teresa suggested we check out a derelict building on the south side of Billings, a neighborhood grocery that had been empty for years, its exterior walls covered with graffiti. It was a dump, and I thought she had lost her mind.

We contacted a realtor and took a tour of the concrete block building. Since it had sat empty for several years, the power had been cut off, so we made our tour by flashlight; it was a spooky place.

But the price was good. A building inspector looked the place over and told us that, essentially, it was a sound building, and the roof was in pretty good shape. The insides didn't matter much, since we would be renovating the interior anyway. So we bought the place.

We knew that, as an organization working for the conservation of natural resources, we wanted our new home to reflect our values. We wanted a home that used salvaged materials, recycled materials, less toxic materials; a home that conserved energy and water.

We decided to try for certification as a LEED building. LEED stands for Leadership in Energy and Environmental Design, a points-based certification program run by the U.S. Green Building Council. We hoped to reach LEED Gold.

The first step in renovating this old grocery store was to clear out the interior. We advised our contractor that we wanted as much waste as possible kept out of the city landfill. Recovered metal was sent to a local recycling company. Two large rooms in the building had been refrigerated, and were both heavily insulated, with walls and ceilings made of tongue-and-groove fir boards. Inside those walls, the contractor found over 13 tons of horsehair insulation. The boards that lined those rooms were saved, eventually becoming our door frames, window frames, baseboards, and a fence outside. The horsehair insulation went to a local composting company.

Recycling and reuse were fundamental to the renovation. We were diligent about minimizing waste – of all the wood, metal, concrete, and old insulation that came out of this old building, more than 90% of it never went to the landfill. It was reused, recycled, or composted.

We acquired 33 oak doors from a firm that was renovating a 100 year-old building downtown. Those doors had 100 years' worth of varnish and paint on them; our volunteers spent several Wednesday nights and Saturday mornings stripping the paint and varnish off those lovely oak doors with a citrus-based stripper.

Shelves and cabinets in the building were manufactured from wheat straw and sunflower seed shells. Cubicles and other furnishings were purchased second-hand. The sinks in the rest rooms were donated, and the stalls were made out of recycled plastic.

The lot was landscaped with plants that don't require a lot of water, and a drip irrigation system minimizes water use.

Making our new office energy efficient and as reliant as possible on renewable energy meant renovating it as a system, and making all the parts of that system work together. This included our insulation strategy, our ventilation, our use of natural light to reduce our electrical needs, employing a low-tech radiant heat system in the floors, using solar collectors to pre-heat the water for that system, using other solar collectors to generate electricity, using an evaporative cooling system instead of air conditioning. We installed "light shelves" on the windows to minimize unwanted heat while maximizing the amount of light entering the building. Clerestories on the roof – an old building strategy – let natural light into the interior of the building. There are no incandescent lights in the building, which means reduced electricity use.

The urinal in the men's room requires no water. The parking lot is surfaced with pulverized glass, small chunks of glass that no longer have sharp edges, and that allow moisture to enter the soil below instead of flowing into the city's storm sewer system. French drains accomplish the same thing on landscaped areas. The paints and varnishes in the building are low in volatile organic compounds, which means they release far less toxic gas into the air than conventional paints. Our contractor purchased as much material as possible within a 500-mile radius to reduce energy use in transportation.

A member donated professional landscape design services and lots of plants. In addition to cleaning those 33 oak doors, members volunteered their time and work to pull nails from the fir boards in the building and to run wiring to our work stations. Members donated rock from their ranches for the landscaping; they and other volunteers gathered up and hauled all those rocks into town. Several volunteers dug hundreds of holes for our plants. Another member welded a bike rack.

We christened our new office "Home on the Range." The mayor and one of Montana's U.S. Senators came to the ribbon-cutting, and a local Lutheran pastor offered a blessing for the building and the people who work in it.

After keeping track of our energy use for a year, it became clear that this concrete block building built in 1940 had become something special. Home on the Range was using only 21% of the energy that would be used by a new, comparably sized office building constructed to modern building codes. And we had done it for less money than that traditional building would have cost.

The U.S. Green Building Council doesn't award LEED certification based on what we tell them. An independent commissioning agent reviews the information and verifies it to USGBC. When that process was complete, Home on the Range did not receive the LEED Gold certification we had sought; it was awarded the highest possible certification – LEED Platinum.

Home on the Range was the first LEED Platinum in Montana, and only the 41st in the United States. It was a comparatively small project, was completed on a tight budget, and has served to showcase the many possibilities for energy-efficient buildings (or green buildings, or whatever you prefer to call them). Since it was built, five more LEED Platinum buildings – three renovations and two new buildings – have been certified in downtown Billings. Not bad for an old Montana cow town.

And we keep moving forward; a new solar array of 75 collectors was added to the property in 2016 on the tenth anniversary of the building's opening.

Contractors, architects, and architectural students have toured Home on the Range to learn about the many strategies that can improve the efficiency of a building and reduce waste and the consumption of natural resources.

Improving the efficiency of a building requires architects, designers, engineers, contractors, and suppliers. It creates jobs, saves energy, and conserves natural resources. Every efficient building like this represents a step toward America's energy independence.

CHAPTER FORTY-SIX

There's Something Wrong

Amphibians are disappearing from wide areas around the world, and we don't know why. The world's oceans can no longer provide all the fish we want to take from them.

···

The crisis over the national debt is not new. We've been warned about it for decades by presidents, economists, and business people. But for those decades, we – as a people – have found it easier to put off doing anything about it.

The same thing is happening with the natural world and even our built-up environment. Whether we're looking at threats to natural places or rivers or public health or the decision-making practices of our government, a crisis is on its way.

The night sky is disappearing for many Americans. Our planet's climate is changing, and most scientists think they know why.

Oh, and here's something not too many people talk about. When I was born, the world's population was about 2.5 billion people. <u>Just in my lifetime, we've nearly tripled the number we're asking the earth to support</u>. Do we really think we can continue to feed a world that adds an infinite number of new mouths to feed? What if all of them want the "standard of living" that Americans have come to expect? Even if we can feed an infinite number of people, what will the lives of our grandchildren be like, in an ever-more-crowded world? I don't know the answer, but I know we can't ignore this one.

Only 3 percent of the world's water is fresh water, and nations and regions are increasingly facing water shortages. But at the same time, we're finding more and more ways to pollute our water, and more excuses for allowing our fresh water to be polluted. Decades ago, we took the phosphates out of laundry detergent. But now we're using fresh water to inject a stew of toxic chemicals underground to extract oil and natural gas. Many of those chemicals (and much of the water) stay in the ground – forever removed from the hydrologic cycle. But some of the chemicals are brought to the surface with the gas. As I write this, the nature of those chemicals is still a secret from you and me because the natural gas industry persuaded Congress in 2005 to exempt them from the Safe Drinking Water Act. In the meantime, some people who live near gas-drilling fields have had the unsettling experience of holding a lighted match to their tap water and seeing their water catch fire.

An assessment by the Defense Intelligence Agency in 2012 reported that water shortages worldwide will destabilize countries important to America's economic and security interests as those countries struggle to find enough water to grow food, run industry, generate electricity, and extract fossil fuels. Water rights between nations will be more jealously guarded, and water infrastructure will likely become a target for terrorists.[1]

Amphibians are disappearing from wide areas around the world, and we don't know why.

The world's oceans can no longer provide all the fish we want to take from them.

There's a big dead zone in the Gulf of Mexico, caused by everything we put into the Mississippi River as it flows through the heart of America.

The largest "landfill" in the world is a floating patch of garbage, twice the size of Texas, in the Pacific Ocean. There's another big patch in the Atlantic Ocean, too, floating among the seaweed of the Sargasso Sea. It's not just that it's garbage; much of the garbage is plastic, and that plastic is made of toxic chemicals. As they slowly break down, they will introduce more toxic chemicals into the seas. Once the plastic particles become small – about the size of a grain of salt – they are colonized by bacteria. Some of the bacteria are disease-causing pathogens, and we have provided a new means for them to travel long distances and to become part of the food chain.[2]

Coral reefs are dying off throughout much of the world.

Most of America's food production is controlled by corporate monopolies.

Honeybees, which pollinate a third of the food we eat, are declining precipitously.[3] And we don't know why. The best guess scientists have come up with, though, is a class of pesticides – neonicotinoids – that is heavily used on corn crops.[4]

There is so much chemical pollution everywhere on the earth that all of our bodies contain industrial chemicals, most of which we don't know all that much about, but some of which we know cause cancers, disrupt how our bodies work, and create other life-changing afflictions.

Since the beginning of the industrial age, levels of highly toxic mercury in the oceans have more than tripled.[3]

In 25 years' time, the world's population of monarch butterflies has fallen by more than 90 percent.

This list could go on and on. Here in Montana – and other places west of the 100th Meridian – water is connected to just about everything. We saw coal bed methane drillers planning to drain our aquifers and dumping salty wastewater into streams and onto the soil – until citizens forced a change. We see coal strip mines tearing aquifers apart. We see companies trying to privatize our water. We see oversized rural subdivisions polluting ground water with too many septic systems and depleting aquifers with too many wells too close together. We see metal mines discharging pollution that can ruin rivers. (Water protection laws have made it a lot better than it used to be when mines dumped anything they wanted, wherever they wanted.) We see those deep wells for natural gas where they inject a brew of toxic chemicals into the ground, with a large portion never recovered... we've seen the experiences of people in other states whose water wells became contaminated after deep gas drilling came to their neighborhood.

The mindset of the bankers and Wall Street gamblers who caused the Great Recession of 2008 is the same mindset that ruins wild places or endangers public health. It's the mindset that believes America means money rather than liberty. It's the mindset that believes I'm entitled to anything I want, never mind how it affects my country or my countrymen. It's the mindset that convinces a politician to vote for whatever gets him the most campaign contributions, never mind how it affects the country or its people.

Our inability to deal with the national debt – though we had been warned about it for decades – is no different than our inability to deal with threats to America's environment. And the day will come when we can put it off no longer.

Fuzzy Math

Almost always, protecting the environment is regarded as an expense, an expense that has no corresponding value.

…………………………………………………………………..

An increasing number of economists and scientists are making an important point that most of us don't think about very often – that we depend on the plants and animals and other life forms with which we share the planet, that they have a very real economic value which goes largely uncalculated. [1]

This includes the food and fiber we get from wild sources, along with raw materials and pharmaceuticals from plants and animals and microbes and fungi. Plants and animals and other forms of life process dead organisms, enrich the soil, filter the water, remove carbon dioxide from the air and create oxygen, anchor the soil, prevent floods, pollinate many of our crops, and so on.

Of course, we also have to include the services we receive from non-living nature – the climate that makes agriculture possible, the hydrologic cycle that makes water available for our use, the geological structure that makes good water accessible to us, the processes that create soil, without which we would all be in serious trouble.

If you believe our existence on earth is merely a marketplace full of goods and services, then what's the economic value of all that work? What's the economic loss if all that work were to cease?

And why don't we make those services part of our economic calculations? That value is rarely, if ever, accounted for. Almost always, protecting the environment is regarded as an expense, an expense that has no corresponding value.

Whenever we talk about protecting the environment – reclaiming mined land, preventing pollution of the water and the air, protecting key habitat for wildlife – all we hear about is how much it costs. We never hear in public discourse that a healthy and diverse environment has value. We never hear a mining company acknowledge that reclaiming the land is restoring value which the mining company took away during its operations. We also never hear that the money a mining company is required to spend on reclamation is money that buys products and employs people.

We never hear that clean air regulations reduce infant mortality and increase real estate values. Instead, we only hear how expensive it is to protect the environment, how it reduces some polluter's profit margin, and what a bad thing that is.[2]

There is still a well-worn pathway in our minds where clean air is unlimited and unending. We have more than enough air for everybody, people say, so it has no market value. We have more than enough fresh water, people say, so it has no market value (unless humans add to that value by bottling it or piping it somewhere).

But think of a water well that serves the needs of a home or a ranch. Obviously, that water has a value to the family that depends on it. If they had to replace that water from another source, it would come at a price.

But what about the rest of the aquifer from which that water comes? Let's say that no other domestic wells use the aquifer – just the one ranch house. Is the rest of the aquifer without value? Of course not. If the rest of the aquifer were polluted, then that one well would eventually bring polluted water to the ranch family. If the rest of the aquifer were depleted, that one well would eventually go dry.

Of course, we should add in the fact that ground water is often connected to surface water. The water in deep aquifers can travel great distances, and sometimes reaches the surface far away. The water in shallow aquifers often feeds springs. Sometimes it's connected to streams, either feeding a stream or accepting water from it. Polluted ground water can result in polluted rivers.

We modern people are very accustomed to thinking that human intervention is what gives value to anything in nature. And yet it's precisely the absence of human intervention that gives value to certain pieces of the world (maybe the Great Sand Dunes or maybe a spot like the woods I played in as a boy).

Of course, – and we must not forget this – the world is more than a marketplace. It's full of life forms that have evolved with us, that were made by the same Creator, and that live with the same climate and the same water that we do.

Plants and animals and the places where they live have an economic value, but dollars are not the only measure of value. We would never teach our children that everything is measured in dollars, because we know it's not true.

A few months before he was assassinated in 1968, Sen. Robert Kennedy reminded an audience about the flaws in the way we value things. (Note to reader: In this passage, Kennedy refers to two mass murderers in the 1960s: Charles Whitman, who shot 48 people on the University of Texas campus, killing 16, and Richard Speck, who raped and murdered eight student nurses in Chicago.)

Too much and too long, we seem to have surrendered community excellence and community values in the mere accumulation of material things. Our gross national product. – if we should judge America by that – counts air pollution and cigarette advertising, and ambulances to clear our highways of carnage. It counts special locks for our doors and the jails for those who break them. It counts the destruction of our redwoods and the loss of our natural wonder in chaotic sprawl. It counts napalm and the cost of a nuclear warhead, and armored cars for police who fight riots in our streets. It counts Whitman's rifle and Speck's knife, and the television programs which glorify violence in order to sell toys to our children.

Yet the gross national product does not allow for the health of our children, the quality of their education, or the joy of their play. It does not include the beauty of our poetry or the strength of our marriages; the intelligence of our public debate or the integrity of our public officials. It measures neither our wit nor our courage; neither our wisdom nor our learning; neither our compassion nor our devotion to our country; it measures everything, in short, except that which makes life worthwhile. And it tells us everything about America except why we are proud that we are Americans.[3]

CHAPTER FORTY-EIGHT

Brown Pollution, Brown Trout

This is a lesson we are slow in learning, that a lot of really bad pollution doesn't show up in photographs.

One of the stupidest remarks I've ever heard came from the mouth of a Montana state senator in the mid-1990s. He was being interviewed on the radio and the subject of pollution came up. The senator said to the interviewer, "I know pollution when I see it. Pollution is brown."

Of course, pollution is not "brown." Some of it is, but much of it is colorless, odorless, and tasteless. And some of that colorless, odorless, tasteless pollution can kill people.

Yet many of us still think all pollution is visibly dirty. We visualize smokestacks belching black smoke, and that's not what most smokestacks look like nowadays. We visualize industrial sewers spewing visibly dirty waste into rivers, and we don't see as much of that nowadays.

You may have seen photographs of mountain streams colored orange by mining pollution. While this orange coloration indeed shows us one effect of pollutants coming from a mine site, there are worse pollutants that don't discolor anything. This is a lesson we are slow in learning, that a lot of really bad pollution doesn't show up in photographs.

And some pollution has different effects depending on where it is. For instance, we can safely drink water that could ruin a trout fishery or a field of alfalfa. I watched as a TV reporter drank a glass of discharge water from a coal bed methane well, making what he thought was a powerful demonstration that the discharge water is harmless. The point he never grasped was that the main problem with the discharge water is its salt content. He could safely drink it, but that water can raise hell with soil and plants if downstream irrigators put it on their fields year after year.

In 1996, there was a ballot measure in Montana that dealt with water pollution from metal mines. Someone in the mining industry's campaign conceived a plan to discredit environmental groups by demonstrating that environmentalists tolerated water standards in their own offices that they wouldn't allow for the mining industry's discharges. The idea was this – since most environmental groups rented office space in old buildings, and since most old buildings had pipes with lead in the solder, it would be easy to show that the water in those offices had a high level of lead.

And, yes, old office buildings do have lead in their pipes. So does my 1940 house. When you live or work in an old building, it's understood that you should let the water run a minute before drinking it if it's been a few hours since the last time water has run.

So the mining industry group hired a commercial lab to visit the offices of environmental groups, take a water sample, and test it to show that the lead levels were higher than the standards environmental groups wanted applied to mining company discharges.

If the water is good enough for environmentalists to drink, the logic went, it should be good enough for mining companies to discharge into Montana's mountain rivers. The day their water sampling guy came to Northern Plains' office – this was before we got our new office – I happened to be the only person there. When this guy walked in and headed straight for the men's room – I had no idea who he was – I asked him if there was someone he was there to see. He said he was there to take a water sample, and that he wasn't allowed to say who the test was for. My first instinct was that this sounded fishy, but I decided to let the guy do his job and take his sample. Of course, he didn't run the water from the faucet before taking the sample. And, of course, the sample tested high for lead. The test was designed for exactly that outcome.

But even if the test hadn't shown a high level of lead, it would have missed the point. Montana's mountain streams are trout fisheries, and pollution levels that would be acceptable in drinking water could ruin a trout fishery. During a staff meeting later on, my boss, Teresa, remarked, "It's not like we're trying to raise rainbow trout in the toilets."

(My co-worker Dennis Olson, replied, "No, just browns.")

If we want trout in our world, we need cold, oxygenated, super-clean rivers in our mountains. Clear water isn't clean enough. Drinking-quality water isn't clean enough. In this modern age, our world is full of chemicals that we can't see or smell or taste, but that can do damage to people and other living things. Some of these pollutants can do that damage in amounts we can barely trace. This idea that pollution is brown, or sudsy, or foul-smelling, this is a throwback to a much simpler time.

12 Things I've Learned from Being an Environmentalist

1. <u>Nothing changes by itself</u>, especially nothing important.

2. <u>You are not alone</u>. If you have concerns about some issue, chances are that other people do, too. I've seen people with legitimate and reasonable concerns censor themselves because they assumed everybody else in town would disagree with them and disapprove of them as people. Some will, some won't. But you are a citizen, and you have the right to speak. Nothing will get better if you say nothing.

3. <u>Stampedes result in poor decisions</u>. When the nation gets into a mad rush toward some decision – to mine coal as fast as possible maybe, or to rush into a war – there is little tolerance for anyone who stands in the way. But it's exactly at those times when we all need someone to stand up and force us to slow down a bit. Some of these "herd" decisions have long-lasting effects, and we shouldn't stampede into them. They remind me of the way Plains Indians were able to drive herds of buffalo over cliffs, buffalo jumps, because the herd was doing what herds do – following everyone else.

4. <u>The truth is not enough</u>. Simply telling people the facts won't ensure that people will listen to you. And the party with the most information isn't necessarily the party telling the most truth. In the end, political change is about winning. That means work, strategy, persistence, fundraising, and more work.

5. <u>Even people you respect won't agree with you on everything</u>. If you belong to an organization, nobody in that organization will agree with you

about everything because it's just not how the world works. If we challenge the way things are, or challenge anyone powerful, it will create controversy. Expecting to change the way things are without creating controversy is expecting the impossible.

6. <u>An environmental organization can't do its work unless people support it financially</u>. It costs money to do what they do... if you believe in what they do, you need to at least make a donation.

7. <u>If you spend enough time with a subject, you will know more about it than you ever thought possible</u>. I've seen people develop huge levels of expertise just by immersing themselves in a subject.

8. <u>You can't be an expert on everything</u>. If people know you as an environmentalist, some of them might expect you to be conversant about every "environmental" issue, or to have an opinion on everything. It's not possible.

9. <u>Like the rest of the human race, you won't live a perfect life</u>. And, sure enough, someday some guy will tell you that you don't have a right to complain about fossil fuels if you drive a car. Most places in America are built for cars, and cars are the only way most people can get around in a community of any size. Yes, I drive a car. It gets good gas mileage, and I drive conservatively. I won't allow someone to silence me with a red herring argument that I can't say anything unless my life is perfect. Who lives life perfectly? And just who is demanding that you do?

10. <u>Opportunities are where you find them</u>. Sometimes an issue looks like a lost cause. Let's say you just see a confrontation between a small band of citizens and a large international corporation; the outcome may seem a foregone conclusion. But things happen. Sometimes the law happens. Sometimes politics happens. Sometimes public opinion happens. Sometimes the marketplace happens. As that desert rat Edward Abbey told us, "Be of good cheer. All may yet be well. There's many a fork, I think, in the road from here to destruction."[1]

11. <u>One organization can't be all things</u>. More than once, I've been asked, "Why can't all the environmental groups get together and work as one?" There are a lot of organizations out there, working in different ways and on different issues, and some people who generally support protecting the environment get a little frustrated. Wouldn't it be easier, they think, if there were just a few organizations? But it will never be that easy. There is no single "best" model for an environmental organization. Some, like the organization where I work, have a core belief that citizen volunteers must lead and citizen volunteers must speak in order to achieve meaningful change. I personally believe in that model. But other organizations approach things in different ways, and some of those approaches may be valid as well. Different groups have different constituencies. They look at the same issue in different ways. They have different ideas of what makes an effective strategy. They have different perspectives of what goals to pursue. They have different personalities, visions, and experiences. Sometimes, all these differences compete with one another, and sometimes they can complement one another. But they can't all become one group, and we shouldn't even want them to.

12. <u>We can't afford to be stupid or ignorant</u>. If we are going to solve the problems we face today – I mean all of us, we the people – we have to deal in facts. But every step of the way, we must ensure that our better nature – our honor, love of justice, concern for our fellow man, sense of responsibility, and so on – are stronger than the greed, intolerance, pride, envy, and other deadly sins that seem to lurk within most of us. Our values tell us where we should go. The facts help us find the way there.

CHAPTER FIFTY

25 Simple Things to Remember

1. It's wrong to pee in the pool.

2. Pollution is a market failure. It has no place in a free market.

3. Our financial lives are not morally separate from the rest of our lives.

4. You can't just walk away from politics.

5. Corporations have great power over our lives.

6. Unlike American people, large corporations have no intrinsic loyalty to our nation.

7. Corporations are not people. People are people.

8. Money is not speech. Speech is speech.

9. Nature has value that isn't measured in dollars. So do justice, love, truth, fidelity, kindness, honor, patience, liberty, humility, courage, restraint, and hope. So do people.

10. Burning something in an incinerator doesn't make it disappear. Whatever we burn may change form but it doesn't disappear.

11. Just because you can't smell, taste, or see a substance doesn't mean it can't hurt you.

12. Solar energy is good for more than generating electricity. Solar systems can heat air and liquids, and they can be mechanically "active" or "passive." They can be built onto our houses as well as in large industrial complexes.

13. Politicians and public agencies often forget who they are supposed to be working for.

14. Pollution represents waste; reducing pollution means reducing waste, and this often turns out to be profitable.

15. Coal pollutes the air we breathe more than any other fuel.

16. We are seriously messing up many parts of our planet. Some of them are specific places, but other parts – our atmosphere in particular – are everywhere and affect everyone.

17. An ounce of prevention is worth a pound of cure. This is true of personal hygiene, car maintenance, and global climate change. Think it will cost too much to stave off climate change? Wait till you see what it costs to fix it or live with it.

18. All fossil fuels are finite. They will all run out.

19. We Americans have more in common than we may think we do. We need to allow ourselves to recognize those things, and stop treating other Americans as if they have no right to be heard.

20. To repeat what Wendell Berry said,

    The great centralized economic entities of our time do not come into rural places in order to improve them by "creating jobs." They come to take as much of value as they can take, as cheaply and as quickly as they can take it.

21. If we allow environmental protections to be scuttled, some people and companies will make money, and the rest of us will pay the price.

22. Technology, alone, will not save us.

23. Good things rarely happen unless people work hard to make them happen.

24. Protecting the environment is about justice.

25. A journey of a thousand miles begins with the first step. To reach our future, sooner or later we have to start.

CHAPTER FIFTY-ONE

25 Things I Want for America

When we say we love America, we must love her traditions of liberty and her shining mountains.

....

It's not that I want you to like me or to like any other environmentalist. It's that, if you discount everything environmentalists say because you believe environmentalists are bad people, then you and the rest of our nation will fail to hear things that we all need to hear and understand.

I don't know at what point in his life or for what reason my dad decided that he hated African Americans. He never really heard or cared about anything that Martin Luther King, Jr., had to say. Dad was OK with black people as entertainers and athletes, so long as they didn't talk about anything serious. But he would never have paid a shred of respect to people like Dr. Percy Julian, who synthesized cortisone to treat arthritis; or Alex Haley, whose book *Roots* transformed the way many Americans came to look at their families. He would have thought he had no use for the likes of Dr. Charles Richard Drew, who set up the first blood bank; or Ralph Bunche, who negotiated the 1948 Arab-Israeli truce; or Marian Wright Edelman, who founded the Children's Defense Fund. Because of what Dad <u>thought</u> he knew about African Americans, he would never have believed that Gen. Colin Powell could have successfully planned the Persian Gulf War; or that Toni Morrison could have won the Nobel Prize in Literature.

Because of what he believed about African Americans and their abilities, the world – had he controlled it – would have gone without accomplishments like these. He would not have allowed African Americans into the positions from which they could exercise an influence over medicine, literature, politics, or national security.

Many Americans, because of what they have been told about environmentalists, will not listen to what those environmentalists are saying – not about the value of America's natural heritage, not about the health of our food or water or air, not about the inevitable necessity of using energy from the sun and wind to power our nation.

It's time to re-examine that position. Environmentalists probably aren't right about everything, but neither are they wrong about everything. And they wouldn't bother about any of it if they didn't love their country.

More important, some of the concerns of environmentalists are crucial to the future of the nation.

Not all environmentalists want the same things. Here are 25 things I personally want:

1. I want a substantial piece of the American land to be protected so that Americans in the future will be able to take comfort in the glory and beauty of our nation. I don't want this opportunity to be taken away from Americans by the nationwide ruination of pure water, the silence of wild places, the vistas, the wildlife, and the dark night skies of our country.

2. I want America's wildlife – the big and the little, the fierce and the shy – to have places to live... not just zoos, but real pieces of America. They are part of our land, part of our heritage. Americans fought to save the bison and the bald eagle. We need to fight to save our polar bears and desert tortoises.

3. I want family-scale farms and ranches to survive and prosper in America. Compared to corporate farms – which is what we'll end up with if we're not careful – family farms and ranches are better for the environment, produce healthier food, strengthen the communities nearby, and give us a stronger marketplace and stronger economy.

4. I want Americans to have access to locally grown food – food that didn't have to travel halfway across the country (or from another continent). In doing this, we'll be supporting those family-scale farms and ranches, and we'll keep more dollars in our communities.

5. I want our soil and water – and our bodies – to be protected from contamination by toxic materials that are dumped into the environment just because that's the cheapest short-term way to deal with them.

6. I want our food to be protected, too – for example, we should not be feeding antibiotics to farm animals as a feed supplement.

7. I want less stuff to be wasted. The more we waste, the more problems we create. Pollution is waste, and a culture of reducing waste would also help us think in ways that reduce pollution.

8. I want an end to the practice of externalizing the costs of pollution onto the general public and our natural resources. Nobody should have the right to do that. It's unjust and it undermines the free market.

9. I want America to rein in the power of the corporation. We need to abandon the fiction that corporations are people. At one time, we as a society controlled the activities of corporations; they were chartered for specific purposes and for limited periods of time. But today, corporations are allowed to exist forever, and for whatever purposes their directors want. Today, a corporation can go into a town like Libby, Montana, and kill hundreds of people, and nobody will spend a day in jail for it. Fine them? It's just another business expense. Corporations – and I'm not talking about small family corporations here – corporations have no national loyalty, no morals, no conscience, no personal responsibility. They are not people, not citizens, and we need to stop thinking they have the same rights that American citizens have. We the people are not powerless to change things.

10. I want our nation to be governed by people who are competent, honest, moral, and wise.

11. I want our policymakers to use the Precautionary Principle as a guide in assessing how we deal with chemicals and other pollution we allow to be released into our surroundings, how we deal with energy, and how we deal with our wild places. I want us to avoid more mistakes so we have fewer messes to clean up.

12. I want America to secure our future by making a serious commitment to generating energy from the sun, the wind, and other renewable sources. We've been subsidizing fossil fuels and nuclear power for generations in this country. We now need to step away from them for our children's sake, and use our ingenuity to build an energy-independent economy. It will not be free of environmental impacts – materials will be mined and products will be manufactured. Just look at some of the controversies over wind farms. But it will be a giant improvement for our environment, for our economy, and for working people. We can do this as a nation, but not if we keep investing in a fossil fuel future.

13. I want a substantial part of our renewable energy to be generated locally and on a small scale. I want to see solar collectors on the rooftops of homes, not just on big buildings and solar generating stations. Solar creates jobs.

14. The cheapest and cleanest energy is the energy we don't use. I want America to get serious about conserving – making the most of the energy we already use. Conservation measures create jobs, and they let us keep more of our energy dollars in our own pockets.

15. Buildings account for around 40% of our energy use. And our buildings are around a lot longer than our cars. I want to see more "green" building practices because they can make big improvements that last for decades. And they create jobs.

16. I want a healthy middle class in America.

17. I want it understood that I am an American citizen, not a "consumer." Who I am is not measured by what I buy.

18. I want a government that works for *me*, the citizen – that protects me from being sickened by pollution, protects my nation's natural heritage from being despoiled, protects my freedom against corporations that want to take away my rights.

19. I want American citizens to have the right to know what's going on – what's being put into our food, what's being discharged into the air we breathe and the water we drink, what's being done to our aquifers.

20. I want my country to be a place where not everything is valued in dollars.

21. I want more of us to live with an eye toward what we are passing on to the next generation of Americans.

22. I want us as a people to recover our ability to think differently, even to live differently. That capacity made our nation and built our freedom, and I worry we are becoming brittle in how we look at things, fearful of embarking on a new journey if we think that journey may challenge us.

23. I want us as a people to recover our ability to disagree with one another without going crazy about it, to listen to each other and maybe even learn from each other.

24. I want justice. Nobody should be allowed to dump poisons into the air that other people breathe, or the water they drink, or the food they eat, or the places where they live.

25. After I die, I hope my country will be a good place for my daughter to live, to work, and to raise a family. I want to leave her a world of justice and tolerance and peace, where the air and water are clean, and where God's creatures still have a home.

America's environment isn't just wilderness areas and national parks, it's also the working landscapes where people raise our food and where some of them steward the natural resources that make our whole nation a better and healthier place to be. We need to understand that our working landscapes – our family farms and ranches – are threatened by many of the same problems and the same forces that threaten our great parks and wilderness areas.

Our environment is also our cities, our workplaces, our homes, our schools. It's the air we breathe, it's wherever we get our water, it's where our kids play. It's the food we serve to our families, and the places where that food was grown.

As Americans, we have important duties when it comes to our environment:

- When we say we love America, we must love her traditions of liberty and her shining mountains.

- Our belief in personal liberty needs to include a belief in personal responsibility.

- As we guard against unbridled government power, we must defend our freedom against unbridled corporate power.

- As much as we value the fruits of hard work, we also have a duty to value justice.

- As we take pride in our history, we should also take pride in our ability to innovate, to find the best way forward to our future.

- If we really value free enterprise, we shouldn't allow the costs of pollution to be shoved off onto our nation's land, water, air, wildlife, and our people.

- If our families are important to us, the world we hand down to the young ones in our families should also be important.

- Our patriotism should include a love of democracy and a love for the glory of our plains, our rivers, our mountains, our forests, and our deserts.

Standing up for America's land and water amounts to standing up for the American people. If our country's natural heritage is lost to pollution or to development that doesn't belong there, then part of our liberty is also lost. If citizens who stand up for America's environment are shoved out of the way or fenced off from the political process, then even more of our liberty is lost.

Protecting America's environment… It may not be our job, but it must be our work. Protecting our land and the plants and animals that live there, our water, our air, our grand wild places, and the right of citizens to defend themselves from polluted water and air – this is not a single contest, and it is not trivial. It is the work of a lifetime, and the well-being of our children and their children depend on us.

God bless America,
Land that I love.
Stand beside her, and guide her
Thru the night with a light from above.
From the mountains, to the prairies,
To the oceans, white with foam
God bless America, My home sweet home.

– Irving Berlin, 1918, 1938

Epilogue

In forty years, I've never met an environmentalist who hates humanity or wants to destroy civilization. I've never met an eco-terrorist. I've never met an environmentalist who is against everything.

It's time to recognize American environmentalists for who they really are: A diverse bunch of people trying to protect something important about our country – perhaps our grand wild places, perhaps the air we breathe and the water we drink, perhaps the fundamental justice of how our nation operates on a day-to-day basis.

That doesn't mean environmentalists don't have their faults – they're human beings. I have faults, you have faults. Let's face it, people aren't perfect.

But that's always been true, and we've still been able to take on the problems we face as a nation. What's different here is that there are loud and adamant voices telling us things like:

- Environmentalists hate America
- Environmental problems aren't real
- America's future depends on letting corporations run the show.

If we want our kids to breathe clean air – *you want that, don't you?* – we need to at least listen to what people say who are trying to keep that air clean. If we want democracy to survive in our nation, we will all have to look beyond the next quarterly statement and the next annual report.

I'm worried. I hope our children and their children don't have to figure out how to live in a world where the climate has been really screwed up, a nation where our glorious wild places have been lost forever, a nation effectively run by corporations instead of a democratically elected government.

I hope the next generation of Americans can thank us for meeting these challenges. I hope they can thank us for seeing something that needed doing and having the courage and resolve to do it.

I believe our nation has a wonderful future ahead if we exercise that courage and that resolve.

Notes

Chapter Three: Nature Fascists

[1] Ron Arnold, quoted in Mark Dowie, *Losing Ground: American Environmentalism at the Close of the Twentieth Century*, The MIT Press, 1995, p. 94.

[2] Stan Adelstein, former South Dakota state representative, quoted in *Rapid City Journal*, "Lawmakers clarify forest bills at crackerbarrel," 1-19-02.

[3] John Stokes, Kalispell, Montana, talk radio host, quoted in "Montana shock jock stokes the fires of fear," *High Country News*, 6-18-01.

[4] John Stokes, quoted in Jim Mann, "Community edgy over radio rhetoric," *Kalispell Daily Inter Lake*, 6-17-01.

[5] Alan Caruba, 9-19-01, *www.tysknews.com/Depts/Environment*

[6] Chuck Cushman, Wise Use Movement spokesman, quoted in *High Country News*, "People for the West launches a 'holy war' against enviros," 6-3-91.

[7] Ron Arnold, quoted in *Rapid City Journal*, "Environmentalism blasted," 5-6-94.

[8] John O. Morris, letter to the editor, *Billings Gazette*, June 20, 2006.

[9] David Holcberg, 7-18-00, "The Environmentalist Evil," *Capitalism Magazine* online, www.capmag.com.

[10] Rush Limbaugh, *The Way Things Ought To Be*, Pocket Books, 1992.

[11] John Lewis, "Nihilism and the War Against Western Civilization," *Capitalism Magazine* online, www.capmag.com, 9-23-01.

[12] People for the West brochure, quoted in *High Country News*, "People for the West fronts for the mining industry," 7-1-91.

[13] Samuel Gipp, quoted in www.texemarrs.com/042000/environ2.htm, "Religious Environmentalists are Menatlly (sic) Ill."

[14] Michael Berliner, 4-16-01, "On Earth Day, Remember: If Environmentalists Succeed, They Will Make Human Life Impossible," *www.aynrand.org*.

[15] Ann Coulter, column, *WorldNetDaily.com*, May 28, 2003.

[16] coal strip miner in Tennessee, quoted by Boomer Winfrey.

[17] Donald Kopp, op-ed in *Rapid City Journal*, 7-31-99.

[18] Ann Coulter, quoted in: "Ann Coulter: Left Is 'out to Destroy the Country,'" by Phil Brennan, *NewsNax.com*, June 25, 2002.

[19] Anonymous post on *Billings Gazette* website, posted July 11, 2012, 11:22 a.m. – http://billingsgazette.com/news/state-and-regional/montana/coal-export-opponents-warn-of-train-congestion/article_8c210e1a-7513-5e1d-b04e-b9f23716357d.html, accessed July 12, 2012.

[20] an elderly Nevada woman yelling from the visitor's gallery when a Republican state senator testified against a Sagebrush Rebellion demand that federal lands be given to

the state; Bill Gilbert and Robert Sullivan, "Alone in the Wilderness," *Sports Illustrated*, Oct. 3, 1983 (v. 59, n. 15), pp. 96-112.

[21] former U.S. Interior Secretary James Watt, speaking at a Cattleman's Dinner in Denver, June 1990, Quoted in Mark Dowie, *Losing Ground: American Environmentalism at the Close of the Twentieth Century*

Chapter Six: The Narrative

[1] Thomas L. Friedman, "America vs. The Narrative," *New York Times*, Nov. 28, 2009

Chapter Seven: A Sampling of Environmentalists

[1] Boyd Charter, quoted by Anne Goddard Charter, in *Cowboys Don't Walk: A Tale of Two*, Western Organization of Resource Councils, 1999.

2 Helen Waller, "To the members..." *The Plains Truth*, Northern Plains Resource Council, v. 8, n. 10, December 1979.

Chapter Eight: Environmentalists Are...

[1] Henry David Thoreau, *Walden*.

Chapter Nine: Nazi Environmentalists???

[1] Alston Chase, *In a Dark Wood: The Fight over Forests and the Rising Tyranny of Ecology*, Houghton Mifflin Company: Boston & New York, 1995, pp. 122-125.

[2] Robert Jay Lifton, quoted in Jon Margolis commentary, "History, science being twisted," *Billings Gazette*, 11-28-94.

[3] Roderick Nash, ed., *The American Environment: Readings in the History of Conservation*, 2nd ed., Addison-Wesley: Reading, MA, 1976.

[4] Hans Huth, *Nature and the American: Three Centuries of Changing Attitudes*, University of California Press: Berkeley & Los Angeles, 1957.

[5] op. cit., Nash.

[6] op. cit., Nash.

Chapter Ten: American Liberty

[1] Associated Press, *Gold mines, a city's pride, leave toxic legacy in South Africa*, Billings Gazette, Mar. 27, 2011.

[2] quoted in Mark Dowie, *Losing Ground: American Environmentalism at the Close of the Twentieth Century*, The MIT Press, 1995, p. 94.

[3] George Will, *Washington Post*, May 31, 1992.

[4] David Roberts, "Underground environmentalism in communist East Germany," *Grist*, Apr. 21, 2011, http://www.grist.org/article/2011-04-21-underground-environmentalism-in-communist-east-germany.

[5] Philip R. Pryde, "Environmentalism and Patriotism," *The Green Elephant* (v. 4, n. 1, Summer 2000.

[6] *Billings Gazette*, "Drinking water unsafe for 300 million in China," Dec. 30, 2005.

[7] Clifford J. Levy, "Government raid targets protest group's computers," *N.Y. Times,* Sept. 12, 2010.

[8] Wallace Stegner, "Coda: Wilderness Letter," in *The Sound of Mountain Water,* E.P. Dutton: New York, 1980, p. 146.

[9] Edward Abbey, "Thus I Reply to Rene Dubos," *Down the River,* E.P. Dutton, 1982.

[10] Theodore Roosevelt, speech in Ossowatomie, Kansas, August 31, 1910; http://www.climateconservative.org/TheodoreRoosevelt.html, accessed Aug. 4, 2012)

[11] op. cit., Philip R. Pryde.

[12] Arlie Hochschild and David Hochschild, "Hooray for the Red, White, Blue, and Green," op-ed in *Los Angeles Times,* 11-11-01.

[13] *BP Statistical Review of World Energy June 2013,* "Oil" section, page 6; http://www.bp.com/content/dam/bp/pdf/statistical-review/statistical_re-view_of_world_energy_2013.pdf, accessed June 1, 2014.

[14] "The Patriotism of Insulation," *House Beautiful,* June 1942, pp. 50-51.

[15] Jeff Plungis, "SUV, truck owners get a big tax break," USA Today, Dec. 18, 2002; http://usatoday30.usatoday.com/money/autos/2002-12-18-suv-tax-break_x.htm, accessed Sept. 30, 2015.

Chapter Eleven: How I Came To Be an Environmentalist

[1] "Black Hills Unseen Money Maker," September 15, 2010, by Austin Hoffman, http://www.keloland.com/newsdetail.cfm?Id=0,104939, accessed Nov. 29, 2013.

Chapter Twelve: Stouthearted Citizens

[1] Talli Nauman, "Mining Companies Show Interest in Uranium in Custer, Fall River," *Custer County Chronicle,* Feb. 1, 1979.

[2] *Gazette-Telegraph* (Colo. Springs, CO), "Day of reckoning near for uranium mill and Canon City," June 28, 1979.

[3] *Billings Gazette,* "USGS to study effect of drill holes on water," Apr. 24, 1979.

[4] Tennessee Valley Authority, *Draft Environmental Statement, Edgemont Uranium Mine,* 1979, p. 162.

[5] Nuclear Regulatory Commission, *Environmental Statement related to operation of Wyoming Minerals Corporation Irigaray Solution Mining Project,* 1978, pp. 6-9.

[6] *High Country News,* Uranium mill shut down after spill," Aug. 10, 1979; *High Country News,* "Tailings, pollution haunt uranium company town," Feb. 22, 1980.

[7] *San Antonio Express-News,* "The poisoning of south Texas," Oct. 2, 1977; North Dakota Department of Health, report on molybdenosis in farm animals, 1970.

[8] Malcolm Ritter, "Initiative backers pick politics over protests," *Rapid City Journal,* Oct. 21, 1980.

[9] Roberta Walburn, "Black Hills quietly opened to exploration," *Minneapolis Tribune,* Sept. 10, 1980.

[10] ibid., Roberta Walburn.

[11] ibid., Roberta Walburn.

[12] *Tri-State Livestock News*, "Ranchers explain why they favor uranium mining initiative," Nov. 1, 1980.

[13] Mark Plenke, "Firm ordered to halt exploration work," *Rapid City Journal*, Sept. 7, 1979.

[14] Malcolm Ritter, "Uranium development issue going to voters," *Rapid City Journal*, Feb. 15, 1980.

[15] Janet Osnes, Energy development issues discussed by panel members," *Rapid City Journal*, Aug. 23, 1979.

[16] David Egner, "Energy Interests fund pro-uranium ads," *Rapid City Journal*, Oct. 29, 1980.

[17] Associated Press, "Uranium battle is mining companies against Black Hills Energy Coalition," Aberdeen *American News*, Aug. 3, 1980.

Chapter Thirteen: Beauty

[1] Brian Shovers, "From Treasure State to Big Sky," *Montana: The Magazine of Western History*, Montana Historical Society, 53 (Spring 2003), pp. 58-64.

[2] Ralph Waldo Emerson, "Nature."

Chapter Fourteen: We Will Rejoice and Be Glad In It

[1] Pope Francis, Encyclical Letter, *Laudato Si' (On Care for Our Common Home)*, par. 84, May 24, 2015

Chapter Sixteen: Justice

[1] Kobre, Ken, "A Last Interview with W. Eugene Smith [1918-1978]," The Master's Exhibition, http://www.nirvana.demon.co.uk/W.E.Smith.txt [April 17, 1999]); also *Trade and Environment Database Case Studies Minamata Disaster,* www.american.edu/TED/MINAMATA.HTM

[2] Edward Broughton, "The Bhopal disaster and its aftermath: a review," Environmental Health, April 6, 2005, http://www.ncbi.nlm.nih.gov/pmc/articles/PMC1142333, accessed March 8, 2015

[3] Cassels, Jamie. *The Uncertain Promise Of Law: Lessons From Bhopal*, University Of Toronto Press Incorporated. 1993

[4] Trade and Environment Database Case Studies: Bhopal Disaster, www.american.edu/TED/BHOPAL.HTM; Editorial: "Toxic Futures," *New Statesman and Society*. Volume 3, Issue 85, January 26, 1990, p.18.

[5] Lois Gibbs, *Love Canal: the Story Continues . . .*, New Society Publishers, 1998.

[6] Sources for this section include:
    - Brown, Matthew, "Libby's tragic legacy," *Billings Gazette*, May 24, 2010.

- Brown, Matthew, "Runoff sweeps asbestos into river," *Billings Gazette*, Nov. 27, 2011.
- Brown, Matthew, Associated Press, "Libby asbestos victims win $43M settlement from state," *Missoulian*, Sept. 16, 2011; http://missoulian.com/news/state-and-regional/article_b2eac84e-e08d-11e0-ae31-001cc4c03286.html, accessed May 22, 2012.
- Devlin, Vince, "Libby residents unsure of outcome on $19.6M W.R. Grace settlement," *Missoulian*, Feb. 2, 2012; http://missoulian.com/news/local/w-r-grace-proposes-m-settlement-with-libby-asbestos-victims/article_06491b3a-4cfe-11e1-91c8-0019bb2963f4.html, accessed May 22, 2012)
- *Dust to Dust*, film by Michael Brown, Michael Brown Productions, 2002.
- Environmental Protection Agency, "Background on the Libby Asbestos Site," www.epa.gov/region8/superfund/libby/background.html
- "EPA to Investigate its Failure to Warn Libby Residents," *Down to Earth* (newsletter of Montana Environmental Information Center), August 2000 (v. XXVI, n. 3).
- Fritz, Jane, "Company Leaves Victims in its Dust," *High Country News*, Apr. 23, 2001.
- "Grace Takes Libby Asbestos Arguments to High Court," *Insurance Journal*, Apr. 18, 2008.
- Johnson, Kirk, "Chemical Company Is Acquitted in Asbestos Case," *New York Times*, May 8, 2009.
- Matthews, Mark, "Libby's Dark Secret," *High Country News*, Mar. 13, 2000.
- McLaughlin, Kathleen, "Commissioners Detail Libby's Health Needs," *Billings Gazette*, July 31, 2001.
- Schneider, Andrew, "A Town Left to Die," *Seattle Post-Intelligencer*, Nov. 18, 1999.
- Schneider, Andrew, "Indictments Give Libby Asbestos Victims Hope," St. Louis Post-Dispatch, published in *Billings Gazette*, Feb. 13, 2005.
- Schneider, Andrew, "W.R. Grace to pay $250 million to clean asbestos from the Montana mining town it contaminated; criminal trial still ahead," http://blog.seattlepi.nwsource.com .
- Schneider, Andrew, "W.R. Grace indicted in Libby asbestos deaths," *St. Louis Post-Dispatch*, published in *Seattle Post-Intelligencer*, Feb. 8, 2005.
- Bob Van Voris & Amy Linn, "W.R. Grace Found Not Guilty in Montana Asbestos Trial," www.bloomberg.com, May 8, 2009, http://www.bloomberg.com/apps/news?pid=newsarchive&sid=a2KONaswwu1Y

- W.R. Grace and Company, "Agreement in Principle is Reached to Settle Objections to Grace's Plan of Reorganization from Libby, Montana Claimants," http://www.grace.com/media/NewsItem.aspx?id=1654938&view=printable, accessed May 22, 2012)
- Williams, Pat (former U.S. Congressman), opinion editorial, *Down to Earth* (newsletter of Montana Environmental Information Center), August 2000 (v. XXVI).

[7] United Church of Christ, *Toxic Waste and Race: A National Report on the Racial and Socioeconomic Characteristics of Communities with Hazardous-Waste Sites*, 1987.

Chapter Seventeen: Big Green

[1] Alex Roth, "PETA's dogma is all bark and no bite: Animal rights group makes the stupid claim that enviros must be vegetarians," (including reader comments, *Grist*, Sept. 14, 2007

[2] Bryan Walsh, "Meat: Making Global Warming Worse," *Time*, Sept. 10, 2008, http://www.time.com/time/health/article/0,8599,1839995,00.html.

[3] Nicolette Hahn Niman, "The Carnivore's Dilemma" (op-ed), *The New York Times*, Oct. 31, 2009

[4] Elisabeth Rosenthal, "To Cut Global Warming, Swedes Study Their Plates," *The New York Times*, Oct. 22, 2009.

[5] Kevin Boyer, "Why cattle grazing does not have to be a climate disaster, *Grist*, Feb. 11, 2016.

[6] Jeanie Alderson, presentation to Northern Plains Resource Council annual meeting, November 2013.

[7] Malcolm Ritter, "Coalition, Alliance: Similar goals, different tactics," *Rapid City Journal*, June 15, 1980.

[8] Roberta Walburn, "Black Hills quietly opened to exploration, *Minneapolis Tribune*, Sept. 10, 1980.

[9] Bryan Jones, "The Black Hills Energy Wars," *Prairie Sentinel*, June/July 1983.

[10] Website of Zoltan Grossman "The Black Hills Alliance," http://academic.evergreen.edu/g/grossmaz/bha.html, accessed June 29, 2014.

Chapter Eighteen: 17 Reasons Environmental Issues Are So Hard to Resolve

[1] George Darrow, quoted in *A Guide to the Montana Environmental Policy Act*, pub. 1998 [rev. in 2004, 2006, 2009] by Legislative Environmental Policy Office, Helena, MT, 99 pp.; http://leg.mt.gov/content/Publications/Environmental/2009mepaguide.pdf.

Chapter Nineteen: Our Only Companions

[1] Olivia Judson, "A Wild Celebration," (op-ed), *New York Times*, December 8, 2009.

[2] Bridget Stutchbury, "Did Your Shopping List Kill a Songbird?" (op-ed), *New York Times*, March 30, 2008.

[3] Lindsey Hoshaw, *New York Times,* "Afloat in the Ocean, Expanding Islands of Trash," Nov. 9, 2009.

[4] Associated Press, "High Levels of toxic metals found in whales," *Billings Gazette,* June 25, 2010.

[5] "A worrisome population decline in the seas," *The Week,* Aug. 20, 2010.

[6] "A Long Job, Too Late to Quit," in *Citizenship Papers,* Shoemaker & Hoard, Washington, D.C., 2003.

[7] Paul Shepard, *The Tender Carnivore and the Sacred Game,* University of Georgia Press, 1973.

[8] Pope Francis, Encyclical Letter, *Laudato Si' (On Care for Our Common Home),* par. 67, May 24, 2015

[9] Betsy Cohen, "Lucky rescue: Cat plucked from Clark Fork after being left for dead," *Missoulian,* Dec. 28, 2005.

[10] Associated Press, "Indiana dad gets 18 months for killing family cat," *USA Today,* Aug. 29, 2008.

[11] Brett French, "Vandals' darting of ducks angers retiree," *Billings Gazette,* Dec. 18, 2010.

[12] Associated Press, *Billings Gazette,* July 21, 2004.

[13] "Eatery takes 'dancing shrimp' off menu," *Billings Gazette,* Sept. 4, 2010.

[14] Associated Press, "College turtle project takes dark twist," *Billings Gazette,* Dec. 28, 2012.

[15] Brett French, "40-year-old fish tale," *Billings Gazette,* 9-18-2007.

[16] Brett French, "Dam Plans," *Billings Gazette,* 10-30-2008; Brett French, "Pallid Proof," *Billings Gazette,* Feb. 12, 2015.

[17] Sandra Steingraber, *Living Downstream,* Vintage Books, 1998.

[18] Reuters News Agency, "Bags suffocated whale," *Salt Lake Tribune,* May 6, 1984.

Chapter Twenty: Free Enterprise

[1] U.S. Bureau of Labor Statistics, *Current Employment Statistics: Highlights, January 2010,* Feb. 5, 2010, http://www.bls.gov/ces/highlights012010.pdf, accessed June 16, 2012.

[2] Gernot Wagner, "Going Green but Getting Nowhere," (op-ed), *New York Times,* Sept. 7, 2011.

[3] Terry L. Anderson & Laura E. Huggins, *Greener Than Thou: Are You Really an Environmentalist?,* Hoover Institution Press, 2008, p. 97.

Chapter Twenty-One: Private Property

[1] Archibald MacLeish, *Land of the Free,* first published in 1938 by Harcourt, Brace.

[2] Wallace McRae, "Eminent Domain" in *Cowboy Curmudgeon,* Gibbs Smith, 1992.

[3] Associated Press, "Developer of power line seeks to condemn land," *Montana Standard*, July 24, 2010; LeAnne Kavanagh, "District judge denies MATL's claim of eminent domain," *Cut Bank Pioneer Press*, Dec. 15, 2010.

[4] from a radio commentary by Sandy Courtnage of the Montana Farmers Union, broadcast on KUFM Public Radio, Feb. 8, 2011.

[5] Hertha Lund, guest editorial, "Eminent domain effort threatens farm and ranch property," *Great Falls Tribune*, March 28, 2011.

Chapter Twenty-Two: Want an Industrial Railroad Through Your Place?

[1] Matthew Brown (Associated Press), "Billionaire strikes deal in fight over Tongue River railroad," *Billings Gazette*, July 22, 2011.

[2] Thomas Michael Power & Donovan S. Power, *The Value of the Otter Creek Coal Tracts to the State of Montana: The Dangers of relying on the Norwest Corporation Appraisal*, July 31, 2009.

[3] Surface Transportation Board, *Draft Environmental Impact Statement: Tongue River Railroad Company Construction and Operation of a New Rail Line in Southeastern Montana*, v. 1, p. 5-2-30 (Table 5.2-17), April 17, 2015.

[4] Surface Transportation Board, *Draft Environmental Impact Statement: Tongue River Railroad Company Construction and Operation of a New Rail Line in Southeastern Montana*, v. 2, (Appendix C), April 17, 2015.

Chapter Twenty-Three: Where Your Home Is

[1] Anne Goddard Charter, in *Cowboys Don't Walk: A Tale of Two*, Western Organization of Resource Councils, 1999.

[2] Jan Falstad, "Swiss company with Russian ties buys into Signal Peak coal mine," *Billings Gazette*, Oct. 19, 2011.

Chapter Twenty-Four: Public Lands

[1] Terry Tempest Williams, *The Open Space of Democracy*, The Orion Society, 2004.

Chapter Twenty-Eight: Gasoline and Groceries

[1] Conoco-Phillips press release, May 11, 2011, *ConocoPhillips Highlights Solid Results and Raises Concerns Over Un-American Tax Proposals at Annual Meeting of Shareholders*, http://www.conocophillips.com/EN/newsroom/news_releases/2011news/Pages/05-11-2011_1.aspx.

[2] Political Economy Research Institute, University of Massachusetts Amherst, *Toxic 100 Air Polluters*, August 2013, http://www.peri.umass.edu/toxicair_current/, accessed March 7, 2015.

[3] *Houston Chronicle*, "Some firms tackle the problem – after a prod," *Nov. 10, 1997*.

[4] *Billings Gazette*, "Valley sheds sulfur dioxide pollution," April 22, 2008; Clair Johnson, "Yellowstone Valley S02 pollution at new low," *Billings Gazette*, May 11, 2009.

5 Associated Press, "Exxon increases estimate of Yellowstone oil spill by 50%, *Billings Gazette*, Jan 20, 2012, http://billingsgazette.com/news/local/exxon-increases-estimate-of-yellowstone-river-oil-spill-by/article_e3f0de2e-f931-50e8-9678-c5f230c9e00d.html, accessed August 26, 2012.

6 "Study finds grocery store meat contaminated," *Billings Gazette*, April 16, 2011, reprinted from the *Los Angeles Times*.

7 *Billings Gazette*, "Meat processor says he's fed up with feds, June 19, 2005; *Billings Gazette*, "Meatpacker aided with lawsuit," March 26, 2005; *Billings Gazette*, "Guest opinion: USDA deregulation penalizes small plants, imperils public health," Nov. 20, 2008.

8 http://media.bioneers.org/listing/the-color-of-sustainability-ladonna-redmond/.

9 Wendell Berry, "Conservationist and Agrarian," in *Citizenship Papers*, Shoemaker & Hoard, 2003.

10 Benedict XVI, Encyclical Letter *Caritas in Veritate*, June 29, 2009, AAS 101 (2009), § 66.

11 Annie Leonard, *The Story of Change*, (film), The Story of Stuff Project, (2012), www.storyofstuff.org/movies/storyofchange .

Chapter Twenty-Nine: Agriculture

1 Wendell Berry, "A Long Job, Too Late to Quit," in *Citizenship Papers*, Shoemaker & Hoard, 2003.

2 Wendell Berry, "Still Standing," in *Citizenship Papers*, Shoemaker & Hoard, 2003.

3 Wendell Berry, *Another Turn of the Crank*, Counterpoint, 1995.

Chapter Thirty: Mining

1 Vinod Khosla, quoted in Tom Freidman column, "Dreaming the possible dream," *New York Times*, March 6, 2010.

2 Heather Abel, "The rise and fall of a gold mining company," *High Country News*, Dec. 22, 1997.

3 Montana Department of Environmental Quality website, http://deq.mt.gov/recovery/remediation/ZortmanLandusky/default.mcpx on May 30, 2010.

4 Federal Mining Dialogue, http://www.abandonedmines.gov/ep.html, accessed Feb. 7, 2015.

5 "Miners told that environmentalism must be destroyed," *Livingston Enterprise*, May 5, 1994.

Chapter Thirty-One: Good Neighbor Agreement

1 Eric Whitney, "Mining out the middleman," *High Country News*, July 31, 2000.

Chapter Thirty-Two: Overzealous Regulation?

1 William K. Reilly, quoted in Charles Duhigg, "That Tap Water Is Legal but May Be Unhealthy," *New York Times*, December 17, 2009.

[2] Charles Duhigg, "That Tap Water Is Legal but May Be Unhealthy," *New York Times*, December 17, 2009.

[3] Eve Byron, "WQB's enforcement officer is being muzzled," *Helena Independent Record*, July 17, 1994.

[4] Robert H. Boyle, "James Watt and Other Environmental Hazards," in "Scorecard" ed. by Robert W. Creamer in *Sports Illustrated*, Aug. 10, 1981.

[5] "Watt's New Land Board Unbalanced, Foes Say," *Billings Gazette*, Feb. 12, 1982.

[6] Jonathan Thompson, "As Interior Turns," *High Country News*, Dec. 22, 2008.

[7] Rebecca Clarren, "The Sick and Tired West," *High Country News*, Dec. 22, 2008.

[8] Rebecca Clarren, "The Sick and Tired West," *High Country News*, Dec. 22, 2008.

[9] Juliet Eilperin, "U.S. exempted BP's Gulf of Mexico drilling from environmental impact study," *The Washington Post*, May 5, 2010.

[10] Marisa Taylor, "Since Spill, Feds Have Given 27 Waivers to Oil Companies in Gulf," McClatchy Newspapers, May 10, 2010, http://www.mcclatchydc.com/2010/05/07/93761/despite-spill-feds-still-giving.html, accessed May 28, 2012.

[11] Associated Press, "Regulator apologizes for pro-drilling cake," *Billings Gazette*, May 22, 2010.

[12] Jason DeParle, "Minerals Management Service Has a Mandate to Produce Results, *New York Times*, Aug. 7, 2010.

[13] Associated Press, "Statistics tell different story of EPA enforcement," *Billings Gazette*, May 31, 2012.

Chapter Thirty-Three: Sue the Bastards

[1] Carol Nash, quoted in "Living with Oil and Gas," an online project of the Western Organization of Resource Councils, https://www.facebook.com/livingwithoilandgas , Feb. 18, 2016.

Chapter Thirty-Four: Environmentalist as Obstructionist

[1] Todd Wilkinson, "Where do you draw the line?" *High Country News*, Jan. 21, 2008.

[2] Ed Swartz, in a speech to the Western Organization of Resource Councils, June 6, 2009, Grand Junction, Colorado.

Chapter Thirty-Five: False Choices

[1] Dan Testa, "Holding His Ground: MEPA Author Critical of Proposed Changes to Environmental Law," *Flathead Beacon*, Mar. 29, 2011, http://www.flatheadbeacon.com/articles/article/holding_his_ground/22450, accessed Nov. 16, 2012.

[2] Montana Code Annotated 75-1-103.

[3] *A Guide to the Montana Environmental Policy Act,* p. 14,pub. by Montana Legislative Environmental Policy Office, by John Mundinger and Todd Everts 1998, rev. in 2004 by Larry Mitchell, rev. in 2006 by Todd Everts, rev in 2009 and 2013 by Hope Stockwell,

http://leg.mt.gov/content/Publications/Environmental/2009mepaguide.pdf, accessed Feb. 7, 2015.

Chapter Thirty-Six: Frequently Asked Questions

[1] Rear Admiral David Titley (ret.), quoted in interview by Eric Holthaus, "'Climate change war' is not a metaphor," *Grist*, April 22, 2014, http://grist.org/climate-energy/climate-change-war-is-not-a-metaphor/?utm_source=newsletter&utm_medium=email&utm_term=Daily%2520April%252022&utm_campaign=daily, accessed April 22, 2014.

[2] David Roberts, "My quest for a family car has ended , and the winner is...," *Grist*, May 16, 2012, http://grist.org/article/my-quest-for-a-family-car-has-ended-and-the-winner-is/, accessed May 12, 2012.

3 Susan Gregory Thomas, "Why Broke-Ass is a patriot," *Grist*, June 30, 2011.

4 Wade Sikorski, "On Mad Bombers," *Theory & Event* (v. 1, n. 1), 1997.

5 Isaac Arnsdorf, "On Terror Alert: Inside Big Oil's Fight to Build Keystone," *Bloomberg Business*, Feb. 24, 2015, http://www.bloomberg.com/news/articles/2015-02-24/on-terror-alert-inside-big-oil-s-fight-to-build-keystone, accessed Feb. 27, 2015.

6 ibid., Isaac Arnsdorf.

Chapter Thirty-Eight: Wilderness

[1] Multiple-Use and Sustained-Yield Act of 1960 [Public Law 86-517], Sec. 2.

[2] "Flambeau," in *A Sand County Almanac*, Oxford University Press, 1949.

[3] Wallace Stegner, "The Gift of Wilderness," in *One way to Spell Man*, Doubleday & Company, Inc., 1982.

[4] Wallace Stegner, "The Gift of Wilderness," in *One way to Spell Man*, Doubleday & Company, Inc., 1982.

[5] Edward Abbey, "Thus I Reply to Rene Dubos," *Down the River*, E.P. Dutton, 1982.

[6] Edward Abbey, "Thus I Reply to Rene Dubos," *Down the River*, E.P. Dutton, 1982.

Chapter Thirty-Nine: One Montana Coal Mine

[1] http://www.landgrant.org/corps.html, accessed April 26, 2012.

[2] Letter from Montana's then-Governor Brian Schweitzer, April 2, 2010.

[3] Montana Department of Environmental Quality, *Scoping Report: Otter Creek Mine, Powder River County, Montana*, April 2013 (Revised June 2013), p. 2.

[4] *Road to Little Bighorn* (timeline of historic events 1400-2003), John Doerner (chief historian, Little Bighorn Battlefield Nat'l Monument), Friends of the Little Bighorn Battlefield, http://www.friendslittlebighorn.com/Roadtolittlebighorn.htm , accessed June 5, 2016.

[5] Bureau of Land Management, *Draft Environmental Assessment for Compliance with Section 503 of the Department of the Interior and Related Agencies Appropriation Act of 1998 [Public Law 105-83]*, February 2002; *Otter Creek Coal, LLC, Application for Prospecting Permit X2011334, Otter Creek Tracts, Powder River County, Montana*, prepared by Hydrometrics, Inc., Billings. MT.

[6] http://www.educationjustice.org/states/montana.html, accessed July 21, 2012.

[7] Thomas H. Jones, "State Lotteries and the Financing of Public Education," *Public Justice Report* / Center for Public Justice, Sept.-Oct. 1994; Rodney E. Stanley & P. Edward French, "Can students truly benefit from state lotteries: a look at lottery expenditures towards education in the American states," *The Social Science Journal*, 40 [2003], pp. 327-333; Tony Messenger, "Missouri auditor says gambling law shortchanges schools," www.stltoday.com, Sept. 24, 2010; Greg Janda, "Q: Gambling for Education? Lottery won't cover education budget gap,"www.nbcdfw.com [Dallas-Fort Worth], March 15, 2012: Montana Office of Public Instruction, *Understanding Montana School Finance and School District Budgets*, January 2011, http://opi.mt.gov/pdf/schoolfinance/budget/UnderstSchlFin.pdf.

[8] Charles S. Johnson, "Ed budget chair: U-system brass should advocate for natural resource development," *Billings Gazette*, Jan. 23, 2013.

[9] 1,300,000 million tons recoverable reserves = 2,600,000,000,000 pounds; 8,940 Btu/lb. x 2,600,000,000,000 pounds = 23,244,000,000 million Btus. Carbon dioxide emission factor for Montana sub-bituminous coal = 213.4 pounds of CO_2 per million Btus. [Heating value for Sub-bituminous C coal from "Heating Values of Standard Grades of Coal," http://www.engineeringtoolbox.com/coal-heating-values-d_1675.html, accessed May 26, 2012; emission factor from B.D. Hong and E. R. Slatick, "Carbon Dioxide Emission factors for Coal," Energy Information Administration, *Quarterly Coal Report,* January-April 1994, DOE/EIA-0121[94/Q1] {Washington, DC, August 1994}, pp. 1-8, accessed May 26, 2012.

[10] Zachary Davies Boren & Lauri Myllyvirta, "2015: The year global coal demand fell off a cliff," Climate Spectator, Nov. 10, 2015, http://www.businessspectator.com.au/article/2015/11/10/energy-markets/2015-year-global-coal-demand-fell-cliff, accessed Dec. 13, 2015.

Chapter Forty: Why I Don't Believe In Climate Change

[1] Associated Press, "Study: Arctic growing darker, warming earth," *Billings Gazette*, Feb. 18, 2014.

[2] Hugh Montgomery, Peng Gong, Anthony Costello, et.al., "Health and climate change: Policy responses to protect public health," *The Lancet*, v. 386, n. 10006, Nov. 7, 2015, pp. 1861-1914, http://www.thelancet.com/journals/lancet/article/PIIS0140-6736%2815%2960854-6/fulltext, accessed Dec. 9, 2015.

[3] Intergovernmental Panel on Climate Change, *Climate Change 2007: Synthesis Report*, adopted at IPCC Plenary XXVII, Valencia, Spain, November 12-17, 2007.

[4] Intergovernmental Panel on Climate Change, *Climate Change 2013: The Physical Science Basis, Contribution of Working Group I to the Fifth Assessment Report of the Intergovernmental Panel on Climate Change*, Cambridge University Press, New York, pp. 142-144.

[5] Wade Sikorski, Ph.D., *Before It Is Too Late: The Climate Crisis and Economic Development*, 2011, p. 18.

[6] American Association for the Advancement of Science, AAAS Climate Science Panel report, *What We Know: The Reality, Risks and Response to Climate Change*, March 18, 2014, p. 2; http://whatweknow.aaas.org/wp-content/uploads/2014/07/whatweknow_website.pdf..

[7] Neela Banerjee, Lisa Son & David Hasemyer, "Exxon: The Road Not Taken," *Inside Climate News* (Part 1 of 9-part series), Sept. 16, 2015.

[8] Cited in Paul R. Epstein, et. al., "Full cost accounting for the life cycle of coal," *Annals of the New York Academy of Sciences*, Feb. 2011, pp.73-98.

[9] Rebecca Lindsey, "No surprise, 2015 sets new global temperature record," National Oceanic and Atmospheric Administration, Jan. 19, 2016; https://www.climate.gov/news-features/featured-images/no-surprise-2015-sets-new-global-temperature-record, accessed Mar. 13, 2016.

[10] National Academy of Sciences press release: "Strong evidence on climate change underscores need for actions to reduce emissions and begin adapting to impacts," May 19, 2010.

[11] American Meteorological Society, *Climate Change: An Information Statement of the American Meteorological Society* [Adopted by the AMS Council on 1 February 2007] *Bull. Amer. Met. Soc.*, 88.

[12] National Geographic Society website, *Causes of Climate Change* http://environment.nationalgeographic.com/environment/global-warming/gw-causes.

[13] National Aeronautics and Space Administration, Goddard Space Flight Center, *Earth Impacts Linked to Human-Caused Climate Change*, http://www.nasa.gov/centers/goddard/news/topstory/2008/human_impact.html.

[14] American Geophysical Union, Position Statement: *Humans Impact Climate, and the Scientific Community has the Responsibility to Educate and Communicate the Implications of Climate Change to the Public and Policy Makers*, Adopted by the American Geophysical Union December 2003; Revised and Reaffirmed December 2007, February 2012; *http://www.agu.org/sci_pol/pdf/position_statements/AGU_Climate_Statement.pdf*.

[15] American Association for the Advancement of Science, AAAS Climate Science Panel report, *What We Know: The Reality, Risks and Response to Climate Change*, March 18, 2014, p. 2; http://whatweknow.aaas.org/wp-content/uploads/2014/07/whatweknow_website.pdf..

[16] General Gordon R. Sullivan , quoted in *National Security and the Threat of Climate Change*, report published by CAN Corporation, 2007.

[17] Thomas L. Friedman, "Going Cheney on Climate," *New York Times*, Dec. 9, 2009.

[18] American Association for the Advancement of Science, AAAS Climate Science Panel report, *What We Know: The Reality, Risks and Response to Climate Change*, March 18, 2014, p. 8; http://whatweknow.aaas.org/wp-content/uploads/2014/07/what-weknow_website.pdf.

[19] American Association for the Advancement of Science, AAAS Climate Science Panel report, *What We Know: The Reality, Risks and Response to Climate Change*, March 18, 2014, p. 8; http://whatweknow.aaas.org/wp-content/uploads/2014/07/what-weknow_website.pdf.

[20] Neela Banerjee, "Scientist proves conservatism and belief in climate change aren't in-compatible," *Los Angeles Times*, Jan. 5, 2011.

[21] Associated Press, "Global warming has one more believer," *Billings Gazette*, Oct. 31, 2011.

Chapter Forty-One: It's Not Just an Environmental Problem

[1] David Roberts, "'Environmentalism' can never address climate change," *Grist*, Aug. 9, 2010.

[2] John M. Broder, "Climate Change Seen as Threat to U.S. Security," *New York Times*, Aug. 8, 2009.

[3] U.S. Department of Defense, *FY 2014 Climate Change Adaptation Roadmap*, June 2014.

[4] *National Security and the Threat of Climate Change*, report published by CNA Corporation [Center for Naval Analyses], 2007.

[5] Retired Navy Rear Admiral David Titley, quoted in interview by Eric Holthaus, "'Climate change war' is not a metaphor," *Grist*, April 22, 2014, http://grist.org/climate-energy/climate-change-war-is-not-a-metaphor/?utm_source=newsletter&utm_medium=email&utm_term=Daily%2520April%252022&utm_campaign=daily, accessed April 22, 2014.

[6] Retired Vice Admiral Dennis McGinn, "Montana should embrace clean energy development," Guest column, *Missoulian*, Oct. 22, 2009, accessed Oct 22, 2009.

Chapter Forty-Two: Clean Coal

[1] Terry C. Whiteside, Gerald W. Fauth III, and Richard H. Streeter; *Heavy Traffic Ahead: Rail Impacts of Powder River Basin Coal to Asia by Way of Pacific Northwest Terminals*, Report prepared for Western Organization of Resource Councils, July 2012; updated by Terry C. Whiteside and Gerald W. Fauth III; *Heavy Traffic Still Ahead;* Report prepared for Western Organization of Resource Councils, February 2014.

[2] Sally Jacobsen, "Energy v. the environment in Montana," *New Scientist*, July 26, 1973, pp. 186-187; Thomas Bass, "Moving Gary, Indiana, to the Great Plains," *Mother Jones*, July 1976, pp. 34-38, 56-58.

[3] Sally Jacobsen, "Energy v. the environment in Montana," *New Scientist*, July 26, 1973.

[4] L.J. Turner email to Steve Paulson, Oct. 24, 2012.

[5] Boyd Charter, quoted in *Cowboys Don't Walk*, by Anne Goddard Charter, Western Organization of Resource Councils, 1999.

[6] Wendell Berry, *A Continuous Harmony: Essays Cultural and Agricultural*, Harvest Books, 1972.

[7] Janet Keating, in a speech to the Northern Plains Resource Council annual meeting; Billings, Montana; Nov. 10, 2012.

[8] Matthew L. Wald, "Fossil fuels' cost is in billions, study says," *New York Times*, Oct. 20, 2009.

[9] Conrad Schneider and Jonathan Banks, *The Toll From Coal, An Updated Assessment of Death and Disease from America's Dirtiest Energy Source*, Clean Air Task Force, Sept. 2010.

[10] Paul R. Epstein, et. al., "Full cost accounting for the life cycle of coal," *Annals of the New York Academy of Sciences*, Feb. 2011, pp.73-98.

[11] Paul R. Epstein, et. al., "Full cost accounting for the life cycle of coal," *Annals of the New York Academy of Sciences*, Feb. 2011, pp.73-98; Alan H. Lockwood, et. al., *Coal's Assault on Human Health*, report by Physicians for Social Responsibility, November 2009.

[12] John Collins Rudolf, "Tallying coal's hidden cost." *N.Y. Times Green Blog*, Feb. 17, 2011.

[13] Paul R. Epstein, et. al., "Full cost accounting for the life cycle of coal," *Annals of the New York Academy of Sciences*, Feb. 2011, pp.73-98.

[14] Shaila Dewan, "Tennessee Ash Flood Larger Than Initial Estimate," *New York Times*, Dec. 26, 2008; NASA Earth Observatory, "Coal Ash Spill, Tennessee," http://earthobservatory.nasa.gov/NaturalHazards/view.php?id=36352; *Scientific American*, "Earth Talk: The Lasting Damage of the Tennessee Coal Ash Spill," May 19, 2009.

[15] Shelley Vinyard & Lauren Randall, *Dirty Energy's Assault on Our Health: Mercury*, p. 8, Environment America Research and Policy Center, January 2011.

[16] J.I. Levy, J.D. Spengler, D. Hlinka, & D. Sullivan, *Estimated Public Health Impacts of Criteria Pollutant Air Emissions from the Salem Harbor and Brayton Point Power Plants*, Harvard School of Public Health, 2000; cited in Epstein et.al.

[17] Howard Berkes, "Mine Disaster Probe Finds Intimidation, False Papers," National Public Radio, July 6, 2011, http://www.npr.org/2011/06/29/137504341/federal-investigators-massey-falsified-safety-records, accessed Dec. 26, 2015; Mark Memmott, "West Virginia Mine Superintendent Pleads Guilty to Fraud," National Public Radio, March 29, 2012, http://www.npr.org/sections/thetwo-

way/2012/03/29/149609996/west-virginia-mine-superintendent-pleads-guilty-to-fraud, accessed Dec. 26, 2015.

[18] Office of Surface Mining Reclamation and Enforcement, *Annual Evaluation Report for the Regulatory Program / Montana*, Casper Field Office, September 2012.

Chapter Forty-Three: It Didn't Happen By Itself

[1] Conrad Schneider and Jonathan Banks, *The Toll From Coal, An Updated Assessment of Death and Disease from America's Dirtiest Energy Source*, Clean Air Task Force, Sept. 2010.

Chapter Forty-Four: Taking Precaution

[1] Ian Urbina, "Think Those Chemicals Have Been Tested?" *New York Times*, April 13, 2013.

Chapter Forty-Six: There's Something Wrong

[1] McClatchy Newspapers, "Report: Water woes will be on rise," *Billings Gazette*, March 23, 2012.

[2] Louis Sahagun, "An ecosystem of our own making could pose a threat," *Los Angeles Times*, December 28, 2013.

[3] Seth Borenstein, *Associated Press*, "Bee disappearance accelerating, USDA survey says; study looks at pesticide," March 25, 2010.

[4] Eryn Brown, "Pesticides suspected in mass die-off of bees," *Los Angeles Times*, March 29, 2012.

[5] Associated Press. "Study: Oceans more tainted with man-made mercury," *Billings Gazette*, August 7, 2014.

Chapter Forty-Seven: Fuzzy Math

[1] Chelsea Harvey, "Economists keep saying we should put a price on nature. Now they've finally done it," *Washington Post*, Feb. 8, 2016, https://www.washingtonpost.com/news/energy-environment/wp/2016/02/08/scientists-have-come-up-with-a-way-to-put-a-price-on-nature/?wpmm=1&wpisrc=nl_green, accessed Feb. 23, 2016.

[2] Motoko Rich and John Broder, "A Debate Arises on Job Creation and Environment," *The New York Times*, Sept. 4, 2011.

[3] Robert F. Kennedy, address, University of Kansas, Lawrence, Kansas, March 18, 1968.

Chapter Forty-Nine: 12 Things I've Learned from Being an Environmentalist

[1] Edward Abbey, "Floating," in *Down the River*, E.P. Dutton, 1982.